# THE BOOK OF GREAT
# Breakfasts and Brunches

# THE BOOK OF GREAT
# *Breakfasts* and *Brunches*

TERENCE JANERICCO

VNR VAN NOSTRAND REINHOLD
New York

Copyright © 1993 by Van Nostrand Reinhold

Library of Congress Catalog Card Number 92-46781
ISBN 0-442-01355-8

I⟨T⟩P  Van Nostrand Reinhold is an International Thomson Publishing company.
       ITP logo is a trademark under license.

Printed in the United States of America

Van Nostrand Reinhold                          International Thomson Publishing Gmbl
115 Fifth Avenue                               Königswinterer Str. 418
New York, NY 10003                             53227 Bonn
                                               Germany

International Thomson Publishing              International Thomson Publishing Asia
Berkshire House,168-173                       221 Henderson Bldg. #05-10
High Holborn, London WC1V 7AA                 Singapore 0315
England

Thomas Nelson Australia                       International Thomson Publishing Japan
102 Dodds Street                              Kyowa Building, 3F
South Melbourne 3205                          2-2-1 Hirakawacho
Victoria, Australia                           Chiyoda-Ku, Tokyo 102
                                              Japan

Nelson Canada
1120 Birchmount Road
Scarborough, Ontario
M1K 5G4, Canada

16  15  14  13  12  11  10  9  8  7  6  5  4  3  2

**Library of Congress Cataloging-in-Publication Data**

Janericco, Terence.
    The book of great breakfasts and brunches / Terence Janericco.
        p.   cm.
    Includes index.
    ISBN 0-442-01355-8
    1. Breakfasts. 2. Brunches. I. Title.
TX733.J357   1993
641.5'2—dc20                                    92-46781
                                                CIP

# Contents

# Recipe Contents

## Chapter 2     BISCUITS, DOUGHNUTS, MUFFINS, AND OTHER QUICK BREADS

## Chapter 3    YEAST BREADS, COFFEE CAKES, AND PASTRIES

## Chapter 4    EGGS

## Chapter 8    FISH

## Chapter 9    MEATS

## Chapter 10    VEGETABLES AND PASTA

# Preface

Breaking fast is how we all start the day. Some of us rise as if being slowly drawn out of a deep well and others go at it by leaping tall buildings at a single bound. However we arise, we soon need to eat. For many a cup of coffee suffices while others add a glass of juice, a piece of fruit, a slice of toast; cereal is certainly on many a menu. Others select more elaborate fare. Bacon and eggs have a bad name these days, but there are still those who happily start the day with them, while others eat steak, apple pie, or that favorite treat, cold pizza!

In other countries breakfast often differs dramatically from the American practice. The Dutch indulge in bread and cheese. The Italians like a cup of deep, rich coffee and a freshly made crisp, hard roll. The French prefer a brioche or croissant with their morning *café au lait*. We find this relatively easy to accept and incorporate into our diet. Eastern cultures start the day with salted fish in *congee*, a long-cooked rice gruel. This is about as appealing to us as a hearty bowl of oatmeal is to them, I am sure.

Americans have become breakfast-conscious in the last few years because of the writings of many food editors and nutritionists. Some information is wrong, some of it misleading, and much of it built on the latest scientific report exaggerated out of proportion. These writers want a single solution to our dietary needs. If we eat oat bran, they imply, we shall live forever in perfect health. There are many of us who have a far more realistic view. Yes, good health is important, but not when the achievement removes the quality of life. We do not want every meal to be a study in nutrition and a chore. We want to dine well, enjoying varied food flavors and sensations. We accept creamed lobster as a treat, not daily fare. We know that there is nothing wrong with bacon and scrambled eggs once in awhile. We appreciate that various grains are not only good for us, but can also be a treat when they are not forced upon us. We adore hearty breads made with whole grains while we still love croissants. Perhaps what we appreciate best is that a balanced diet allows us to eat what we want—providing we do so in moderation.

There are writers who stress that a hearty breakfast is the way to start the day and it is true. But hearty for one may be bare subsistence for another. Steak and apple pie for breakfast (an old New England custom, also found in many farming communities) makes sense if you are about to go out and plow the back forty, or if it is a late breakfast that combines breakfast and lunch. If you do serious physical labor for four or five hours before the next meal, cereal, fruit, meat, and a vegetable with toast or another starch makes sense. If you are driving to the office and writing at the computer for four hours, a breakfast of cereal and fruit is more suitable. Add a slice of toast, unless you know the coffee wagon is due at 10 A.M.

I believe that what is most important, is that you allow time for breakfast. Starting the day with a half-eaten piece of toast and two swallows of hot coffee can hardly begin your day favorably. Sitting down for a few minutes to eat that toast or cereal, and to savor that coffee, can be a wonderfully relaxing start to the day.

# BRUNCHES

Fortunately no matter how hectic life is during the week, most of us can take one or two mornings a week and turn them into relaxing events. We can invite guests to join us, or simply provide a different meal for the family. When this occurs later in the morning and involves heartier food, breakfast, in theory at least, becomes brunch. It is true that brunch can replace two meals, if properly timed, but if you plan a 9:00 A.M. brunch, no one is going to be fooled.

The first item to consider in giving a brunch is the time. If you serve it before 11:00, it is really going to be more of a breakfast and the food should be more breakfast-like. After 11:00 A.M., the meal is more apt to be a luncheon with some breakfast foods. You can start with juice and have heartier items, such as egg dishes, that still make it more breakfast than lunch. The smart host will choose a menu and a time to suit his or her lifestyle. If you get up at 6:00 A.M. and start every day with a bang, an 8:00 or 9:00 breakfast-brunch can work well. You can get everyone off to the slopes before the lifts get full. If you know that facing the world before 9:00 A.M. is a problem, then give your brunch at 11:00 or 12:00 or even 1:00. The well-organized host prepares the day before. Getting up at 5:00 A.M. to start the croissants can test the patience of anyone.

Make an effort to keep some food light in feel, if not in fact. (The word "light" in regard to food has almost lost its meaning. Some people will laud the "light" doughnut, while others will condemn the "heavy" crêpe. Light has become the password for permissibility. If you can say it is light, then you can eat it almost guilt-free.) Provide a bowl of cut up fruit and some plain bread along with the coffee cakes.

For most people, brunch is an occasion to entertain. It allows a host to feed hordes of people casually. Everything does not have to match: use whatever dishes you have, but please use real dishes. Paper is suitable for picnics, but never at home. You do not need to use silver. You can give your brunch a distinctive country look using floral china, pots of daisies, and lots of wooden and brass serving dishes; or a contemporary city feel with black dishes, grey napkins, brightly colored anemones on stainless steel or glass serving dishes. You can even evoke Victorian elegance with the best china and glassware served with all the family silver and bowls of full-blown roses. In other words, you can give many brunches and easily have a different mood for each.

Set the table the night before. Review the recipes and decide which ones can be done ahead and to what point. If they require a lot of last-minute attention, this may not be the time to use those recipes. You can, for instance, do much of the preparation of Eggs Benedict a day ahead. On the other hand, soufflés need to be prepared shortly before serving. Fried eggs are cooked to order.

For the most part brunches are buffets. They allow the late-risers to eat a light breakfast while the early-risers chow down on heartier fare. You can make it formal, with servers passing hors d'oeuvre before you serve the cold poached salmon, or you can gather all your friends in the kitchen for a make-your-own omelet or crêpes party.

If you work well with others, assign kitchen duties. If you do not, plan ahead and prepare ahead. Remember that brunches are usually informal affairs and that you should be able to put most of the food out so that people can help themselves. Arrange pitchers of juices in an ice-filled bin and pile the breakfast breads in a basket. Plan a menu that you can handle easily. If you have selected foods that require a lot of last-minute preparation and you are alone, you will hate the party, your guests, and everything else. Fortunately, with a little planning and a relaxed attitude you can make the occasion as much fun for yourself as for your guests.

*Beverages*

For most of us breakfast starts with the aroma of a steaming beverage. In America and most European countries that is coffee, although in parts of Europe and South America the aroma of hot cocoa is preferred. But worldwide, tea is the choice of the greatest number of people. Whatever the beverage, make it fresh with the finest ingredients. Instant coffee, tea, or cocoa is truly never acceptable. When you provide these you are telling your guest, even if *you* are the guest, that you do not care enough. True coffee drinkers will appreciate the effort of carefully selected, freshly ground beans. If you buy ground beans, buy small quantities. Better yet grind your own beans. The coffee will be fresher and you can sample different varieties, and create blends to suit your preference.

All too often, tea lovers, especially in the United States, are treated as second class citizens. In this country we throw a bag into a cup, add hot water, and call it done. Tea drinkers deserve as much attention as any other guest, and brewing a pot of tea is even simpler than brewing a pot of coffee. Simply pour boiling water into the pot to heat it, then add a spoonful of tea, and freshly boiling water. Let the guest decide when it has steeped. You can blend teas to suit your taste, but if it is not your forte, remember that generally tea drinkers drink real tea and do not consider every root and herb soaked in hot water, tea!

In the United States, adults are apt to leave the cocoa to the kids unless they are on a skiing weekend. But cocoa has its fans, and as an option for brunch may bring more takers than you would suspect. An added advantage for the brunch cook is that it can be made ahead and reheated, an action not recommended for coffee or tea. You can make cocoa as sweet and creamy or as dark and bitter as you prefer.

Of course for many, brunch means something more potent than coffee, tea, or cocoa. In fact many alcoholic drinks have become standard fare at brunch time. Bloody Marys and Screwdrivers made with vodka, Orange Blossoms and Ramos Fizzes made with gin, or Mimosas and Kir Royales made with champagne are all examples of spirited ways to start a brunch.

Generally, brunch drinks are based on fruit juices and a liquor. Since some people do not want a strong drink, or do not care to drink at all, offer some alternatives. Champagne or any other white wine is always well-received. This is the time to serve some less well-known wines of the Rhine and Mosel regions, a welcome change for the guest who automatically asks for Chardonnay.

Wines that are fuller in fruit and less acidic are the best choice. Try some better rosés from France or a sparkling Vouvray. If the meal is to include some hearty dishes, a Beaujolais or other young red will appeal. For the non-drinkers, Bloody Mary mix without the liquor, and fruit juices provided as mixers are good options, as is mineral water.


# COFFEE

Coffee, one of the most common beverages, is often poorly prepared. The host grabs any brand from the shelf, and makes it with little care or concern. Good coffee, though not difficult, does take care. There are dozens of machines available, from paper filters set in cones over a container, to elaborate and expensive machines that produce differing types of coffee, including boiling milk. Select the machine that works best for you and produces the type of coffee you like to drink. An espresso machine for someone who hates strong coffee is a mistake. Most of the machines work and the problem is not the equipment, but the coffee itself.

In years gone by, I used a filter-lined plastic cone set over a pot. I poured boiling water over the grounds and the coffee dripped into the container. Since then, I have gone on to an automatic coffee machine. It has a filter, but the machine takes care of the water and the pouring. I find the result as good as the hand-poured method and a lot more convenient.

Coffee varies in flavor according to the area in which it grows and the amount of roasting it receives. Some beans are richer and more full-flavored than others: some are lightly roasted, and others are roasted longer to obtain deeper, richer flavors. Spend some time sampling different coffees to see if there is a standard blend that appeals to you, or try mixing one variety and roast with another. My favorite combination is one quarter espresso, one quarter French Roast and one half Columbian Supremo. I mix the whole beans in a container and grind them as needed. This produces a rich, full-flavored coffee with medium body. Some coffee drinkers may find this blend too full-flavored. Ordinarily I drink regular coffee, but in my catering business so many clients have requested decaffeinated coffee that I have produced the same blend with decaffeinated beans. I find that those who prefer decaffeinated coffee are pleased and those who prefer regular coffee never even ask.

In preparing for a party, know that one pound of beans yields 50 cups even when the prices rise. Some restaurants have been known to attempt to get 60 to 70 cups from a pound as prices rise. Anyone who likes coffee can tell the difference. If you use a standard coffee blend you may find that a particular brand is too strong or too weak in these proportions, and you might wish to make adjustments.

Coffee deserves some care, especially once the beans are ground. They lose their aroma and flavor in a relatively short period. Store opened containers of ground coffee in the freezer and spoon out what you need as you need it. Coffee beans keep longer at room temperature, but even they will last longer if stored in the freezer. There are purists who will insist that coffee should be ground no more than 5 minutes before brewing, and that the beans be no more than a week old. There are others who say grinding ahead removes bitterness. Grinding your own beans, as you need them, is easy with one of the inexpensive grinders so readily available.

## COFFEE

2 quarts cold water                          ⅔ cup coffee beans

Place the water in a kettle and bring to a full boil. Finely grind the beans and place in a filter over a pot. Pour on ½ cup boiling water to moisten the grounds. When they are soaked and the liquid drained, add more water, ½ cup at a time.
Serve at once.

Yield: 8 cups

NOTE

The filter can be fine sheeting placed in a sieve, if you do not have a large paper filter. If you are using an automatic coffee machine, use the same quantities and let the machine do the work, or follow the instructions that come with the machine.

Coffee is at its best served and drunk within half an hour of preparation. This is not always possible with large groups. Once the coffee is made, remove and discard the grounds. It is better to let the coffee cool and reheat gently than to try to keep it hot. Do not bring to a boil or it will be bitter.

Serve coffee with cream and sugar. Heavy cream makes the richest coffee but many people have acquired a taste for medium or light cream or even skimmed milk. For a change offer sweetened whipped cream, dusted with cinnamon, nutmeg or cloves, or flavored with vanilla.

For large groups, mix 1 quart of milk with 1 cup of heavy or medium cream for 50 servings. This will satisfy most people. Since more and more people drink their coffee black, I have found that this is more likely to serve 75 persons than 50.

## FLAVORED COFFEES

The true coffee lover drinks coffee straight, with no additives other than perhaps some cream and sugar. Occasionally they may prefer coffee made with cinnamon, or even laced with a liqueur. Flavored coffees with almonds, hazelnuts, and so on, are really more a gimmick than a serious drink and often the flavor is less than pleasing. I strongly recommend that you serve unflavored coffee and then provide flavorings for guests to suit their tastes. Supplying a liqueur tray with Cognac, rum, whiskey, hazelnut, or orange liqueur, with bowls of cream and sugar and shakers of cinnamon and nutmeg can be a fun presentation and makes it possible for everyone's needs to be met.

## ICED COFFEE

Prepare freshly brewed coffee and allow it to cool to room temperature. Add ice to taste and serve with sugar and cream.

# TEA

There are at least as many blends and types of tea as coffee and there are even more types of herbal concoctions sold as teas. These may or may not please the true tea drinker. Orange pekoe is the standard variety found in supermarkets, and in most tea bags, although in recent years more varieties of tea have appeared on market shelves. True tea lovers despise tea bags as much for their appearance as for the flavor. Shops that sell premium coffee generally sell premium teas well, including variations of tea leaves with other flavorings such as orange and ginger.

### Herbal Teas

There are many *tisanes* such as camomile that have a relaxing effect and are delicious. There are also dozens of mixtures sold commercially with apples and cinnamon and mint, and so on, that are not as pleasing to my taste. If offering tea to a guest, offer real tea unless you know they prefer an herbal concoction.

Keep teas in an airtight canister once opened and use within a year at the very longest. If you do not know how long you have had the tea, it is probably time to replace it. Teas flavored with other ingredients are more likely to lose their potency quickly.

---

## TEA

2 quarts cold, fresh water                    8 teaspoons loose tea leaves

Bring the water to a boil.
Pour 2 cups of water into the pot and swirl the water to heat the pot and drain. Add the tea leaves to the pot and pour on the remaining water. Cover and steep 3 to 5 minutes. Strain and serve with sugar, lemon, or milk.

Yield: 8 cups

People lace tea with liquor, as with coffee, but it is not as common. Provide a decanter of Cognac or rum and let guests add it if they want. Honey is a delicious sweetener.

### ICED TEA

Traditionally you prepare iced tea by letting hot tea cool to room temperature and adding ice, or making strong hot tea and pouring it over ice. The first method often produces a cloudy tea and the latter is often weak and bitter.

You can make excellent iced tea with cold water. This is often called Sun Tea, because the container of the tea is placed in the sun until it brews. But, the sun is not necessary to the result, though it does not hurt. Place one teaspoon or bag of tea for each cup of water in a jar. Let sit at room temperature for about 4 hours. Chill until ready to serve.

# COCOA

Cocoa is common in Latin America, Spain, and Portugal as a breakfast drink while the rest of us think of it as a soothing beverage to drink after intense physical activity in cold weather. It does have extraordinary appeal and makes a wonderful start to a winter brunch.

As with coffee and tea, using pure cocoa will provide a more pleasing drink than the packaged mixes. You can control the amount of sugar and the type of liquid, to make a version distinctly your own. It takes no more than a few minutes to prepare cocoa, so time is not really a consideration.

### *Milling*

Whether you use your own preparation or store bought, a common problem is the skin that forms on top. Children find this particularly repulsive. To prevent the skin from forming, beat the hot cocoa with a rotary beater, wire whisk, or hand-held electric mixer to create a foam on the top. This is called *milling*.

---

## COCOA

3 tablespoons cocoa
¼ cup sugar, or to taste
Pinch of salt

¾ cup boiling water
4 cups milk, or 2 cups milk
    and 2 cups cream

In a 2-quart saucepan, mix the cocoa, sugar, and salt. Stir in the boiling water and cook, stirring over medium heat for 2 minutes. Stir in the milk and heat, beating with a rotary beater, wire whisk, or electric mixer until hot and the top is foamy.
Serve immediately.

Yield: 6 cups

NOTE

Cooking the cocoa in the water before the adding the milk helps to cook the starch for a better-tasting drink. Serve cocoa with a bowl of whipped cream, sweetened and flavored with vanilla, cinnamon or cloves, or flavor the cream with rum or Cognac.

Adjust the amount of sugar to suit your taste, and add cream for a richer cocoa. For children—of all ages—float a marshmallow or two on top.

Cocoa can be prepared the night before, refrigerated and reheated over low heat the next morning. Be sure to remove any skin and do the milling just before serving. Like tea and coffee, cocoa can benefit from a lacing of Cognac, rum, orange liqueur, or kirsch.


# COLD DRINKS

### Non Alcoholic Beverages

Many hosts like to offer a cold drink with a difference. It is right to serve orange juice or Bloody Mary mix without the addition of Champagne or vodka and indeed, in this way, many hosts show sensitivity to those guests who might not want to start the day with coffee, tea, or alcohol. Also, brunch parties often include children, and clearly something other than caffeine and alcoholic drinks are required for them.

But some hosts prefer to offer non-alcoholic beverages that are more creative than plain orange juice. Remember that this is breakfast and you need to keep it simple. Cranberry, pineapple, apricot nectar, tomato, and vegetable juices are only a few of the offerings available at your local market. If there are a number of children, keep the choices rather plain. You can offer orange juice, which is a sure thing, and then perhaps a mixed fruit drink, say cranberry-apple, for some of the more adventurous children. Many younger adults prefer mixed fruit drinks, the more exotic, the better, it would seem. Again many commercial preparations are on the market and they can be the simplest answer to the problem.

### Glasses

Tradition often dictates which glass to use for which drink. Punch cups, old-fashioned, or highball glasses are typically used for certain drinks, wine glasses for others, and pilseners for beer. Fortunately we are less rigid, and for brunch the rules are always casual. I prefer to use an over-sized (18 ounce) wine glass for everything, whether a martini, still wine, or Champagne. I do not fill the glass, but prepare the standard-size drink and just leave the extra room.

## Ice

Of course an attentive host will always have ice on hand to chill water, if nothing else. Many of the drinks call for ice without stipulating them in the recipe in the same manner that many recipes require water without listing it.

## Sugar Syrup

Ideally prepare sugar syrup by heating 2 cups of sugar in a saucepan with 1 cup of water until the sugar dissolves, and let it cool to room temperature. If you are in a hurry you can dissolve the sugar by stirring in cold water.

## CRANBERRY APPLE PINEAPPLE DRINK

1 quart cranberry juice
3 cups apple juice
8-ounce can pineapple
    cubes with the juice

½ cup lemon juice
1 quart ginger ale
1 quart soda water

Chill all the ingredients. In a bowl or pitcher, mix the cranberry juice, apple juice, pineapple cubes and juice, lemon juice, ginger ale, and soda water.

Yield: 20 5-ounce servings

Prepare just before serving to preserve the sparkle.

## CRANBERRY ORANGE LIME DRINK

1 quart cranberry juice
1 quart orange juice
½ cup lime juice

Sugar syrup to taste (see
    page 9)
1 quart soda water, optional

In a bowl or pitcher, mix the cranberry juice, orange juice, and lime juice. Sweeten to taste with sugar syrup and chill. If desired, just before serving add the soda water to give it sparkle.

Yield: 8 to 12 servings

## GRAPEFRUIT LIME DRINK

1 quart grapefruit Juice
juice of 8 limes (1 cup)
sugar syrup to taste (see
   page 9)

2 tablespoons minced fresh
   mint leaves
mint sprigs for garnish

In a container, mix the grapefruit juice, lime juice, syrup, and minced mint. Stir and chill for 2 hours. Strain into a pitcher and serve over crushed ice and garnish with a sprig of mint.

Yield: 8 servings

Can be prepared 2 days before serving.

## LEMONADE

6 lemons, halved
2½ quarts water

2 cups sugar syrup (see
   page 9) or to taste

Squeeze the juice from the lemons. In a pitcher combine the lemon juice, halves of 3 lemons, water, and sugar syrup to taste. Mix well and chill.

Yield: 10 to 12 servings

## ORANGE PAPAYA DRINK

1 quart papaya juice
2 cups orange juice
¼ cup lime juice

Sugar syrup (see page 9), optional
1 quart soda water, optional

In a pitcher or bowl, mix the papaya, orange, and lime juices with sugar syrup. Chill and serve. If desired, add the soda water just before serving.

Yield: 6 to 8 servings

---

# PINEAPPLE ORANGE LIME DRINK

1 quart pineapple juice
2 cups orange juice
¼ cup lime juice

1 quart ginger ale
sugar syrup to taste

In a bowl or pitcher, mix the pineapple, orange, and lime juices. Just before serving, add the ginger ale and sweeten with sugar syrup if needed.

Yield: 8 servings

---

# CARDINAL

Cardinal is the name for a classic sauce of raspberry and strawberries. Here is a flavorful drink from the same ingredients.

12 ounces fresh or frozen
    raspberries
1 pint fresh or frozen straw-
    berries

sugar syrup to taste
1 quart soda water

In a processor, purée the raspberries and strain through a sieve. Discard the seeds.
Hull the strawberries and purée in the processor and strain.
Combine the raspberry and strawberry juices and sweeten with the syrup. Chill. Just before serving, stir in the soda water.

Yield: 8 servings

# PUNCH

*Alcoholic and Non-alcoholic*

A brunch is often the perfect occasion to serve punch. Set the bowl in a convenient location—well away from the food—and let the guests help themselves.

When preparing punch it helps to remember that the word comes from India and means five. The original versions had 5 ingredients: sugar, lime juice, water, and 2 juices, for example. When made with alcohol the mixture became sugar, lime juice, brandy, and a wine. Although today we do not adhere to this formula as rigidly, it is always wise to remember not to add too many different juices, because instead of a pleasing marriage of flavors the result will taste sweet and the flavors murky.

For those occasions when you wish to create a punch, consider the number of guests and provide accordingly. A punch recipe for 50 servings is unnecessary for a handful of friends. Simply combine the ingredients in a pitcher. For larger groups dig out the crystal punch bowl or your prettiest casserole. Use a wine cooler or any other attractive large container and serve the punch in that.

Punches are often based on a "mother," usually a citrus-flavored sugar syrup mixture. (The sugar-lime mixture mentioned above.) You may prepare this a day or two before to allow the flavors to meld. At serving time, add the sparkling ingredients, soda water, or ginger ale for nonalcoholic punches, and sparkling wine or Champagne for alcoholic versions. The base is called a "mother" because of all the children it can produce.

### Punch Garnishes

Many people like to garnish the punch and forget that the object is to drink it. This writer has always found the addition of melting sherbet less than pleasing. How anyone could consider several flavors and colors of sherbet, melting in a sweet icy mass in a bowl of liquid appealing is truly beyond me. If the sherbet does not melt, then how are you to consume it? Ice rings, on the other hand, are appealing and possibly flavorful.

### To Prepare an Ice Ring

In a ring mold, pour about ½ inch of water and freeze. Add an arrangement of grapes, strawberries, or other small fruits or berries and add about ¼ inch of water and freeze. The object is to freeze the fruits in place. When frozen, fill the mold to the top and freeze completely. When ready to serve, dip the outside of the mold into a bowl of hot water and invert into the punch bowl. Pour the punch over the ice ring.

You may substitute flowers for the fruits if desired. Roses, nasturtiums, and other small flowers work very well. But check with your florist to make sure that the flowers you plan to use are not toxic. Plastic or silk flowers are not acceptable. You can use a tall empty #10 food can as a mold and make a whole bouquet the arrangement for a large block of ice. Some hosts prefer to freeze a complementary juice for the mold so melting water does not dilute the punch.

## TROPICAL PUNCH

½ cup sugar                           2 cups pineapple juice
½ cup lime juice                      1 quart ginger ale
2 cups papaya juice                   1 banana, thinly sliced

In a container, mix the sugar and lime juice until the sugar dissolves. Stir in the papaya and pineapple juices and chill. Just before serving pour the mixture into a punch bowl and add ice and banana slices.

Yield: 12 servings

The base can be prepared 2 days before serving.

## NECTAR OF THE GODS

½ cup sugar                           10 ounces frozen raspber-
¼ cup lime juice                        ries, puréed and strained
¼ cup lemon juice                     1 cup orange juice
2 cups apricot nectar                 1 quart sparkling water
2 cups pear nectar                    1 pint raspberries or small
                                        strawberries

In a container mix the sugar, lime, and lemon juices until the sugar dissolves. Stir in the apricot nectar, pear nectar, raspberry purée, and orange juice. Chill.
Just before serving, pour the mixture into a punch bowl and add the ice and sparkling water. Garnish with the strawberries.

Yield: 12 servings

The base can be prepared 2 days before serving.

---

## SUMMER PUNCH

3 oranges
3 lemons
1 cinnamon stick
2 quarts water
2 cups sugar
1 quart strong tea

1 quart orange juice
1 8-ounce can crushed pine-
    apple
2 quarts ginger ale
2 limes, thinly sliced
2 tablespoons crushed mint

Pare the rind from the oranges and lemons and place in a large
    saucepan with the cinnamon stick and water. Simmer 15 min-
    utes, add the sugar, and stir until the sugar dissolves. Add the
    tea and chill.
Squeeze the juice from the oranges and lemons and add to the tea
    base with the quart of orange juice, cranberry juice, and pine-
    apple. Chill.
Just before serving, pour into a punch bowl and add the ginger
    ale, lime slices, and mint.

Yield: about 50 cups

The base can be prepared 2 days before serving.

---

## CALCUTTA PUNCH

1 quart strong tea
1 cup simple syrup
1 quart orange juice

1 quart apricot nectar
1 quart pineapple juice
2 quarts soda water

In a punch bowl, mix the tea, simple syrup, orange juice, apricot
    nectar, pineapple juice, and soda water. Add a large block
    of ice or 3 trays of ice cubes. Float fruit in the punch if
    desired. Or make an ice ring with strawberries and orange
    slices.

Yield: 50 servings

## VARIATION
Add 1 pint to 1 quart of rum, for an extra lift.

---

# CHAMPAGNE PUNCH I

2 pints apricot brandy          2 quarts ginger ale
1 bottle sauternes               6 bottles of Champagne

Chill all the liquors well.
If desired prepare an ice ring with kiwis, sliced limes, and strawberries.
In a punch bowl, place the ice and pour over the apricot brandy,
   sauternes, ginger ale, and Champagne.

Yield: about 50 servings

---

# CHAMPAGNE PUNCH II

10 oranges                       sugar to taste
1½ teaspoons bitters             5 bottles Champagne
½ cup Cointreau

Squeeze the juice from the oranges. Stir the bitters into the orange
   juice with the Cointreau, and stir in sugar to taste.
If desired make an ice ring with orange slices and mint leaves. Place
   the ring into the punch bowl and pour on the orange mixture.
   Just before serving, add the Champagne.

Yield: 50 servings

---

# ALCOHOLIC BEVERAGES

Although starting the day with spirits is not the norm, brunches
are parties where it is most appropriate. Certain drinks are as much
a part of a brunch as coffee or tea. Bloody Mary's and Screwdrivers

are *de rigeur* at most brunches. The white wine crowd will want their wine, but often enjoy a dash of raspberry or cassis syrup for additional flavor.

It is possible to substitute liquors in drinks. For instance drinks made with "white liquors" like gin, rum, or vodka can be interchanged easily. The same applies with "brown liquors" like Scotch, Irish, bourbon, or rye whiskies. Hence the Gin Orange Blossom becomes the Vodka Screwdriver and the Rye Manhattan becomes the Scotch Rob Roy.

## PRAIRIE OYSTER

Before you serve anything to your guests, a head straightener, stomach settler, or pick-me-up may be in order. The following morning-after recipe has been in the literature for over a hundred years. The author does not attest to its efficacy.

1 egg yolk
1 teaspoon catsup
1 teaspoon Worcestershire
  sauce

¼ teaspoon vinegar
black pepper to taste
dash of cayenne or Tabasco

Slide the yolk into an old fashioned glass without breaking the yolk. Add the catsup, Worcestershire sauce, and vinegar. Season with pepper and cayenne.
Drink down in one gulp without breaking the yolk.

Yield: 1 drink

## ALBEMARLE FIZZ

1 tablespoon lemon juice
½ tablespoon
  confectioners' sugar

1 ounce gin or vodka
6 ounces soda water
1 teaspoon raspberry syrup

In a blender or cocktail shaker, combine the lemon juice, sugar, and gin. Blend well. Pour into an 8 ounce glass, fill with ice cubes and add the soda and raspberry syrup.

Yield: 1 drink

# GIN FIZZ

3 ounces gin
1½ ounces lemon juice

1 teaspoon confectioners'
    sugar
2 ounces soda water

In a blender, or cocktail shaker, combine the gin, lemon juice, and
    sugar. Blend well and pour into a 10-ounce ice-filled glass and
    add the soda.

Yield: 1 drink

## VARIATION

### GOLDEN FIZZ

Add 1 whole egg to the blender in the Gin Fizz recipe and finish
as directed.

Yield: 2 drinks

# ORANGE GIN FIZZ

3 ounces gin
3 ounces orange juice
1½ ounces lemon or lime
    juice

1 teaspoon confectioners'
    sugar
2 ounces soda water

In a blender or cocktail shaker, mix the gin, orange juice, lemon
    or lime juice, and sugar. Blend well. Pour into an ice-filled glass
    and add the soda.

Yield: 1 drink

# BRONX COCKTAIL

1 ounce gin
1 ounce orange juice

½ ounce sweet vermouth
½ ounce dry vermouth

In a blender or cocktail shaker, combine the gin, orange juice,
    sweet vermouth, and dry vermouth. Blend well and pour into
    an 8-ounce glass filled with ice.

Yield: 1 drink


NOTE

This is a strong drink. For brunch you may prefer to increase the orange juice. Some mixers like to add a splash of soda.


## RASPBERRY COCKTAIL

This is a delicious, but potent drink. One, perhaps two per person will be more than sufficient.

1 cup fresh raspberries          8 ounces dry white wine
6 ounces gin                     6 fresh raspberries
½ ounce kirsch

In a bowl, mash the raspberries lightly. Add the gin and let
    macerate for 2 hours. Strain, pressing on the raspberry pulp
    to extract the juices. Put the raspberry juice into a blender
    with the kirsch, wine, and 8 ice cubes. Blend until the ice is
    crushed. Pour into cocktail glasses and top with a raspberry.

Yield: 6 drinks


## RICKEYS

Rickeys, similar to fizzes, are mixed instead of blended.

3 ounces gin, rum, bour-         ½ ounce lemon juice
    bon, or Calvados             soda water
1 ounce lime juice               1 slice lime

In an 8-ounce glass, place 3 ice cubes. Add the liquor, lime juice,
    and lemon juice. Stir well and add soda to fill the glass. Garnish
    with the lime slice.

Yield: 1 drink

# SINGAPORE SLING

3 ounces gin
½ ounce Cherry Heering
½ ounce lemon juice

water or soda water
1 orange slice

Place 2 or 3 ice cubes in an 8-ounce glass. Add the gin, Cherry Heering, and lemon juice. Fill with water or soda water and garnish with the orange slice.

Yield: 1 drink

# DAIQUIRI

3 ounces light rum
¾ ounce lime juice

1 teaspoon confectioners' sugar
1 teaspoon Cointreau

In a blender mix the rum, lime juice, sugar, and Cointreau. Add 1 ice cube and blend until smooth. Pour into a 6-ounce glass.

Yield: 1 drink

## VARIATIONS

### FROZEN DAIQUIRI

Add 1 cup crushed ice to the Daiquiri recipe and blend until mushy.

### FRUIT DAIQUIRI

Add half a fresh peach, half a banana, or ½ cup strawberries to the blender before blending.

# KNICKERBOCKER SPECIAL

2 ounces rum
1 teaspoon Cointreau
1 slice fresh pineapple
1 teaspoon orange juice

1 teaspoon lemon juice
1 teaspoon raspberry syrup
1 pineapple stick

In a blender, mix the rum, Cointreau, pineapple, orange, lemon, and raspberry juice. Add 3 ice cubes and blend well. Pour into an 8-ounce glass and garnish with the pineapple stick.

Yield: 1 drink

---

## PINEAPPLE FIZZ

3 ounces light rum
2 tablespoons minced fresh
   pineapple

1 teaspoon confectioners'
   sugar
3 ounces soda water

In a blender, mix rum, pineapple, and sugar. Blend until almost smooth. Pour into ice-filled 8-ounce glass and add soda water.

Yield: 1 drink

---

## RUM FLIP

3 ounces rum, brandy, port
   or sherry
1 egg

1½ teaspoons
   confectioners' sugar
Nutmeg to taste

In a blender, mix the rum, egg, and sugar. Blend well. Pour into an ice-filled, 8-ounce glass. Sprinkle with the nutmeg.

Yield: 1 drink

---

## SUNSHINE, OR SUNRISE

This drink was originally prepared with rum and called Sunshine. When bartenders started to use tequila, they changed the name to Sunrise.

4 ounces orange juice

2 ounces rum or tequila

In a mixing glass, mix the orange juice and rum, and pour into an ice-filled, 8-ounce glass. Garnish with slice of lime if desired.

Yield: 1 drink

# BLOODY MARY

4 ounces chilled tomato
   juice
3 ounces vodka
2 teaspoons lemon juice

2 drops Worcestershire
   sauce
2 drops Tabasco sauce
black pepper to taste
celery stick, optional

In a large (12-ounce) wine glass, mix tomato juice, vodka, lemon
   juice, Worcestershire and Tabasco sauces, and black pepper.
   Mix well. Add 2 to 3 ice cubes and a celery stick.

Yield: 1 drink

NOTE

You can use lime juice instead of lemon, and substitute gin, rum,
or aquavit for the vodka. I always add ½ teaspoon grated horseradish. Make the mixture in quantities without the liquor and add that
to taste for a large party, or leave it out for those guests who prefer
"Virgin Marys."

# BULL SHOT

4 ounces cold strong beef
   bouillon

3 ounces vodka
salt and pepper to taste

In an ice-filled mixing glass, mix the bouillon and vodka. Season
   with salt and pepper and mix well. Strain into a large stemmed
   wine glass.

Yield: 1 drink

NOTE

The bouillon must be fat free or this will be unsightly and unpleasant.

# SALTY DOG

4 ounces vodka
3 ounces grapefruit juice

¼ teaspoon confectioners'
   sugar

In an ice-filled mixing glass, mix vodka, grapefruit juice, and sugar.
Shake until the sugar has dissolved. Strain into an 8-ounce wine
glass and add an ice cube.

Yield: 1 drink

---

# DE RIGUEUR

2 ounces scotch                    1 ounce honey
1 ounce grapefruit juice

In a blender, mix the scotch, grapefruit juice, and honey. Add 2
ice cubes and blend well. Pour into an old-fashioned glass.

Yield: 1 drink

---

# WHISKEY SOUR

3 ounces whiskey, gin,             1 teaspoon confectioners'
  brandy, rum, or Calvados           sugar
1 ounce lemon juice                1 maraschino cherry
                                   1 slice orange

In a blender, mix the whiskey, lemon juice, sugar, and 3 ice cubes.
Blend until mixed. The ice will be chunky. Strain into a stemmed
glass and add the cherry and orange slice.

Yield: 1 drink

---

# WARD 8

3 ounces bourbon                   soda water
1 ounce lemon juice                1 orange slice
½ ounce grenadine

In a blender, mix the bourbon, lemon juice, grenadine, and 3 ice
cubes. Blend until mixed; the ice will be chunky. Strain into a

large wine glass. Fill with soda water and garnish with orange slice.

Yield: 1 drink

---

# BRANDY ALEXANDER

2 ounces brandy, gin, or vodka

1 ounce crème de cacao
1 ounce heavy cream

In a blender mix the brandy, crème de cacao, cream, and 3 ice cubes. Blend until mixed; the ice will be chunky. Strain into a 6 ounce glass.

Yield: 1 drink.

---

# BREAKFAST EGG NOG

½ cup milk
2 ounces brandy
1 ounce Cointreau

1 egg
1 teaspoon superfine sugar
nutmeg to taste

In a blender, mix the milk, brandy, Cointreau, egg, sugar, and 3 ice cubes. Blend until well mixed: the ice will be chunky. Strain into a large stemmed wine glass. Sprinkle with the nutmeg.

Yield: 1 drink

---

# JACK ROSE

3 ounces applejack
1 ounce lemon juice

½ teaspoon grenadine

In a blender, mix the applejack, lemon juice, grenadine, and 3 ice cubes. Blend until well mixed: the ice will be chunky. Strain into a cocktail glass.

Yield: 1 drink

## MIMOSA OR BUCKS FIZZ

Originally a Bucks Fizz, this has become more commonly known as a Mimosa. Whatever the name, it is a delicious way to get your vitamin C.

2 ounces chilled orange          6 ounces chilled champagne
    juice

Pour the orange juice into a 10-ounce glass and add the champagne.

Yield: 1 drink

## VERMOUTH CASSIS

3 ounces French vermouth          soda water
1 ounce crème de cassis

Fill a 10-ounce glass with ice, pour on the vermouth and cassis. Fill the glass with soda water.

Yield: 1 drink

## KIR

1 teaspoon crème de cassis          6 ounces dry white wine

Pour the cassis into a wine glass and fill with wine.

Yield: 1 drink

## KIR ROYALE

1 teaspoon raspberry li-          6 ounces champagne
    queur

Pour the raspberry liqueur into a champagne glass with champagne.

Yield: 1 drink

# HOT ALCOHOLIC BEVERAGES

---

## HOT BUTTERED RUM

3 ounces rum
1½ teaspoons
    confectioners' sugar
1-inch piece cinnamon stick

1 cup hot milk
1 teaspoon butter
grated nutmeg to taste

Rinse a 12-ounce mug in very hot water and shake dry. Place the rum, sugar, and cinnamon stick in the mug and stir to dissolve the sugar. Add the hot milk and top with butter and sprinkle with nutmeg.

Yield: 1 drink

NOTE
You may substitute water for the milk but the milk provides a more soothing drink.

---

## IRISH COFFEE

There are many variations on the theme of coffee combined with a liquor, topped with whipped cream. Feel free to substitute your favorite liquor to create your "International" coffee.

1 teaspoon sugar
5 ounces strong hot coffee

1½ ounces Irish whiskey
2 tablespoons whipped
    cream

Rinse an 8-ounce stemmed goblet in very hot water. Shake dry. Place the sugar in the glass and add the coffee and whiskey. Stir to dissolve the sugar. Top with whipped cream.

Yield: 1 drink

# HOT TODDY

3 ounces rye, bourbon,
  rum, or brandy
1 strip lemon peel
1 whole clove

3-inch piece cinnamon stick
sugar to taste
boiling water

Rinse an 8-ounce glass in very hot water. Shake dry. Place the
  whiskey, lemon peel stuck with the clove, cinnamon stick, and
  sugar in the glass. Fill the glass with the boiling water.

Yield: 1 drink

NOTE

Substitute dark rum to make grog.

# VIN CHAUD (GLUHWEIN)

1 slice lemon
2 cloves
2 tablespoons sugar

1 cinnamon stick
1 cup red wine

Stud the lemon slice with the cloves. In a saucepan, mix the sugar
  and cinnamon stick and cook over moderate heat, stirring until
  the sugar melts. Add the wine and bring just to a boil.
Strain into a heated mug and serve garnished with the lemon slice.

Yield: 1 drink

# Biscuits, Doughnuts, Muffins, and Other Quick Breads

$A$ doughnut and coffee to start the day is an old American tradition, that has lost some, but certainly not all, of its appeal. We may not have doughnuts every day, but all those doughnut shops around the country show that we still eat them—a lot of them. Even those shops have found that there is a need to have a breakfast or snack bread with less fat, and have begun to serve muffins regularly. And biscuits have long been a staple for a quickly prepared bread. In addition, there are dozens, if not hundreds, of recipes for banana, date, orange, and other fruit-flavored breads made without yeast.

Quick breads assemble quickly and some bake almost as quickly, unlike yeast breads that can take several hours of rising before they are ready to bake. Doughnuts, muffins, and biscuits are all ready for baking within a very few minutes. They can literally be prepared and served within a half hour, or less. Other so-called quick breads have a greater resemblance to bread and though they assemble quickly, the cooking time can be an hour or longer.

The advantage to these breads is that because they are often fruit-based, they will keep longer at room temperature. Doughnuts, muffins, and biscuits start to lose quality immediately after baking. Within an hour doughnuts and biscuits are still edible but not even close to their quality when first cooked. Muffins, on the other hand, will last several hours, but although edible the next day, they are far less appetizing. Quick breads made with fruits often improve in texture and flavor if made the previous day. If you are having a large crowd, you can make doughnuts, muffins, and biscuits ahead and freeze them when they reach room temperature. (Like all breads, they freeze well.) Reheat them in a microwave oven for about 30 seconds and they will be almost as good as if fresh out of the oven.

With a little careful planning you can serve freshly made quick breads whenever you want. Measure the ingredients the night before and assemble them on the counter in the order needed. Prepare the baking pans. The next morning they can be ready almost before the coffee has finished brewing.

## BISCUITS

Biscuits are both the easiest and most difficult of breads to prepare. Rub a fat into some flour, add a small amount of liquid, and shape. Bake for a few minutes and they are done. Still, if you are not careful you will have bullets instead of featherlight breads. The secret is to work quickly and lightly. Unlike most yeast breads, where diligent kneading will produce a finer texture, with biscuits kneading makes them tougher. For perfect biscuits follow these guidelines:

- Preheat the oven. It must be hot to give the proper push to the dough.

- Do not be too concerned if some fat pieces are a little larger than others.

- Do not be too concerned if the dough is not evenly moist.

- Most important, do not try to shape the uncut dough too smoothly. Overworking the dough toughens it. It is better to knead the dough no more than 8 to 10 times to create a relatively cohesive dough, and then pat that into the desired thickness.

- Cut the biscuits as close together as possible and rework the scraps as little and as lightly as possible. Some cooks prefer to pat the dough into a square about an inch to an inch and half thick and cut it into 2-inch squares or diamonds, instead of rounds. Bake immediately.

## BAKING POWDER BISCUITS

| | |
|---|---|
| 2 cups flour | ½ cup butter |
| 2 teaspoons baking powder | ⅔ cup milk |
| 1 teaspoon salt | |

Preheat the oven to 450° F. Butter a baking sheet. In a bowl, or the bowl of a food processor, mix the flour, baking powder, and salt.

With your fingertips, a pastry blender or in a processor, cut the butter into the flour until it forms coarse meal. With a fork, or quick on/off turns of the processor, add the milk and mix to form a soft, slightly damp dough.

Turn onto a lightly floured surface and knead by pushing and pressing the dough onto itself about 6 to 8 times. Do not try to make it too smooth.

Pat into a cake ½ inch thick. It can be square or round. Cut into 2-inch round or square biscuits and place on the prepared baking sheet.

Bake for 15 to 20 minutes until they are puffed and light golden brown.

Yield: 24 biscuits

## VARIATIONS

You can flavor the basic biscuit with other ingredients and shape it differently. Try making diamonds or crescents for a change. To make crescents, use the round cutter and cut half way into the dough. Make the next cut halfway above that and the shape will be a crescent.

## CINNAMON ROLLS

Add 1 tablespoon of sugar, 1 teaspoon cinnamon, ¼ teaspoon nutmeg, and a pinch of ground cloves to the dry ingredients. Make the dough and turn onto a lightly floured board. Roll into a rectangle ¼ inch thick. Dust the surface with ½ cup softened butter. In a bowl, mix 4 tablespoons sugar, 1 teaspoon cinnamon, and ¼ teaspoon nutmeg. Sprinkle over the buttered pastry. Roll from the long side into a jelly roll and cut into 1 inch thick slices. Place, cut side down on a buttered baking sheet. The rolls should just barely touch on the baking sheet. Bake at 375°F for 25 to 30 minutes or until golden.

## VARIATION

Add 1 cup chopped walnuts, pecans, and/or raisins to the pastry before rolling.

## HERBED BISCUITS

Add ½ cup minced parsley, chives, thyme, and/or dill to the dry ingredients.

## ONION ROSEMARY BISCUITS

In a large skillet, heat 3 tablespoons bacon drippings over low heat, add 2 cups minced onion, 1½ teaspoons rosemary, ¾ teaspoon pepper, and ¼ teaspoon salt. Cook until the onion is tender, stirring for about 8 minutes. Cool. Set aside ¼ cup onion mixture and stir the remainder into the milk and add to the flour. Dab biscuits with remaining onion just before baking.

## CHEESE BISCUITS I

Add 1 cup grated Parmesan or cheddar cheese to the dry ingredients.

## CHEESE BISCUITS II

1 cup sifted flour
½ cup whole wheat flour
½ cup rye flour
1 tablespoon sugar
1 tablespoon baking powder
¾ teaspoon ground cumin
   seeds
½ teaspoon salt
⅛ teaspoon cayenne pepper

6 tablespoons butter
1½ cups grated Gruyère or
   Havarti cheese
⅓ cup minced parsley
¾ cup milk
1 egg blended with 1 tablespoon cream
poppy seeds

Preheat the oven to 450°F. Butter a baking sheet.

In a bowl, or a food processor, mix the flour, whole wheat flour, rye flour, sugar, baking soda, cumin, salt, and cayenne pepper together. With your fingertips, a pastry blender or a processor, cut the butter into the flour mixture until it resembles coarse meal. Add the milk and stir until evenly moistened.

Turn onto a lightly floured board and knead about 8 to 10 times. Pat into a ½ inch thick square and cut into 1½ inch squares. Arrange on baking sheet about ½ inch apart. Brush with the egg-cream glaze and sprinkle with poppy seeds.

Bake until light brown about 12 to 16 minutes.

Yield: about 24 biscuits

## BASIL CREAM BISCUITS

Cream is often used to replace the butter and milk in a recipe. These are particularly delicious.

2 cups flour
¼ cup minced fresh basil
1 tablespoon baking powder
1 teaspoon salt

1 teaspoon cracked black
   pepper
1 to 1½ cups heavy cream
⅓ cup butter, melted

Preheat the oven to 425°F.

In a bowl, or a food processor, mix the flour, basil, baking powder, salt, and pepper.

Slowly stir in 1 cup of cream and add more cream if required to make a dough that gathers into a ball. Do not overwork. If using a processor, use on/off turns to make the dough. Do not work to a smooth ball on top of the blade.

Turn onto a lightly floured board and pat the dough into a ½-inch thick square and cut into 16 squares. Dip each square into melted butter, coating completely. Transfer to an ungreased baking sheet about 1 inch apart.

Bake until lightly browned, about 12 to 16 minutes. Serve immediately.

Yield: 16 biscuits

---

# BUTTERMILK CHIVE BISCUITS

Buttermilk gives biscuits a slight tang. These are delicious even without the chives.

| | |
|---|---|
| 3 cups sifted flour | ½ teaspoon baking soda |
| 2 tablespoons baking pow-<br>der | 2 tablespoons minced chives |
| | 1 cup butter |
| 1 tablespoon sugar | ¾ cup buttermilk |

Preheat the oven to 400°F.

Butter a baking sheet.

In a bowl, or a food processor, mix the flour, baking powder, sugar, baking soda, and chives.

With your fingertips, a pastry blender or a processor with on/off turns, cut in the butter until the mixture resembles coarse meal. Stir in the buttermilk to make a soft dough. Use on/off turns of a processor until just moistened.

Turn onto a lightly floured board and knead 6 to 8 times and place on the baking sheet. Pat into an 8 by 12 inch rectangle. Cut into 2 inch squares, but do not separate.

Bake for about 20 minutes or until risen and golden. Serve immediately.

Yield: 24 biscuits

# SCONES

These are a first cousin to biscuits and made in much the same way.

# GRIDDLE SCONES

Griddle scones are a cross between a biscuit and a pancake and are truly delicious. When you want to start the day with a hot quickly made bread, put these at the top of the list.

2 cups flour
1 teaspoon baking soda
½ teaspoon cream of tartar
½ teaspoon sugar

¼ teaspoon salt
¼ cup butter
1¼ cups buttermilk
1 large egg

In a bowl, mix the flour, soda, cream of tartar, sugar, and salt.

Work in the butter to make the consistency of coarse meal. Add the buttermilk and egg and mix into a soft dough.

Heat a well-seasoned or lightly-greased griddle or heavy skillet. Drop the dough by heaping tablespoons to make 3–4 scones. Spread with the back of a spoon to flatten.

When golden on one side, turn and cook the other until golden and the center seems firm to the touch.

Remove and keep warm while cooking the remainder. Serve plain with butter or jam.

Yield: 24 rolls

# CURRANT SCONES

2½ cups flour
6 tablespoons sugar
1½ teaspoons baking pow-
    der
¼ teaspoon salt
¾ cup chilled butter cut
    into pieces

1⅓ cups dried currants
½ cup buttermilk
6 tablespoons heavy cream
½ teaspoon baking soda
1 egg beaten with 2 table-
    spoons cream

Preheat the oven to 325°F.

Butter 2 baking sheets

In a processor, or by hand, blend flour, sugar, baking powder, baking soda, and salt. Add butter and process until the size of small peas.

Add currants and with machine running add buttermilk and heavy

cream and process just until the dough gathers together. Or, stir
the liquids in by hand.

Place on sheet of waxed paper cover with another sheet and roll
¾ inch thick. Cut into 2 inch rounds. Reroll scraps. Arrange on
baking sheets, 2 inches apart.

Brush with egg cream glaze and bake until tops are lightly
browned, about 25 minutes.

Yield: about 30 rolls

---

# SAFFRON SCONES

⅛ teaspoon saffron threads
½ cup milk
1 egg
2 cups flour
½ cup sugar

1 tablespoon baking powder
¼ teaspoon salt
1½ sticks butter
⅓ cup currants

Preheat the oven to 425°F.

With your fingertips, crush the saffron into a small bowl and add
the milk and egg. Mix to blend.

In a large bowl combine the flour, sugar, baking powder, and salt.
Cut 1 stick butter into the flour mixture until it resembles coarse
meal. Stir in the currants.

In a small saucepan, melt 4 tablespoons butter and cool. Pour
the saffron mixture into the flour and quickly stir into a
dough.

The dough will be wet and sticky. On a well floured board pat the
dough into an 8-inch square, ½ inch thick. Cut into 4 squares
and cut each square into a diagonal. Arrange on a baking sheet,
1 inch apart and brush with melted butter.

Bake in upper third of the oven for 13 minutes or until lightly
browned.

Yield: 16 rolls

# DOUGHNUTS

There are two types of doughnuts: those made quickly with baking
powder as the leavening, and those made with yeast. Yeast dough-

nuts take several hours to rise. This chapter includes both types, though other yeast breads are in a separate chapter.

Baking powder doughnuts like other quick breads are best when served immediately after cooking. Yeast doughnuts remain fresher longer, but still are at their best within minutes of cooking. If you choose to make baking powder doughnuts ahead, freeze immediately and reheat in a 350°F oven for about 5 minutes, or in a microwave oven for about 30 seconds so they are warm when served.

Baking powder doughnuts, like biscuits, require careful handling. Too much, or too firm handling will produce a tough product.

# PLAIN DOUGHNUTS

Remember to handle the dough very lightly and knead as little as possible.

| | |
|---|---|
| 4 cups flour | 2 eggs |
| 1 cup sugar | 1 egg yolk |
| 1 tablespoon baking powder | 1 cup milk |
| ½ teaspoon ground cinnamon | ¼ cup melted butter |
| ½ teaspoon salt | oil for deep frying |

Preheat the fat in a large skillet to 375°F. In a bowl, combine the flour, sugar, baking powder, cinnamon, and salt.

In a small bowl, beat the eggs, egg yolk, and milk until blended. Gently stir the liquid ingredients into the dry, with the melted butter. Mix until just moistened. Turn onto a well floured board and pat into a flat cake.

Roll gently to a 1 inch thickness. Cut with a floured doughnut cutter. Cut the scraps into 1 inch balls. (It is best not to reroll the dough.) Cook the small pieces separately.

Fry the doughnuts until golden on one side, turn and fry the second side. Drain on paper toweling.

Yield: 18 doughnuts

Once fried, serve within an hour or freeze until ready to serve.

NOTE

The dough is very soft and can easily be patted into shape without using a rolling pin.

VARIATIONS

Flavor the doughnuts by rolling the fried doughnuts in sugar or cinnamon sugar, frosting with confectioners' sugar and water mixed to desired thickness, dip in a glaze made with a thin mixture of confectioners' sugar and water.

CRULLERS

Pat the dough into ¼ to ½ inch thickness, and cut into strips about 1 inch wide and 8 inches long. Fold in half and twist the ends to make a spiral. Fry as for doughnuts.

# OLLIE BOLLEN OR OLYKOEK (DUTCH, FRUIT-FILLED DOUGHNUTS)

These are made with yeast so do not be afraid to knead diligently. Unlike the plain doughnuts, which would get tough, these will have a finer texture.

| | |
|---|---|
| 1 cup milk, scalded | 3½ cups sifted flour |
| 1 teaspoon salt | brandied raisins or orange |
| ¼ cup sugar | currant filling, see below |
| 3 tablespoons butter | oil for frying |
| 1 package dry yeast | confectioners' sugar |
| 1 egg, well beaten | |

In a mixing bowl, mix the milk, salt, sugar, and 1 tablespoon of butter. Sprinkle on the yeast and let it proof for 10 minutes. Stir in the egg, remaining butter, and 1½ cups flour to make a stiff batter. Beat well. Gradually stir in the remaining flour.

Turn onto a floured board and knead until smooth and elastic, about 8 to 10 minutes. Add more flour if needed.

Place the dough in a buttered bowl and cover with a sheet of plastic wrap and a towel. Set in a draft-free place and let rise until doubled in bulk, about 2 to 3 hours. Punch down and knead for 2 minutes.

Cut off small pieces of dough about 2 tablespoons in size. Shape into balls and poke a dent in the center of each. Put ¼ to ½ teaspoon of brandied raisins in each hole and pinch the edges together to enclose the raisins. (If desired, you can knead all the fruit into all the dough and shape into small balls.)

Let the balls rise on a lightly floured tray until doubled in bulk, about 20 to 30 minutes.

Heat the oil to 375°F. Fry the balls until golden, turning to brown all sides, about 3 minutes. Drain on paper toweling and roll in confectioners' sugar while still warm. Serve within 2 hours, or freeze for future use.

Yield: about 36 doughnuts

## BRANDIED RAISINS

Soak 1 cup raisins in just enough brandy to cover, for 24 hours. Use them as a dessert topping or as a filling in coffee cakes also. They keep up to 4 months.

## ORANGE CURRANT FILLING

In a bowl, mix ½ cup chopped currants, ¼ cup chopped raisins, ¼ cup chopped candied orange peel, and 2 tablespoons grated lemon peel.

# YEAST-RAISED DOUGHNUTS

Remember that yeast doughs get better with kneading, unlike quick bread doughs which become tough.

| | |
|---|---|
| 2 packages dry yeast | 2 egg yolks |
| 2 tablespoons sugar | 1 teaspoon grated lemon |
| 1 teaspoon salt | rind |
| 1 cup warm milk | ¼ cup soft butter |
| 1 egg | oil for frying |
| 3 to 4 cups flour | |

In a bowl, sprinkle the yeast over ¼ cup warm water. Add the sugar and salt, cover and proof for 10 minutes. Stir in the milk, egg, egg yolks, and lemon rind and mix well. Add enough flour to make a medium-firm dough. Work in the soft butter. Knead the dough until smooth and elastic. (This can be done in a food processor if preferred.)

Place the kneaded dough in a large bowl, dust lightly with flour, and cover the bowl with plastic wrap and a dish towel. Set in a draft free place until doubled in bulk, about one hour. Punch down, cover and let rise a second time, about 45 minutes. Punch the dough down and divide into 36 pieces.

Shape the dough as desired, see below. Place on a floured sheet and let rise until doubled in bulk, about 20 to 30 minutes.

Heat the oil to 375°F. Fry a few pieces at a time until golden on one side, turn and fry the second side. Remove from the fat and drain on paper toweling.

Yield: 36 doughnuts

Serve within a few hours for the best flavor, or freeze for future use.

## SHAPING

### JELLY DOUGHNUTS

Roll each piece into a ball and let rise. Once cooked and cooled, use a long-nosed pastry tube (called a Bismarck tube), inserted into the center, to fill with a jelly of your choice. Roll in granulated sugar.

### NUGGETS

Cut the pieces in half and roll into small balls. Fry and roll in sugar before serving.

### RAISED DOUGHNUTS

Spread the dough onto a floured board and pat to about ¼ inch thick. With a doughnut cutter, cut into doughnuts. Let rise until doubled in bulk and fry. Drain on paper towels and serve.

### GLAZED DOUGHNUTS

Make a thin icing of water and confectioners' sugar and dip each doughnut into the icing. Place on a rack and let dry for an hour to set the coating. If desired, roll the glazed doughnuts in chopped nuts, coconut, or chocolate sprinkles.

# MUFFINS

In recent years muffins have become a most popular breakfast bread. You can vary the recipes to suit your particular wishes. Substitute some whole wheat flour for white flour, add nuts, raisins, vegetable purées like pumpkin or grated carrots to make a muffin of your choice. The original, cupcake-like version with added fruit has become the second choice in today's search for the most pleasing and often healthful muffin. You can bake muffin mixtures in loaf pans to serve as quickbreads, if desired.

---

## BASIC BERRY MUFFINS

2 cups sifted flour
1 tablespoon baking powder
3 tablespoons sugar
½ teaspoon salt
1 egg, beaten

1 cup milk
3 tablespoons melted butter
1 cup berries (see note)
½ cup flour

Preheat the oven to 400°F.
Butter 12 2½-inch muffin cups.
In a bowl, mix the flour, baking powder, sugar, and salt. Beat in the egg, milk, and butter until well blended. Do not overbeat.
Toss the fruit with the flour and fold into the batter. Fill the muffin cups ⅔ full.
Bake 20 to 30 minutes or until golden and a skewer inserted in the center comes out clean. Remove from the oven, let stand 5 minutes then unmold. Serve warm.

Yield: 12 muffins

Can be frozen after baking.

NOTE

Select any berry such as blueberries, strawberries, or raspberries. Or use pitted cherries or cut up fruit such as apples, pears, or bananas, or use nuts. Season the batter with a teaspoon of cinnamon or ¼ teaspoon of nutmeg.

## SOUR CREAM POPPY SEED MUFFINS

2 cups flour
¼ cup poppy seeds
¼ teaspoon salt
¼ teaspoon baking soda
½ cup butter

¾ cup sugar
2 eggs
¾ cup sour cream
1½ teaspoons vanilla

Preheat the oven to 375°F.

Butter 12 2½-inch muffin cups.

In a bowl, mix the flour, poppy seeds, salt, and baking soda. Cream the butter and sugar until thick and light. Beat in the eggs, one at a time.

Blend in the sour cream and vanilla and fold in the dry ingredients. Spoon into prepared tin and bake until they test done, about 20 minutes. Cool in tin for 5 minutes. Remove and cool.

Yield: 12 muffins

Can be frozen.

## CARROT MUFFINS

½ cup raisins
2 cups flour
1 cup sugar
2 teaspoons baking soda
2 teaspoons cinnamon
½ teaspoon salt
2 cups grated carrots

1 green apple, grated
½ cup chopped pecans
½ cup shredded coconut
3 eggs
½ cup vegetable oil
2 teaspoons vanilla

Preheat the oven to 350°F.

Butter 16 2½-inch muffin cups.

Soak raisins in hot water for 30 minutes and drain.

In a bowl, mix flour, sugar, baking soda, cinnamon, salt, raisins, carrots, apple, almonds, and coconut.

In another bowl, beat the egg with the oil and vanilla to blend. Stir into the flour mixture until just combined. Divide among the muffins cups.

Bake until muffins are golden brown and they test down, about 20 to 22 minutes. Cool 5 minutes. Remove from pans.

Yield: 16 muffins

Can be frozen.

---

# LEMON MUFFINS

1¾ cups flour
¾ cup sugar
1 tablespoons grated lemon rind
1 teaspoon baking powder
¾ teaspoon baking soda
¼ teaspoon salt
1 cup yogurt or sour cream

6 tablespoons melted butter, cooled
1 egg
1 tablespoon lemon juice
⅓ cup lemon juice
¼ cup sugar
2 teaspoons grated lemon rind

Preheat the oven to 400°F.
Line 12 muffin cups with liners.
In a bowl mix the flour, sugar, lemon peel, baking powder, baking soda, and salt.
In another bowl mix the yogurt, butter, egg, and lemon juice. Stir into the dry ingredients and turn into muffin cups.
Bake until golden, about 20 minutes. Cool in pans for 5 minutes.
In a small saucepan prepare a glaze by combining the lemon juice, sugar, and lemon peel, and heat until the sugar is dissolved.
Remove muffins from pan and place on a rack and pierce the tops with a skewer. Drizzle glaze over each muffin and cool.

Yield: 12 muffins

Can be frozen.

---

# PUMPKIN WALNUT MUFFINS

2 eggs
½ cup dark brown sugar
¼ teaspoon cinnamon
¼ teaspoon grated nutmeg
¾ cup pumpkin purée

3 tablespoons melted butter
1½ cups flour
1½ teaspoons baking powder
¾ cup chopped walnuts

Preheat the oven to 400°F.

Butter 12 2½-inch muffin cups.

Break eggs into a bowl and beat lightly. Add the sugar and stir. Add the cinnamon, nutmeg, pumpkin, and butter. Blend well.

Mix flour and baking powder and beat into the egg mixture. Fold in the walnuts.

Pour into muffin tin and bake for 20 to 25 minutes.

Yield: 12 muffins

Can be frozen.

NOTE

For enriched flavor, toast the walnuts.

---

# BASIC BRAN MUFFINS

2 tablespoons butter
¼ cup sugar
1 egg, beaten
1 cup bran

¾ cup milk
1 cup flour
2½ teaspoons baking pow-
   der
Pinch of salt

Preheat the oven to 400°F.

Butter 12 2½-inch muffin cups.

In a bowl, cream the butter and sugar until light and fluffy. Beat in the egg until well mixed. The mixture will look curdled. Combine the bran and milk and stir in the egg mixture.

In a bowl, mix the flour, baking powder, and salt and stir into the liquid ingredients until just moistened. Do not overbeat. Fill muffin cups ⅔ full.

Bake 25 to 30 minutes or until the muffins are brown and pull away from the sides of the pan. Serve warm.

Yield: 12 muffins

Can be frozen and reheated.

## VARIATIONS

### BANANA BRAN MUFFINS

Fold 3 diced bananas into the mixture with the dry ingredients.

### BERRY BRAN MUFFINS

Fold ½ cup blueberries, cherries, raspberries, or other berry into the mixture with the dry ingredients.

### RAISIN BRAN MUFFINS

Substitute dark brown sugar for the white sugar and stir in ¾ cup seedless raisins. Add nuts if desired.

### DATE BRAN MUFFINS

Add 1 cup chopped dates and ⅓ cup currants to the ½ cup flour and fold into the batter at the end.

### MAPLE PECAN MUFFINS

Substitute ½ cup dark brown sugar for the white and ¼ cup maple syrup for ¼ cup milk. Add a pinch of allspice and 1¾ cups broken toasted pecans to the dry ingredients.

---

# MOUNTAIN TRAIL BRAN MUFFINS

These muffins are high in sugar and fats, just what you need when scaling the Matterhorn.

| | |
|---|---|
| ½ cup oil | 1 teaspoon baking soda |
| 1 cup brown sugar | ½ teaspoon salt |
| 1 egg | ¼ teaspoon cinnamon |
| 2 tablespoons molasses | ¼ teaspoon nutmeg |
| 1½ cups flour | ⅛ teaspoon cloves |
| ½ cup wheat germ | 1½ cups bran |
| ¼ cup sesame seeds | ½ cup raisins |
| ¼ cup chopped walnuts | 1 cup buttermilk |

Preheat the oven to 400°F.

Butter 12 2½-inch muffin cups

In a bowl beat the oil, sugar, egg, and molasses together. Add the flour, wheat germ, sesame seeds, walnuts, soda, salt, cinnamon, nutmeg, cloves, bran, raisins, and buttermilk until just blended.

Place in muffin cups and bake for 25 to 30 minutes.

Yield: 12 muffins

## SOUR CREAM BRAN MUFFINS WITH RAISINS

1 cup butter
1 cup dark brown sugar
½ cup molasses
3 eggs
2½ cups flour

1 tablespoon plus 1 tea-
   spoon baking soda
½ teaspoon salt
2½ cups bran flakes
2½ cups sour cream
1¼ cups raisins

Preheat the oven to 375°F.

Butter 24 2½-inch muffin tins.

In an electric mixer, cream the butter and sugar until light and
   fluffy. Add the molasses a little at a time, beating thoroughly so
   the batter is smooth. Add the eggs, one by one until incorporated.

Sift together the flour, baking soda, and salt. Add to the batter
   alternately with the bran and sour cream, ending with the flour.
   Remove beaters and fold in the raisins.

Divide among the muffin cups. Bake for 24 to 30 minutes or until
   puffed and firm. Let cool in the cups and unmold.

Yield: 24 muffins

## BASIC CORN MUFFINS

1 cup yellow cornmeal
1 cup sifted flour
¼ cup sugar, optional
½ teaspoon salt

4 teaspoons baking powder
1 egg, lightly beaten
1 cup milk
¼ cup melted butter, or oil

Preheat the oven to 375°F.

Butter 12 2½-inch muffin cups.

In a bowl, mix the cornmeal, flour, sugar, salt, and baking powder.
   Mix in the egg, milk, and butter to moisten the ingredients. Do
   not overbeat. Turn into the prepared pan.

Bake for 15 minutes or until golden and they test done. Let cool
   5 minutes. Unmold and serve warm.

Yield: 12 muffins

Can be frozen.

## VARIATIONS

### CORNBREAD

Pour the batter into an 8-inch square pan and bake for 30 minutes.

### DOUBLE CORN MUFFINS OR BREAD

Add 1 cup kernel corn to the batter with the milk.

### CHEESE MUFFINS OR CORNBREAD

Add 1½ cups grated cheddar cheese to the dry ingredients.

### HERBED MUFFINS OR CORNBREAD

Add 1 teaspoon dried oregano and 1 teaspoon dried basil to the dry ingredients. Or add 1 tablespoon minced dill to the batter.

---

# APPLE CORN MUFFINS

2 cups flour
½ cup cornmeal
⅓ cup brown sugar
1 tablespoon baking powder
½ teaspoon salt

1 cup milk
1 egg, lightly beaten
4 tablespoons butter, melted
1 apple, peeled, chopped

Preheat the oven to 425°F.
Lightly butter 12 2½-inch muffin cups.
In a bowl, blend the flour, cornmeal, sugar, baking powder, and
    salt. In another bowl combine the milk, egg, and butter. Add
    the milk and apple to the flour mixture and fold until
    combined.
Fill cups and bake 30 minutes or until the tops are golden.

Yield: 12 muffins

---

# CORN MUFFINS WITH SPICED HAM

¾ cup sour cream
2 tablespoon oil
¾ cup corn kernels

1½ ounces Tasso or other
    spicy ham, diced
¼ red pepper, chopped

1½ teaspoons minced cori-
ander
2 eggs
¾ cup cornmeal
3 tablespoons flour

2¼ teaspoons baking pow-
der
¼ teaspoon cayenne pepper
½ teaspoon salt
2 teaspoons sugar

Preheat the oven to 400°F.
Butter 12 2½-inch muffin cups.
In a bowl, combine the sour cream, oil, corn, ham, pepper, and
coriander. Beat in the eggs.
In another bowl mix the cornmeal, flour, baking powder, cayenne,
salt, and sugar. Add to the sour cream mixture and stir to
combine.
Pour into prepared tins and bake until golden, abut 20 minutes.
Cool 5 minutes before unmolding.

Yield: 12 muffins

Can be frozen.

## QUICKBREADS

These can be sweet or savory. The composition is very similar to
muffins, except that the batter is baked in a single pan. Most muffin
recipes can be prepared as breads and vice versa. The baking time
will be the difference. Muffins take from 12 to 25 minutes as a rule
and breads from 40 to 60 minutes. When done, a skewer inserted
into the center should come out dry.

## ANCHOVY MOZZARELLA BREAD

2⅔ cups flour
4 teaspoons baking powder
½ teaspoon salt
4 ounces anchovies,
drained and diced

6 ounces grated mozzarella
cheese
2 eggs
1 cup milk
2 tablespoons sugar

Preheat the oven to 350°F.
Butter a 9 × 5 × 3-inch loaf pan.
In a bowl, combine the flour, baking powder, and salt. Mix well.

Add the anchovies and mozzarella and mix well. Make a well in the center of the dry ingredients and beat in the eggs, milk, and sugar. Mix the dough until all ingredients are well moistened. Do not overbeat.

Pour into the prepared pan and bake for 1 hour. Cool to room temperature before serving.

Yield: 1 loaf

Can be frozen.

---

# SALAMI CHEESE LOAF

3 cups flour
2 tablespoon sugar
1½ tablespoons baking powder
1½ teaspoons salt
1 teaspoon fennel seeds
¼ teaspoon baking soda

3 tablespoons grated Parmesan cheese
11 ounces cream cheese,
   softened
1 cup milk
2 eggs, lightly beaten
¼ cup oil
1 cup diced Genoa salami

Preheat the oven to 375°F.

Butter a 9 × 5 × 3-inch loaf pan.

In a large bowl, mix the flour, sugar, baking powder, salt, fennel seeds, baking soda, and Parmesan together. In a mixer or processor cream the cream cheese until smooth and gradually beat in the milk to make a smooth mixture. Add the eggs and oil.

Stir into the dry ingredients and fold in the salami until well moistened. Do not overbeat.

Pour into the pan and bake 1 hour or until it tests done. Cool in the pan for 5 minutes. Serve warm.

Yield: 1 loaf

Can be frozen.

NOTE

Use cold, thinly sliced, for sandwiches.

## OATMEAL RAISIN BREAD

1½ cups whole wheat flour
1½ cups rolled oats
1½ cups buttermilk
1¼ cups raisins

¾ cup firmly packed light
    brown sugar
2 eggs, lightly beaten
2 teaspoons baking soda
2 teaspoons baking powder

Preheat the oven to 350°F.
Butter a 9 × 5 × 3-inch loaf pan.
In a bowl, mix the flour, oats, buttermilk, raisins, sugar, eggs,
    baking soda, and baking powder, until fully moistened. Do not
    overbeat.
Turn into the loaf pan and bake 1 hour or until it tests done. Cool
    in the pan for 4 minutes. Unmold onto a wire rack and cool.

Yield: 1 loaf

Can be frozen.

## BOURBON PECAN BREAD

½ cup butter
½ cup dark brown sugar
2 eggs
2½ teaspoons baking powder
2 cups flour

salt to taste
½ cup maple syrup
½ cup bourbon
1½ cups chopped pecans
confectioners' sugar

Preheat the oven to 350°F.
Butter a 9-inch tube pan.
In a mixer, or processor, cream the butter and sugar. Add the eggs
    until combined.
In another bowl, mix the baking powder, flour, and salt. Beat into
    the creamed butter alternately with maple syrup and the bour-
    bon. Fold in the pecans.
Turn into the pan and bake for 45 to 50 minutes or until it tests
    done. Cool in the pan for 10 minutes. Unmold and let cool
    completely. Serve sprinkled with confectioners' sugar.

Yield: 1 large cake

Can be frozen.

# LEMON NUT BREAD

1½ cups flour
1 teaspoon baking powder
2 eggs, lightly beaten
¼ pound melted butter
1 cup sugar

salt
½ cup chopped walnuts
grated zest of 1 lemon
juice of 1 large lemon
⅓ cup sugar

Preheat the oven to 350°F.
Butter an 8½ × 4½ × 2½-inch loaf pan.
In a bowl, combine the flour and baking powder and mix well. Add the eggs, butter, 1 cup sugar, salt, nuts, and lemon zest and beat together. Turn into the pan and bake for 50 minutes or until it tests done. Meanwhile in a small bowl, mix the lemon juice and ⅓ cup sugar until the sugar dissolves.
Let the bread cool in pan 5 minutes. Then pour the glaze over the top. Let cool 10 minutes longer and unmold.

Yield: 1 loaf

Can be frozen.

# ORANGE TEA BREAD

½ cup plus 1 teaspoon butter
¾ cup sugar
1 egg, lightly beaten
3 cups flour

1 tablespoon baking powder
1 cup milk
grated rind of 2 oranges

Preheat the oven to 350°F.
Butter a 9 × 5 × 3-inch loaf pan.
In a bowl, cream the butter and sugar until light and fluffy. Beat in the egg.
In a bowl, mix the flour and baking powder and beat into the butter mixture alternately with the milk. Stir in the orange rind.

Turn into the prepared pan and bake for 50 minutes or until it
   tests done.

Yield: 1 loaf

Can be frozen.

## SPICED COFFEE CAKE

| | |
|---|---|
| 2 eggs | ¼ teaspoon ground carda- |
| 1 cup sugar | mom |
| ½ cup butter | Pinch of salt |
| ½ cup heavy cream | 1¼ cups flour |
| ½ teaspoon cinnamon | 2 tablespoons |
| ½ teaspoon baking soda | confectioners' sugar |

Preheat the oven to 350°F.
Butter an 8-inch springform pan and set aside.
In a food processor, blend eggs and sugar 1 minute. Add the butter
   and blend 1 minute. With machine running, pour in the cream
   and mix 10 seconds. Add the cinnamon, baking soda, cardamom, salt, and flour. Incorporate with 3 or 4 turns.
Pour into the pan and bake about 40 minutes, or until it tests done.
   Let cool in the pan for 5 minutes and unmold. Sift the
   confectioners' sugar over the top.

Yield: 6 servings

Can be frozen.

## TOASTED COCONUT BREAD

Coconut for breakfast? Yes, try it. This is a wonderful bread.

| | |
|---|---|
| 1 cup grated unsweetened | ½ teaspoon salt |
| coconut | 1 cup milk |
| 2 cups flour | ¼ cup vegetable oil |
| ¾ cup sugar | 1 egg, well beaten |
| 1 tablespoons baking pow- | 1 teaspoon vanilla |
| der | |

Preheat the oven to 350°F.

Butter and flour a 9 × 5 × 3-inch loaf pan.

Spread the coconut on a baking sheet and bake until lightly browned, about 3 to 5 minutes. Transfer to a bowl.

In a large bowl, combine the flour, sugar, baking powder, salt, and coconut. Mix in the milk, oil, egg, and vanilla and stir until blended.

Pour into the pan and bake until golden, about 55 to 60 minutes. Cool in the pan for 5 minutes and unmold. Let cool before slicing.

Yield: 1 loaf

Can be frozen.

---

# BLUEBERRY BREAKFAST BREAD

2 cups flour
2¼ teaspoons baking powder
½ teaspoon salt
2 tablespoons sugar

1 egg
1 cup milk
3 tablespoons butter, melted
2 cups blueberries or cranberries

Preheat the oven to 350°F.

Butter an 8-inch square baking pan.

In a bowl mix the flour, baking powder, salt and sugar. Add the egg, milk, and butter and mix well. Fold in the blueberries and pour into the prepared pan.

Bake for 20 minutes or until it tests done.

Yield: 9 servings

Can be frozen.

NOTE

You can dress up this cake with a streusel topping. In a bowl combine ¼ cup sugar and 1 teaspoon lemon zest until the sugar absorbs the lemon flavor. Add ¼ cup flour, and cut in 2 tablespoons butter until the mixture resembles coarse meal. Sprinkle over the top just before baking.

## PUMPKIN BREAD

1 teaspoon cinnamon
1 teaspoon baking powder
½ teaspoon nutmeg
½ teaspoon baking soda
½ teaspoon salt
¼ teaspoon ground cloves
¼ teaspoon ground ginger

dash allspice
3 cups flour
½ cup vegetable oil
¼ cup yogurt or sour cream
1 egg
1½ cups sugar
1¼ cups pumpkin purée
½ cup chopped walnuts

Preheat the oven to 350°F.
Butter a 9 × 5 × 4-inch loaf pan.
In a bowl, sift the cinnamon, baking powder, nutmeg, baking soda,
    salt, cloves, ginger, allspice, and flour and set aside.
In a separate bowl, mix the oil, yogurt, eggs, sugar, and pumpkin
    until smooth. Stir in the flour mixture and fold in the walnuts.
Pour into the prepared pan filling no more than ⅔ full. (Use extra
    dough to make muffins.) Bake about 1 hour. Test for doneness
    after 45 minutes.

Yield: 1 large loaf

Can be frozen.

## BISHOP'S BREAD BUTTERMILK COFFEECAKE

¾ cup butter
2 cups sifted flour
1½ teaspoons baking pow-
    der
1 cup light brown sugar
⅔ cup buttermilk

1 egg, lightly beaten
½ cup finely chopped pe-
    cans, walnuts or almonds
1 teaspoon cinnamon
½ cup currants

Preheat the oven to 425°F.
Butter and flour a 9-inch cake pan.
In a mixing bowl, mix the flour, baking powder, brown sugar, and
    butter together, and rub until the mixture looks like coarse
    crumbs. Set aside ½ cup of the mixture.

Into the remaining mixture, stir the buttermilk, egg, nuts, cinnamon, and currants.

Pour into the pan and sprinkle with the reserved crumb mixture. Bake for 15 minutes, lower the heat to 375°F and bake 20 minutes longer or until it tests done.

Yield: 1 cake

Can be frozen.

---

# BUDAPEST COFFEE CAKE

⅔ cup packed dark brown sugar
1 tablespoon cinnamon
1 tablespoon unsweetened cocoa
2 to 3 tablespoons currants
½ cup chopped walnuts
3 cups sifted flour
1½ tablespoons baking powder

1½ teaspoons baking soda
½ teaspoon salt
¾ cup butter
2 teaspoons vanilla
1½ cups sugar
3 eggs
2 cups sour cream
vanilla icing (see below)

Preheat the oven to 375°F.

Butter a 10-inch turban mold or bundt pan.

In a bowl, combine the brown sugar, cinnamon, cocoa, currants, and walnuts. Set aside.

In another bowl, mix the flour, baking powder, baking soda, and salt. In a mixer cream the butter, vanilla, and sugar until light and fluffy. Beat in the eggs one at a time.

Fold the dry ingredients into the creamed mixture alternately with the sour cream.

Spread a thin layer of batter in the bottom of the pan and sprinkle with ⅓ of the nut filling. Make another layer of batter and sprinkle with another third of the nut mixture. Cover with another layer of batter and sprinkle with the final remaining nut mixture and top with remaining batter. If you have difficulty spreading the batter, drop it by small spoonfuls.

Bake for 55 to 60 minutes or until it tests done. Cool in the pan 5 minutes and unmold. Serve plain or with the vanilla icing.

Yield: 1 cake

Can be frozen.

## VANILLA ICING

In a bowl, beat 2 cups confectioners' sugar, 1 teaspoon vanilla, and 2 tablespoons milk until smooth, adding another tablespoon of milk or more if necessary to make a glaze about the consistency of a cream sauce. Drizzle the icing over the cake while still warm and let it run down the sides.

CHAPTER

3

*Yeast Breads, Coffee Cakes,*
*and Pastries*

*B*rioche, croissants, buttery yeast coffee cakes, and Danish pastries are the *ne plus ultra* of breakfast breads. We think of these and the mouth begins to water. In some areas of the United States there are good pastry shops around where these can be purchased with no difficulty, but for most of us, quality baked goods are only made at home. The offerings in many stores are just not good enough. The pastries, filled with air, remind one more of sponge rubber than of an edible delight.

## BAKING WITH YEAST

Many cooks are wary of yeast breads. Yeast breads seem to have a life of their own, and require years of practice to make a suitable product. Happily this is not true. You can easily learn to make delicious yeast breads, coffee cakes, and Danish pastries with a reasonable amount of care and a certain amount of patience.

These pastries may seem daunting because they need time to rise: in this world of immediate gratification, the wait may seem unacceptable. But if you understand that much of the time is to allow the dough to work without your help; that you can stop the process at several different stages; and that you can make it in large quantities and freeze it for later use, it may become a more appealing activity.

Yeast is a living organism that needs enough warmth and humidity to grow. Too much heat and it will die. Too little heat and you will slow or stop the activity. These characteristics can work to your advantage. You can freeze an unbaked dough until it is more convenient to finish it. Pastries can be frozen unbaked, allowed to thaw, and popped into the oven when needed. You do have to allow time for thawing and for any final rising.

Yeast is best when heated to no more than 100°F to 110°F. If you do not have a thermometer, test the liquid with your finger: it should feel comfortably warm to the touch. If the liquid is too hot for your finger, it is too hot for the yeast. Rising temperature is best at 85°F to 90°F, but it will rise at lower temperatures. It will just take longer. Longer rising is actually a benefit because the yeast has a chance to develop more flavor. If you wish, you can set the dough in the refrigerator to rise overnight. The next morning, punch out the air, knead it a few times, and let it rise on the kitchen counter until ready to shape it for the final rising. An 11 A.M. brunch can have a freshly baked coffee cake without you getting up before dawn.

The safest way to ensure that the yeast is viable and that the liquid you added was not too hot is to proof the yeast. Place the yeast in a container with some, or all of the liquid. The liquid should be warm to the touch, but should not burn. Add a pinch of sugar and stir the mixture and cover with a towel. (If you are using a processor, do this in the bowl and cover with the lid.) Let the mixture stand for about 5 minutes. Look at it and if it looks cloudy and there is motion in the mixture, the yeast is working. (It reminds me of blooming flowers.)

Kneading is the next problem for bakers. Once you learn how, you will develop a rhythm that can almost rock you to sleep. It is necessary to knead enough, and almost impossible for you to over-knead by hand. Many electric mixers are suitable for kneading doughs. Be sure to check the manual to make sure your machine is a heavy-duty machine suitable for kneading yeast doughs. If there is a dough blade, you can assume that it will do the work without damaging the machine. Most food processors can handle small loaves, and larger processors, providing you use the kneading blade, can knead enough for a couple of loaves.

Kneading by hand is simple and very comforting. Place the dough on a lightly floured board. With your fingertips, pick up the edge of the dough furthest from you and bring it over about a quarter of the mass of dough. Press down with the heels of your hands and push the dough about 6 to 8 inches away from you. Give the dough a slight turn, about 2 inches, and repeat. After a couple of motions you will begin to perceive a rocking motion. You can then start to use your whole upper body. Work with a rhythm, rocking back and forth using moderate pressure. It is not necessary to put all your weight onto the dough. If it sticks add a little more flour, but try to add as little extra flour as possible. After a few minutes the dough should start to become smooth and develop elasticity. Knead for at least 6 minutes and do not worry if you have to knead for 10 or 12 minutes. When the dough is smooth, slightly cool to the touch, and springs back when pushed, you have kneaded it enough.

Place the kneaded dough into a bowl and follow the recipe directions about rising. Some recipes call for a buttered bowl, others for a flour-dusted bowl. To cover the dough, I prefer a moist linen towel, but any towel or plastic wrap will do nicely.

Set aside in a draft-free area to rise. The recipe will tell you how long it may take. A warmer area will cause it to rise more rapidly and a cooler room will take longer. Let it rise until doubled in bulk. A simple test is to poke the risen dough with your finger. If the hole remains it has risen enough, if it fills in almost immediately, let it rise longer.

# BRIOCHE

Brioche is kneaded differently from most yeast breads. The dough is exceedingly sticky and cannot be kneaded on a board. The traditional method is to leave it in a heavy bowl. Plunge your hand into the dough, holding onto the bowl with the other hand. Keep raising your dough-filled hand and slapping it down into the bowl until small air bubbles appear on the surface. The kneading is done when the dough pulls off your hand without sticking. This is an arduous process and if you have a processor or an electric mixer that will do the job, this is the time to take advantage of it. A recipe written specifically for the food processor follows this recipe.

---

# BRIOCHE

4 packages dry yeast
¼ cup sugar
2 teaspoons salt
¾ cup warm milk
6 egg yolks, or 3 whole eggs

4 cups flour, approximately
1 cup softened butter
2 egg yolks
2 teaspoons cream or milk
egg wash (see page 289)

In a bowl, proof the yeast by dissolving it in ½ cup lukewarm water. Stir in the sugar and salt to make syrup. Add the milk and eggs and stir well. Beat in 3 cups of flour and the softened butter. Knead the moist, sticky dough thoroughly in a heavy-duty mixer, or by hand.

*If kneading by hand*, leave the ingredients in the bowl. Pick up the dough and slap it down into the bowl and continue to stretch and slap it between the bowl and your fingers. The dough is ready when it is firm and elastic, with bubbles on the surface, and it no longer sticks to your hands.

*If kneading by electric mixer*, follow manufacturer's instructions for a heavy, sticky dough. Let the machine run for several minutes and check periodically to check the condition. When ready, It should fall free from the sides of the bowl and pull free from the dough hook when it is lifted.

*If kneading by food processor,* check the manual to make sure your processor can handle a dough of this sort. Let the dough process for about 2 minutes. Add just enough more flour to make a satiny, smooth dough.

Place the dough in a bowl, dust lightly with flour, cover with plastic wrap and a towel. Let rise until doubled in bulk, about 1 hour. Because of the high butter content it should rise in a cool area. If necessary, refrigerate and allow it to rise longer.

Punch down and let rise again. Chill for at least 2 hours to make it easier to shape.

Preheat the oven to 400°F.

Butter 16 small brioche molds, about 3 inches across the top, or 1 large mold. Cut the dough into 2-ounce pieces and divide those into 1½-ounce and ½-ounce sections. Shape the larger piece into a compact ball and place in the buttered mold. Poke a hole in the center. Shape the smaller piece of dough into a teardrop and put the point into the hole in the brioche. Let rise until doubled in bulk.

Brush with the egg wash and bake for about 20 minutes. A larger brioche bakes in about 60 minutes.

Yield: 16 brioche or 1 large loaf

Can be frozen.


## VARIATIONS

Flavor the dough with cinnamon or nutmeg, or knead in brandied raisins or other fruits, mentioned for Ollie Bollen page 36.


## SHAPES

If you do not have the traditional fluted molds for the brioche, bake it in custard cups, muffin tins, or any other small mold to shape individual brioche. You can braid the dough or bake it in a coffee tin, or a 9 × 5 × 3-inch loaf pan. Fill the tins no more than ⅔ full and let rise to the top of the pan before baking.

## PROCESSOR BRIOCHE

1 package dry yeast
¼ cup milk
1 tablespoon sugar
2 cups flour
1 teaspoon salt

½ cup frozen butter cut
    into 8 pieces
2 eggs, lightly beaten
egg wash (see page 289)

Proof the yeast in warm milk with sugar.

With the blade in place, add the flour, salt, and butter to the
    processor and process until the butter is cut into small pieces.
    Add the yeast and process until combined. Add the eggs and
    process until the dough forms on top of the blades.

Turn onto a lightly floured board and knead until smooth, about
    1–2 minutes. Place in a buttered bowl turning to coat all sides,
    cover, and let rise until doubled in bulk.

Punch down and knead several times.

Preheat the oven to 350°F.

Shape into a loaf or brioche. Let rise until almost doubled.

Brush with the egg wash and bake for 35 to 40 minutes.

Yield: 8 Brioches or 1 small loaf

Can be frozen.

## CHALLAH

1 cup lukewarm water
3 packages dry yeast
4 teaspoons sugar
5 to 6 cups flour
2 teaspoons salt

3 eggs
¼ cup plus 1 teaspoon vege-
    table shortening
egg wash (see page 289)

In a small bowl, mix the water, yeast, and 1 teaspoon of sugar and
    let proof for 5 minutes.

In a large bowl, mix 4 cups of flour, remaining sugar, and salt.
    Make a well and add the yeast mixture, the eggs, and ¼ cup of
    shortening. Stir together and beat for 2 minutes. Add more flour
    to form a dough that can be gathered into a soft ball. Place the
    dough onto a floured board and knead until the dough is
    smooth and elastic.

Shape into a ball and place in a greased bowl, turning to coat. Cover with a kitchen towel wrung out in warm water and let rise for 45 minutes, or until doubled in bulk.

Punch down and knead again. Let rest for 10 minutes.

Brush a baking sheet with the remaining shortening. Divide the dough into 4 equal pieces and shape each piece into a rope about 22 inches long. The ropes should be about 2 inches in diameter in the center and taper to ½ inch ends. Pinch the ends of each rope to form a cross. Lift the ends of two opposite pieces and cross over the center. Repeat with other pair of ropes, always keeping the cross shape. Continue until all the rope is braided. Pinch ends together.

Place the challah on a baking sheet and let rise for 30 minutes.

Preheat the oven to 400°F.

Brush loaf with egg wash and bake for 15 minutes and lower the heat to 375°F. Bake 45 minutes longer or until golden brown and crusty.

Yield: 1 large loaf

Can be frozen.

# PEPPERONI BREAD

3½ cups flour
2 teaspoons sugar
1 teaspoon salt
1 package dry yeast

2 tablespoons butter
¼ cup hot water
½ cup diced pepperoni
oil for pan

Butter a 9 × 5 × 3-inch loaf pan.

In a processor, combine flour, sugar, salt, yeast, and butter. Turn on and add the water gradually, blending until the dough leaves the sides of the bowl. Turn onto a board and knead in the pepperoni. Shape into a ball and let rise in a lightly floured bowl until doubled, about 30 to 40 minutes. Knead gently and shape into an oval and place on the prepared loaf pan. Cover and let double in bulk.

Preheat the oven to 375°F. Slash the top of the loaf in several places. Bake for 35 to 45 minutes, unmold and cool on a rack.

Yield: 1 loaf

## GARLIC POTATO BREAD

1 large potato, boiled and
    grated (about 1½ cups)
1 teaspoon salt
1 garlic clove, crushed
1 cup warm potato water

1 package dry yeast
2 teaspoons sugar
2 cups flour
softened butter

In a bowl, combine the potato, salt, garlic, potato water, yeast, and sugar. Mix well and let proof. Stir in the flour and mix well.

Turn out onto a lightly floured board and knead until smooth and elastic. Place in a buttered bowl and turn to coat all sides. Cover with a towel wrung out in warm water and let rise until doubled in bulk.

Punch down and turn into a buttered 8 or 9-inch cast-iron skillet. Brush top with butter and let rise until doubled in bulk.

Preheat the oven to 450°F. Bake 25 to 30 minutes, or until golden.

Yield: 1 loaf

## HONEY BRAN BREAD

2 packages dry yeast
¼ cup warm water
1 cup milk, scalded
2 teaspoons butter, softened
1 teaspoon salt

½ cup honey
3 tablespoons sugar
1½ cups bran
3½ cups flour

In a large bowl, dissolve the yeast in the water. Stir in the milk, butter, salt, honey, and sugar, and mix well. Stir in the bran and let stand for 5 minutes. Add 3 cups flour and mix well.

Turn onto a lightly floured board and knead the dough until it is relatively smooth and elastic. Place in a buttered bowl and turn to coat the surface. Cover with a towel wrung out in warm water and let rise for 2 hours or until doubled in bulk.

Preheat the oven to 350°F.

Butter a 9 × 5 × 3 inch loaf pan. Punch the dough down, shape into a long loaf, and place in the pan. Let rise until doubled in bulk.

Bake for 55 minutes. Unmold and cool at least 20 minutes before serving.

Yield: 1 loaf

Can be frozen.

---

# PAIN AUX NOIX (WALNUT BREAD)

2 cups lukewarm water
1 tablespoon honey
1 package yeast
3¾ cups whole wheat flour
1 cup flour

2½ teaspoons salt
1¼ cups walnut halves, cut in half
1 egg, beaten with ½ teaspoon salt

In a small bowl, combine the water, honey, and yeast and let proof.

In a bowl, combine the whole wheat and the white flour and make a well.

Pour the yeast into well, add salt and stir gradually, drawing in the flour to make a smooth dough. Add more white flour if needed to make a soft, slightly sticky dough. Turn onto a board and knead 5–10 minutes or until smooth and elastic, adding more flour if it sticks.

Put into an oiled bowl and turn to oil the top. Cover with damp cloth and let rise for 1½ hours or until doubled.

Butter 2 round 7-inch cake pans.

Punch down the dough and knead in the walnuts. Shape the dough into 2 round loaves on a floured board. Set them in the pans and cover with a damp cloth and let rise for 30 minutes or until doubled.

Preheat the oven to 425°F.

Slash the top of each loaf 3 or 4 times and brush with egg glaze. Bake 15 minutes or until the loaves begin to brown. Lower the heat to 375°F. Bake for 30 to 40 minutes or until the loaves sound hollow when tapped. Turn out onto a rack to cool.

Yield: 2 small loaves

Can be frozen.

## BRAIDED OATMEAL BREAD

| | |
|---|---|
| 2 cups water | 3 tablespoons honey |
| 2½ teaspoons salt | 3 cups whole wheat flour |
| 1½ cups rolled oats | 2 cups flour |
| 1 package yeast | 1 egg, beaten to blend |
| ½ cup warm water | additional oats |
| ¼ cup vegetable oil | |

In a saucepan, bring 2 cups water and ½ teaspoon salt to a boil
    and add the 1½ cups oats. Reduce heat to medium and cook 5
    minutes, stirring occasionally. Remove from heat, cover, and set
    aside for 2 hours.
Sprinkle yeast over ½ cup warm water and let proof.
Mix the oil and honey into the oatmeal.
In a large bowl, mix the whole wheat flour, 2 cups flour, and
    remaining 2 teaspoons salt and mix. Beat in the oatmeal and
    yeast mixtures. The dough will be stiff.
Knead until soft and supple, about 10 minutes, adding water, 1
    teaspoon at a time, if dough is dry. Or if sticky add additional
    flour 1 tablespoon at a time.
Butter a large bowl and add the dough turning to coat the surface.
    Cover and let rise until doubled. Punch down, knead lightly, and
    let rise again.
Butter a large baking sheet. Punch dough down and knead until
    smooth.
Cut dough into 3 pieces and shape into 18 inch long ropes. Braid
    the ropes.
Transfer to the baking sheet, cover and let rise until doubled, about
    20 minutes.
Preheat the oven to 350°F.
Brush dough with egg and sprinkle with oats. Bake until browned,
    about 40 minutes.

Yield: 1 large loaf

Can be baked ahead and frozen.

## COUNTRY HEARTH LOAF

| | |
|---|---|
| 1 package yeast | 1 cup warm water |
| 3 tablespoons brown sugar | 2¾ cups flour |

¼ cup cornmeal
¼ cup dry milk
½ cup whole wheat flour
¼ cup rye flour

2 tablespoons oil
1 egg
1½ teaspoons salt
Whole wheat flour

In a small bowl, mix the yeast, sugar, and water and let proof.

In a processor, combine 2½ cups flour, the whole wheat flour, rye flour, cornmeal, dry milk, oil, egg, and salt, and process for 10 seconds. Scrape down and process again. With the machine running, add the yeast and blend until the dough forms a ball. If too wet, add remaining bread flour a teaspoon at a time until it is no longer sticky.

Oil a mixing bowl and transfer the dough to the bowl, turning to coat surfaces. Let rise until doubled in bulk.

Butter a 9 × 5 × 3-inch loaf pan and sprinkle with flour.

Transfer the dough to a lightly floured board and roll into a rectangle and then roll tightly like a jelly roll. Place seam side down in the pan, cover with a damp cloth, and let rise until doubled.

Preheat the oven to 375°F.

Bake 35 minutes, or until golden.

Yield: 1 loaf

Can be frozen.

## CARAWAY RYE BREAD

½ cup lukewarm water
1 package dry yeast
1 teaspoon sugar
2 to 2½ cups flour
2 to 2½ cups rye flour
1 tablespoon salt

1 cup lukewarm milk
¼ cup white vinegar
1 tablespoon butter
½ cup cornmeal, optional
1 egg white
3 tablespoons caraway seeds

Pour ½ cup water into a bowl, sprinkle with yeast, and sugar. Stir to dissolve and let proof for 10 minutes.

In a bowl, mix 2 cups white flour, 2 cups rye flour, and the salt. Stir in the yeast mixture with the milk and vinegar and stir until smooth. Beat until the mixture can be gathered into a ball. Place on a lightly floured surface and knead, sprinkling equal amounts of white and rye flour over the ball to make a medium firm dough. Knead until smooth and elastic.

Rub the inside of a large bowl with the butter, add the dough, and turn to coat evenly. Cover with a towel wrung out in warm water and let rise for 1½ hours, or until doubled in bulk.

Punch down and let rise again until doubled again, about 45 minutes. Sprinkle cornmeal on a large baking sheet and set aside.

Cut the dough in half and shape each half into tapering loaves, about 12 inches long.

Place on baking sheet and make ½ inch deep diagonal slashes about 2 inches apart on top of each loaf. Set in a draft-free place to rise for 30 minutes.

Preheat the oven to 400°F.

Brush the egg white over the tops of the loaves and sprinkle with the caraway seeds. Bake for 15 minutes. Lower heat to 375°F and bake 30 to 35 minutes longer. Cool before serving.

Yield: 2 loaves

Can be frozen.

## BLACK BREAD

| | |
|---|---|
| 2¼ cups water | 2 packages dry yeast |
| 1 ounce unsweetened choco-late | ¼ cup warm water |
| | 1 tablespoon sugar |
| ¼ cup cider vinegar | 1 tablespoon salt |
| ¼ cup dark molasses | 4 cups rye flour |
| 2 teaspoons instant coffee powder | 1 cup bran |
| | 3½ cups flour |
| 2 tablespoons caraway seed | 1 egg white |

Butter a large bowl and a baking sheet.

In a saucepan, heat the water, chocolate, vinegar, molasses, coffee powder, and caraway seed until the chocolate melts.

Dissolve the yeast in a large bowl and let proof. Stir in the chocolate mixture, sugar, and salt. Mix in the rye flour and bran. Stir in 2 cups flour and mix well.

Turn onto a lightly floured board and knead, adding flour as needed until the dough is smooth and elastic.

Transfer to the bowl and turn to coat the surface. Cover with a damp towel. Let stand in draft-free place until doubled in bulk.

Turn onto a lightly floured board. Shape into 3 round or oval loaves, transfer to a buttered or floured baking sheet, and let rise until doubled in bulk.

Preheat the oven to 350°F.

Bake 25 minutes, brush with the egg white and bake until golden, about 20 minutes longer.

Yield: 3 round loaves

Can be frozen.

---

# ORANGE RAISIN BREAD

1½ cups warm water
2 packages dry yeast
½ cup sugar
1 teaspoon salt
¼ cup butter, softened
1 egg plus 1 egg white
2 tablespoons grated orange rind
4½ cups flour

½ cup raisins
1 egg yolk
½ cup light brown sugar, packed
2 tablespoons grated orange rind
3 tablespoons chopped pecans

In a medium bowl, sprinkle the yeast over the water and let proof. Add the sugar, salt, butter, egg, egg white, 2 tablespoons orange rind, and 3 cups of flour. Beat until smooth. Stir in the raisins and the remaining flour.

Place the dough in a buttered bowl and cover with a towel wrung out in warm water. Let rise in a warm place for about 1 hour or until more than doubled in bulk and bubbly.

Lightly butter a 2 quart soufflé dish.

Stir down the dough and beat vigorously for 1 minute. Turn into the soufflé dish and brush the top with the egg yolk.

In a small bowl, combine the brown sugar, grated orange rind, and pecans. Sprinkle on top of the bread.

Let rise for 30 minutes, or until almost doubled in bulk.

Preheat the oven to 375°F.

Bake for 55 minutes. Unmold and cool on a rack.

Yield: 1 loaf

Can be frozen.

---

## EASTERN EUROPEAN NUT ROLL

3 packages dry yeast
½ cup lukewarm water
½ cup sugar
¾ cup warmed milk
½ cup butter, softened
1 teaspoon salt
grated rind of 1 lemon
1 teaspoon vanilla
2 eggs

2 egg yolks
5 cups flour
3 eggs
½ cup sugar
2 cups grated walnuts
½ cup melted butter
grated rind of 2 oranges
½ teaspoon cinnamon
icing, see below

In a large bowl, sprinkle the yeast on the water and let proof. Add
   ½ cup sugar, milk, soft butter, salt, lemon rind, and vanilla. Mix
   well. Beat in 2 eggs and egg yolks. Stir in 2 cups flour and beat
   well. Gradually add enough remaining flour to make a pliable
   dough.
Turn a onto lightly floured board and knead until smooth and
   elastic. Place the dough in floured bowl and cover with a towel
   wrung out in warm water. Let rise until doubled, about 1 to
   1½ hours.
Butter 2 9-inch loaf pans.
Punch down the dough and knead for 3 minutes.
In a bowl, beat the eggs and ½ cup sugar until thick and pale. Stir
   in the nuts, butter, orange rind, and cinnamon.
Roll the dough into a large rectangle, about ⅛ inch thick. Spread
   the filling evenly over the surface and roll like a jelly roll. Cut
   the roll in half and place one half in each pan. Let rise until
   doubled in bulk.
Preheat the oven to 350°F.
Brush the loaves with lukewarm water. Bake for about 45 minutes
   or until golden. Unmold and cool before icing.

Yield: 2 loaves

Can be frozen.

NOTE

Frost after thawing.

---

# ICING

1 cup confectioners' sugar orange juice

In a bowl, mix sugar with just enough orange juice to make a runny icing. Drizzle over the nut rolls.

---

# HOUSKA (CZECH BRAIDED SWEET BREAD)

¼ cup lukewarm water
1 package dry yeast
1 teaspoon plus ½ cup sugar
4½ to 4¾ cups flour
2 teaspoons salt
1 teaspoon grated lemon rind
¼ teaspoon mace
1 cup lukewarm milk

2 eggs plus 1 egg yolk
6 tablespoons softened butter
½ cup finely chopped walnuts or pecans
1 cup raisins
1 egg beaten with 1 tablespoon milk

In a small bowl, mix the water, yeast, and 1 teaspoon sugar and let proof.

In a large bowl, mix 4½ cups flour, remaining sugar, salt, lemon rind, and mace. Make a well in the center and add the yeast mixture, milk, eggs, egg yolks, and 4 tablespoons of butter. Mix to make a medium soft dough. Transfer to a lightly floured board and knead until smooth and elastic, about 10 minutes.

Rub the inside of a bowl with 1 tablespoon of butter and turn the dough to coat evenly. Cover with a towel wrung out in warm water and let rise for about 1 hour or until doubled.

Punch down and knead in the nuts and raisins.

Divide the dough into 5 equal pieces. Roll each piece into rope 12 inches long and 2 inches in diameter. Brush a cookie sheet with remaining butter and place 3 ropes on the sheet. Braid from the center to the ends.

Twist the two remaining ropes together to make a spiral and place on top of the braided dough. Tuck the ends underneath.

Cover with the towel and let rise for 45 minutes, or until doubled.
Preheat the oven to 350°F.
Brush the loaf with the egg mixture and bake until golden, about
    30 to 35 minutes. Cool.

Yield: 1 large loaf

Can be frozen.

---

# KUGELHOPF (ALSATIAN ALMOND COFFEE CAKE)

Also known as Kugelupf or Kougelhopf, there are many different
spellings for this Alsatian specialty. The cake itself is a yeast bread
with raisins and ground almonds. It can be served dusted with
confectioners' sugar or frosted with rum frosting or chocolate
glaze.

| | |
|---|---|
| ½ cup ground almonds | 3¾ cups sifted flour |
| 16 to 20 whole blanched al- | ¼ teaspoon salt |
| monds | 2½ cups warm milk |
| ½ cup raisins | 1 cup soft butter |
| ¼ cup kirsch | 2 eggs |
| 1 package dried yeast | ⅔ cup sugar |
| ¼ cup warm milk | sifted confectioner's sugar |

Butter a fluted kugelhopf mold (any turban or bundt mold will
    suit), and sprinkle with the ground almonds. Arrange the whole
    almonds on the bottom in a decorative pattern.
In a small bowl, soak the raisins in the kirsch. In another small
    bowl, dissolve the yeast in ¼ cup milk.
In a large bowl, mix the flour and salt together. Stir in the milk,
    butter, and yeast.
Beat the eggs until foamy and add the sugar and raisin-kirsch
    mixture. Add to the dough and work until it clears the sides of
    the bowl, adding a little flour if needed.
Place the dough in the mold and let rise to within 1 inch of the top
    of the pan.
Preheat the oven to 325°F.
Bake for 45 to 50 minutes or until golden brown and starts to pull
    away from the sides of the pan. Cool in the pan for five minutes,

unmold and when lukewarm sprinkle with confection-ers' sugar. Or frost with rum or chocolate frosting.

Yield: 1 loaf

---

# RUM FROSTING

1 cup confectioners' sugar          1 tablespoon dark rum

In a bowl, combine the sugar and rum, adding more rum if needed to make a thin frosting. Drizzle over the cooled cake and let it run down the sides of the cake.

---

# CHOCOLATE GLAZE

¼ cup heavy cream                    8 ounces semisweet choco-
1 tablespoon butter                      late, chopped

In a microwave, or a heavy saucepan, bring the cream and butter to a simmer, add the chocolate, and stir until melted. Pour over the cake and twist and turn the cake to coat the surface evenly.

---

# PECAN ROLLS

1 package dry yeast                  4½ to 5 cups flour
½ cup lukewarm water                 ¾ cup melted butter
2 cups milk, scalded                 1½ cups light brown sugar
4 egg yolks                          2 teaspoons cinnamon
1¼ teaspoons salt                    ½ cup raisins
½ cup butter, melted                 ½ cup light corn syrup
¾ cup sugar                          1 cup pecans

In a large bowl, dissolve the yeast in the water and let proof. Stir the milk into the yeast, with the eggs, salt, butter, and sugar. Beat in the flour until the mixture is shaggy. Turn onto a board and knead, adding as much remaining flour as needed to make a smooth and elastic dough.

Place in a buttered bowl and let rise until doubled in bulk. Punch down and let rise a second time.

Roll into a rectangle ¼ inch thick. Spread with ½ cup melted butter. In a bowl mix the ¾ cup brown sugar, raisins, and cinnamon together and sprinkle over the top of the dough. Starting at one long side roll up like a jelly roll and cut into 1¼ inch thick slices.

In a 10-inch cake plan combine the remaining ¾ cup brown sugar, light corn syrup, and the remaining 2 tablespoons melted butter and spread evenly over the bottom. Scatter the pecans over the mixture and arrange the cinnamon buns, cut side down on top of the filling. Let rise until doubled in bulk.

Preheat the oven to 350°F.

Brush the tops of the rolls with the remaining 2 tablespoons of butter.

Bake for 25 minutes or until golden. Place a cake rack over the top of the cake tin and invert. Remove the pan and let cool before serving.

Yield: 12 rolls

Can be frozen.

---

## RICH SOUR CREAM DOUGH

This dough can be shaped and filled in many different ways. Immediately following are recipes for twists and two different coffee cakes. You also can use it to make a coffee cake with the same filling as the Budapest coffee cake, page 53. Use it in place of Danish pastry dough for the various shapes listed there.

| | |
|---|---|
| 2 packages dry yeast | ½ teaspoon salt |
| ¼ cup warm water | 1 teaspoon vanilla |
| 1½ sticks butter, softened | ½ cup milk |
| ¾ cup sugar | 1 cup sour cream |
| 3 eggs | 4-5 cups flour |

In a bowl proof the yeast with the water.

In a mixer cream the butter and the sugar until light and fluffy. Beat in the eggs, 1 at a time. Beat in the egg yolks, salt, vanilla, milk, sour cream, and yeast, until smooth, about 2 minutes.

Gradually beat in 4 cups flour to form a very soft dough. Continue to beat, adding more flour as needed until the dough is smooth and elastic.

Place the dough in an oiled bowl and turn to coat. Cover with a damp towel. Set aside until doubled in bulk, about 45 minutes.

NOTE

The dough can rise in the refrigerator and will keep for up to 3 days. Punch it down whenever it comes close to doubling in bulk.

# BUTTER TWISTS

1 recipe chilled rich sour            2 to 3 cups sugar
   cream dough made with
   only 1 tablespoon sugar

On a lightly floured board, roll the dough into a rectangle about ⅛ inch thick. Sprinkle generously with sugar and fold the dough in thirds like a business letter. Wrap the dough in foil and refrigerate for 20 minutes.

Place the pastry with an open end facing you and roll again to ⅛ inch thick. Sprinkle with sugar and fold again. Chill and repeat the procedure one more time.

Divide the dough in half and roll into 8 × 16-inch rectangles. Sprinkle with sugar and fold in half to make 4 × 16- inch rectangles. Cut into strips, 1 inch wide and 4 inches long. Roll the strips in sugar and twist the ends to create spirals. Chill 30 minutes.

Preheat the oven to 375°F.

Place the strips on baking sheets and press the ends down. Bake for 20 minutes or until golden.

Yield: 6 dozen twists

Can be frozen.

## CINNAMON TWISTS

Add 2 to 3 tablespoons of cinnamon or to taste, to the sugar before rolling it into the pastry.

**NUT AND FRUIT TWISTS**

Sprinkle the pastry with raisins and nuts or candied fruits to your taste, before folding in half and cutting into strips.

# SOUR CREAM COFFEE CAKE WITH HONEY ALMOND GLAZE

1 recipe rich sour cream
   dough
⅔ cup light brown sugar
⅓ cup cream
⅓ cup honey

⅓ cup butter
¼ teaspoon lemon juice
1⅓ cups sliced blanched almonds

Preheat the oven to 375°F.
Butter 2 9-inch cake plans.
Divide the dough in half and shape each into a round loaf. Place
   in the cake pans and let rise until doubled in bulk.
In a saucepan, simmer the brown sugar, cream, honey, and butter
   for 30 seconds. Remove from the heat and stir in the lemon juice
   and almonds. Cool 10 minutes and drizzle evenly over both
   cakes.
Bake for 30 to 35 minutes or until golden. Cool in pans.

Yield: 2 loaves

Can be frozen.

# ORANGE HONEY COFFEE CAKES

1 recipe rich sour cream
   dough
¼ cup melted butter
½ cup butter, softened
grated rind of 1 large orange
⅔ cup honey

⅔ cup chopped walnuts or
   pecans
1 cup raisins
1 egg yolk
1 teaspoon heavy cream
½ cup blanched, sliced almonds

Preheat the oven to 350°F.
Butter two 9 x 5 x 3-inch loaf pans, a single large baking sheet, or
   two 9-inch layer cake pans.

Roll the pastry into a large square, ¼ inch thick. Brush with the melted butter. In a bowl, cream the soft butter, orange rind, honey, and walnuts. Spread over the dough and sprinkle with the raisins. Roll up jelly roll fashion.

With a rolling pin, flatten to a 1-inch thickness. Cut into 3 strips lengthwise and cut the strips in half horizontally. Braid 3 strips into a loaf and repeat with remaining strips. Place the loaves in the loaf pans, or shape free form on the baking sheet, or twist into rings, and place in the layer pans.

In a small bowl, mix the egg yolk, and cream and brush over the loaves. Sprinkle with the almonds. Bake for 45 minutes, or until golden. Unmold and cool on a rack.

Yield: 2 cakes

Can be frozen.

---

# CROISSANTS

Croissants and Danish pastry are similar in technique. The object is to make many layers of butter between many layers of dough. It is important not to overwork the dough. These are difficult to do successfully, but care and practice will bring superb results.

| | |
|---|---|
| 1 package dry yeast | 2 tablespoons sugar |
| 1 tablespoon sugar | 1 cup cold milk, approxi- |
| ½ cup warm water | mately |
| 4 cups flour | ½ pound butter |
| 1 tablespoons salt | egg wash (see page 289) |

In a small bowl, mix the yeast, 1 tablespoon sugar, and water and let proof.

In a large bowl, mix the flour, salt, and remaining sugar. Make a well in the center and stir in the yeast mixture and the milk, working quickly, and lightly stir the ingredients together to make a rough, crumbly mass. Turn onto a counter and let rest 5 minutes. Wash and dry the bowl.

With a pastry scraper, lift the dough onto itself and press down, 8 to 10 times. THIS IS ALL THE KNEADING YOU DO. Place the dough in the bowl and let rise for 2 hours or until doubled in bulk. Punch down.

Wrap the pastry in a plastic bag and shape into a flat, square brick, about 1½ inches thick. Refrigerate at least 20 minutes. Meanwhile, knead the butter to make it smooth, pliable, and waxy. One of the easiest ways is to put the butter in a plastic bag and work it until it is the same consistency as the dough. If the butter becomes too soft or is greasy, put it in the refrigerator to firm. When kneaded, roll the butter, while still in the bag to about ¼ inch thick. The bag will help to shape it into an even rectangle. Refrigerate until firm, but not hard.

When the dough and butter are chilled, cut the butter rectangle in half. Roll the dough on a lightly floured board into a long rectangle, as wide as the butter and 3 times as long as one of the halves. Place one section of butter onto the center of the dough. Pick up one end of the dough and place it over the butter. Place the second half of butter on the dough and cover with the remaining dough.

When rolling, try to keep all the edges as square as possible. Turn the pastry so that an open end faces you. Roll it into a long rectangle. Fold each end to the center and fold it in half again so that it resembles a book. Wrap in floured foil or place in a plastic bag and chill for at least 20 minutes.

Roll and fold again. Let rest in the refrigerator for 3 hours.

Divide the pastry in half and roll each half into a large rectangle about ¼ inch thick. Cut into triangles, about 5 inches on each side.

Roll each triangle toward an opposite point, stretching the point slightly. Place on an unbuttered baking sheet and twist the ends to make a crescent. The center point should point down toward the baking sheet, but not be stuck under the croissant. Let rise for 30 minutes.

Preheat the oven to 400°F.

Brush the croissants with egg wash (see page 289) or 1 egg mixed with 1 tablespoon of heavy cream. Bake for 20 to 25 minutes or until golden.

Yield: 36 croissants

Can be frozen.

## DANISH PASTRY

Danish pastry can be bread-like with thickish layers of dough filled with assorted fillings, or it can be more like a croissant, French puff pastry, and similar to strudel. The Danes call it *weinerbrodt* or Viennese bread. The latter version has crisper, thinner layers of dough for a lighter and flaky Danish pastry. The recipe given here is this version, rather than the more cake-like, or bread-like version mentioned above. This light flaky Danish pastry is similar in technique to croissants.

| | |
|---|---|
| 3½ cups flour | ¼ cup sugar |
| 3 packages dry yeast | 3 tablespoons butter |
| 1 cup milk | ⅛ teaspoon ground carda- |
| Pinch of salt | mom |
| 1 egg | 1½ cups butter |
| 2 egg yolks | |

In a bowl, combine the flour, yeast, milk, salt, egg, egg yolks, sugar, 3 tablespoons of butter, and the cardamom. Mix well until the mixture just holds together.

Turn onto a board and knead about 8 times with a pastry scraper, by lifting and pressing the dough onto itself. Wrap in lightly floured foil, or put into a plastic bag. Shape into a cake about 5 inches square and 1 inch thick. Refrigerate for 20 minutes.

Meanwhile, knead the remaining butter in a bowl of cold water, or in a plastic bag until malleable, but not oily. Shape into a block, about ¾ inch thick. If soft, chill until the same consistency as the dough.

On a lightly floured board, roll the pastry into a 12-inch square. Place the butter in the center with the corners of the butter square pointing to the sides of the pastry square. Lift the corners of the pastry over the butter so that the points meet on top of the butter. Pinch the edges together. Sprinkle lightly with flour and fold the square into a rectangle, three times longer than wide. Fold in thirds like a business letter and wrap in floured foil or put into a plastic bag. Refrigerate for 20 minutes.

Roll and fold again and refrigerate for 1 hour.

The dough is ready to shape into different pastries. Once the pastries are shaped and filled, let them rise for 20 minutes.

Preheat the oven to 400°F.

Bake about 20 minutes or until golden brown.

Yield: 24 to 36 pastries

Can be frozen before, or after, baking.

## SHAPES AND FLAVORS

The pastry can be shaped the same way as the Rich Sour Cream Dough. The fillings for that dough and the fillings below can be used with any shape. My preference is to divide the dough into halves and shape each half differently and fill each shape with a different filling.

## TWISTS

Roll the pastry ¼ inch thick and spread the filling evenly over ½ the dough. Fold in half to cover the filling and cut into ½ inch wide strips. Hold the ends, and twist each strip into a spiral. Place on a buttered baking sheet to rise before baking.

## PRETZELS

Roll the pastry ¼ inch thick and cut into ½ inch wide strips. Shape each strip into a pretzel. Brush the strips with eggwash and sprinkle with sliced or chopped almonds. When baked and cooled, coat with vanilla icing (see page 54).

## TWIN ROLLS (SPECTACLES)

Roll the pastry ⅛ inch thick. Sprinkle with the filling and roll like a jelly roll. Cut into 1-inch thick sections and cut through the center of each section almost to the last layer of pastry. Place on a buttered baking sheet, so that it looks like a pair of "spectacles." Brush with eggwash and bake. When cooled, coat with vanilla icing (page 54), if desired.

## STARS

Roll ¼ of the pastry into a 12-inch wide strip, ⅛ inch thick. Spread with filling and roll like a jelly roll. Cut into ¾ inch thick sections and place cut side down on a buttered baking sheet. With scissors, make 6 cuts around the outer edge toward the center in each piece. Brush with eggwash.

## BUTTERFLIES

Roll the pastry ¼ inch thick and spread with filling. Roll like a jelly roll and cut into 1 inch thick sections. Holding the sections upright, use a thin piece of wood, like a chopstick, or pencil and press down to spread it open to form a butterfly. Place on a buttered baking sheet and brush with eggwash.

## FANS

Roll the pastry 1 inch thick and 9 inches wide. Spread with the filling. Fold in thirds so that the pastry is 3 inches wide. Cut crosswise into 2-inch sections. Make 3 small cuts on the long side of each piece almost but not to the center: like fringing both ends. Place on a buttered baking sheet, twisting the pastry in the center and spreading the sections. Brush with eggwash. When cooled, coat with vanilla icing (page 54), if desired.

## BEAR CLAWS

Shape the pastry as for fans, but cut one side only about ¾ of the way toward the opposite edge. Brush with egg wash. These also can be coated with vanilla icing (page 54).

## FILLINGS

### JAMS

Use about 10 ounces of your favorite jam. Raspberry and apricot are traditional.

---

# ALMOND FILLING

2 cups almonds, toasted
 and ground
6 tablespoons sugar
½ cup fresh bread crumbs

3 tablespoons milk
pinch of cinnamon
½ teaspoon vanilla

In a bowl, combine the almonds, sugar, bread crumbs, milk, cinnamon, and vanilla. Mix well. Add more milk if needed to make the filling creamy.

---

# HAZELNUT FILLING

Sprinkle the pastry with 1 cup shredded toasted hazelnuts and 1 cup cinnamon sugar.

## POPPY SEED FILLING

½ pound poppy seeds                 2 tablespoons heavy cream
½ cup butter                        1 cup chopped walnuts
½ cup honey                         ½ cup raisins
1 teaspoon grated orange
   peel

In a small bowl, cover poppy seeds with boiling water and let stand
   overnight. Drain well. Grind the seeds 3 times with the finest
   blade of a meat grinder, or purée in a processor. In a processor
   or mixer, cream the butter and honey and beat in the poppy
   seeds, orange peel, and cream. Turn into a bowl and fold in the
   walnuts and raisins.

## CHEESE FILLING

¼ cup raisins                       1 teaspoon melted butter
2 tablespoons cognac                1 tablespoon sour cream
1 cup cream cheese                  ½ teaspoon grated lemon
¼ cup sugar                            rind
1 tablespoon flour                  ½ teaspoon vanilla
1 egg yolk

Soak the raisins in the cognac for 20 minutes. Cream the cheese,
   sugar, and flour together. Stir in the egg yolk, butter, sour
   cream, lemon rind, and vanilla. Beat in the raisins and any juices.

CHAPTER

*Eggs*

*B*reakfast, for most people, until recently at least, meant eggs: boiled, scrambled, fried, poached, or made into an omelet. This was the accepted way of starting the day. In recent years, we have turned thoughts to other foods such as cereals and whole-grain breads.

Eggs can not only be prepared in a variety of ways, but also they are delicious. It is mainly in the United States that eggs are relegated to the culinary world of breakfast (now an almost verboten use), and are hard-cooked as a sandwich filling, or as an addition to salad. In other areas of the world, the egg is so highly respected that it takes a prominent role as a luncheon entrée, or as the start to a dinner. Poached eggs are not just dropped onto a slice of toast, but are turned into elaborate hot and cold preparations. Shirred eggs garnished with flavorful accompaniments, and omelets made with a quick, light touch come with a variety of savory fillings.

The egg can be sautéed, poached, broiled, baked, steamed, deep-fried, separated, or emulsified. It is delicious sour or sweet, hot or cold, firm or smooth. It is not only nutritionally sound, but also inexpensive.

Because eggs contain protein, which hardens in heat, they must be treated gently and with respect. They should be soft-cooked, not boiled. Eggs usually take but a brief time to cook, but there are many who want to rush them. The one preparation that requires intense heat is the omelet, which must be cooked so quickly that the eggs do not have a chance to toughen. Omelets take less than a minute to prepare. As simple as egg preparation is, many a dish is unsatisfactory because of rough treatment from the cook. If you treat eggs with care you will be rewarded with a superlative dish.

Plan to serve 2 eggs per person, when eggs are the main course, but for a large menu, a single egg will be sufficient. I recommend large-size eggs for each serving. Jumbo and larger are unnecessary. Many egg dishes call for individual servings: often it is possible to prepare them to serve from a large platter or baking dish. This makes it easier to serve and makes the appearance more impressive.

## SAUCES

Eggs and sauces are a natural pairing. Many sauces are based on, or enriched with, eggs, and the eggs themselves are further enhanced by these sauces. Most often the sauce is a thin coat to enhance the egg, and to bring out the flavor of the food served without masking it. Since some sauces suit many different dishes, I have placed them in a separate chapter for easy reference.

For the best dishes it is important to prepare recipes correctly. Prepare Eggs Benedict, for instance, with toasted English muffins, Canadian bacon, poached eggs, and hollandaise sauce, not toast, ham or bacon, hard cooked eggs, and heated mayonnaise as a student suggested. Oleomargarine is not a substitute for butter. If you cannot use the proper ingredients, then select another recipe. Do not serve guests, nor yourself, scrambled eggs made from some ersatz "egg" product and expect it to be the same.

## POACHED EGGS

You can prepare poached eggs easily. There are just a few secrets to success.

- Use fresh eggs. If in doubt, check the freshness by breaking an egg into a small plate. The yolk should stand high and the white should be viscous and cling to the yolk. There should only be a small amount of watery liquid at the edges of the white. As the egg loses freshness, the yolk flattens and the white gets watery.

- Any pan will do, but the broad surface of a skillet allows for more eggs to poach at one time.

- Use enough water so the eggs will float.

- Add 1 tablespoon of white vinegar to each quart of water to aid in setting the white. If the eggs are truly fresh (no more than 2 days old), this is not necessary, but unless you were present when the eggs were laid, take the precaution of adding the vinegar.

- Heat the water to 185°F. Tiny bubbles will break just below the surface, like bubbles rising in a glass of champagne.

- Break the egg into a custard cup or saucer. Traditionally cooks did this to make sure the egg was not rotten. A better reason to do this is that if you break the yolk, you can set that egg aside for another use.

- Slide the egg into the water and let it poach for 3 to 5 minutes. It does take time to poach; allow the time. The yolk should still be runny and the white fully set.

- Remove the egg with a slotted spoon and drain on a towel. For attractive service, trim any rough edges of white from the egg before serving.

Some people prefer to make molded eggs, using a French egg stand. This is an oval-shaped, pierced pan on small legs, with a long upright tail. The cook places the stand in the water and breaks the egg into it. For more fun, you can use a cookie cutter of any shape (bunnies for Easter, stars for Christmas). Place the cutter in the water and slide the egg into it. When cooked, lift the mold and egg with a spatula onto a plate and use a knife to release the edges of the white from the cutter and unmold.

Poached eggs should have enough liquid to float while cooking. The liquid is usually water, occasionally wine. Eggs cooked enclosed in pans or cups surrounded by a liquid are coddled.

### To Prepare Poached Eggs the Day Before

If you are serving many guests, you can prepare poached eggs the previous night. Poach the eggs as usual, but remove them to a bowl of iced water. Chill overnight. When ready to serve, pour very hot, not boiling water over the eggs and let them stand. Replace the water as often as possible until they eggs have reached about 140°F. Drain and serve.

---

## EGGS BENEDICT

6 English muffins, split and
   toasted
12 thin slices Canadian
   Bacon, broiled

12 poached eggs, drained
¾ cup hollandaise sauce
black olive or truffle cut-
   outs, optional

Arrange 2 muffin halves on each plate, top with the bacon and poached eggs. Coat each egg with a tablespoon of sauce and garnish with the black olive or truffle, if desired. Serve immediately.

Yield: 6 servings

## VARIATIONS

Over the years many chefs have tried to gild the lily or somehow improve on this perfect combination. The most suitable substitute for the Canadian bacon is smoked salmon.

## EGGS BROOKSIDE

3 cups puréed spinach
   (see page 285)
6 slices ham,
   3 inches in diameter

1 tablespoon butter
6 poached eggs
⅓ cup hollandaise sauce
1 teaspoon minced tarragon

Arrange the purée on individual plates. In a small skillet, heat the ham in the butter until just hot and place on top of the spinach. Top with a poached egg. Mix the hollandaise with the tarragon and put 1 tablespoon on each egg.
Serve immediately.

Yield: 6 servings

## EGGS CALIFORNIA

2 10-ounce packages frozen
   artichoke hearts
6 tablespoons butter

12 poached eggs
1 cup hollandaise sauce

Cook the artichokes according to package directions until tender. Drain and chop coarsely. In a small skillet, reheat the artichokes in the butter and arrange on 6 plates. Top with the eggs and coat with the sauce. Serve immediately.

Yield: 6 servings

## OEUFS POCHÉS À LA CRÉCY (POACHED EGGS WITH CARROT PURÉE)

3 cups carrot purée
   (see page 284)
6 poached eggs

⅔ cup mousseline sauce
   (see page 279)

Preheat the broiler. Spread the carrot purée in an 8 × 11 baking dish, or on individual plates. Top with the eggs and coat each egg with 2 tablespoons of sauce. Brown under the broiler. Serve immediately.

Yield: 6 servings

---

## OEUFS POCHÉS À LA BÉARNAISE (POACHED EGGS WITH BEARNAISE SAUCE)

This is similar to the recipe above, except that the potato purée and eggs are coated with a béarnaise sauce, which has a sharper and more complex flavor than a hollandaise.

2½ pounds potatoes, peeled
6 tablespoons butter
½ cup milk
¼ pound butter, melted

12 poached eggs
¾ cup béarnaise sauce
salt and pepper to taste

Preheat the oven to 450°F.
In a saucepan, cook the potatoes in boiling, salted water to cover until tender. Drain, and rice the potatoes into a bowl. Beat in 6 tablespoons butter and the milk to make a smooth purée. Season with salt and pepper. On a well buttered baking sheet, or cocottes, pipe 6 large nests, with a 16-inch pastry bag fitted with a # 5 open star tip. Bake until golden brown and fully heated. Transfer to serving dishes, if necessary, and fill with the eggs. Coat with the sauce. Serve immediately.

Yield: 6 servings

---

## POACHED EGGS BORGIA

6 large firm tomatoes
salt and pepper to taste

12 poached eggs
1 cup béarnaise sauce

Preheat the oven to 350°F.
Cut the tomatoes in half and season with salt and pepper.
    Arrange in a baking dish and bake 12 to 15 minutes or until

very hot. Top with the eggs and coat with the sauce. Serve immediately.

Yield: 6 to 12 servings

## OEUFS POCHÉS HENRI IV (POACHED EGGS HENRY THE FOURTH)

The credit for Sauce Béarnaise usually goes to this King of France, but others credit it to a restaurant outside Paris.

12 poached eggs                          1½ cups béarnaise sauce
6 croustades (see page 286)

Preheat the broiler. Place the eggs on the croustades and coat with the sauce. Brown under the broiler. Serve immediately.

Yield: 6 servings

## OEUFS POCHÉS JENNY LIND (POACHED EGGS JENNY LIND)

6 sautéed croutes (see page          6 poached eggs
   286)                              ¾ cup béarnaise sauce
1½ cups cauliflower purée
   (see page 284)

Spread the croutons with the purée and top with a poached egg. Coat the eggs with the sauce. Serve immediately.

Yield: 6 servings

## OEUFS POCHÉS AURORE (POACHED EGGS AURORA)

6 croutes (see page 286)             1½ cups sauce Aurore (see
6 poached eggs                          page 276)
salt and pepper to taste             4 hard cooked egg yolks,
                                        sieved, optional

On serving plates arrange the croutes, top with the eggs, and season with salt and pepper. In a small saucepan, heat the sauce Aurore and spoon over each egg. Sprinkle with egg yolk, if desired. Serve immediately.

Yield: 6 to 12 servings

## OEUFS POCHÉS À LA FLORENTINE (POACHED EGGS FLORENTINE)

Eggs Florentine are perhaps the second most popular brunch dish.

1½ pounds cooked spinach
1½ cups Mornay sauce (see page 276)
12 poached eggs

⅓ cup grated Gruyère or Parmesan cheese
⅓ cup buttered bread crumbs, optional

Preheat the broiler.
Squeeze any excess moisture from the spinach and mince finely. Mix the spinach with ¾ cup Mornay sauce and spread on the bottom of one baking dish or individual dishes. Arrange the eggs on top and coat with the remaining Mornay sauce. Sprinkle with the cheese and bread crumbs if using. Broil until golden. Serve immediately.

Yield: 6 to 12 servings

## OEUFS POCHÉS À L'ANDALOUSE (POACHED EGGS ANDALUSIAN)

6 green peppers
6 cups rice pilaf (see recipe below)
12 chicken livers

3 tablespoons butter
12 poached eggs
¾ cup tomato sauce (see page 280)

Cut the peppers in half and blanch in boiling, salted water to cover for 2 minutes. Drain and arrange on serving plates. Fill the peppers with the rice pilaf. In a skillet, sauté the livers in the butter until medium. Slice the livers and arrange on the rice.

Top each pepper with a poached egg and coat with the sauce Serve immediately.

Yield: 6 to 12 servings

NOTE:

If desired, prepare peppers and rice ahead and reheat in a 350°F oven until hot.

# RICE PILAF

3 cups tomato sauce (see page 280)
3 cups chicken or beef stock
salt and pepper to taste
3 cups raw rice
3 tablespoons butter, softened.

In a 3 quart saucepan, bring the tomato sauce and the stock to a boil. Season with salt and pepper. Add the rice and stir until it returns to a boil. Simmer, covered 20 minutes, or until the rice has absorbed the liquid and is tender. Fold in the butter with a fork.

# POACHED EGGS WITH ANCHOVY TOAST AND GRILLED TOMATOES

2 ounces anchovy fillets, mashed
7 tablespoons butter, softened
6 slices bread, toasted
6 tomatoes, cut in half
2 tablespoons minced basil
12 poached eggs
salt and pepper to taste

In a bowl, cream the anchovies and 4 tablespoons butter until light and fluffy. Spread on the toast.
Dot the tomatoes with the remaining butter and sprinkle with the basil. Broil 5 minutes.
Arrange the toasts and tomatoes on a platter and top the toast with eggs. Season with salt and pepper. Serve immediately.

Yield: 6 to 12 servings

## TSCHIMBUR (POACHED EGGS WITH GARLIC YOGURT SAUCE)

3 cups yogurt
3 garlic cloves, minced
salt and pepper to taste

12 poached eggs
¼ cup butter
3 tablespoons paprika

In a saucepan, warm the yogurt with the garlic, salt, and pepper, but do not boil. Arrange the eggs on serving plates and coat with the sauce. In a small saucepan, heat the butter and paprika until fragrant. Pour over the eggs and serve immediately.

Yield: 6 to 12 servings

## OEUFS POCHES À LA BOELDIEU (POACHED EGGS BOELDIEU)

4 tomatoes, peeled, seeded, and diced
2 tablespoons butter
Salt and pepper to taste
2 tablespoons minced parsley

6 bread cases, toasted
6 poached eggs
1½ cups velouté sauce (see page 276)

In a skillet, over high heat, saute the tomatoes in the butter until the liquid evaporates. Season with salt, pepper, and parsley. Spoon the tomato mixture into the bread cases, top with poached egg, and nappe with the sauce. Serve immediately.

Yield: 6 servings

## POACHED EGGS ON CRAB CAKES WITH LIME HOLLANDAISE

1 pound crabmeat
1 cup crushed unsalted saltines
1 teaspoon dry mustard

1 egg, lightly beaten
salt and pepper to taste
3 tablespoons mayonnaise

2 tablespoons minced parsley
¼ cup minced parsley
½ cup vegetable oil

6 poached eggs
Lime Hollandaise (see page
 278)

Pick over the crab meat discarding any shell or cartilage. Place in
 a bowl. Add the cracker crumbs, mustard, egg, salt, pepper,
 mayonnaise, and parsley and blend gently. Shape into flat cakes.
 Refrigerate until ready to cook. In a skillet heat the oil and sauté
 the cakes until golden on both sides. Place the cakes on individual serving plates and top with a poached egg. Coat with sauce
 and serve immediately.

Yield: 6 servings

## COLD POACHED EGGS

Although not well known, there are many recipes for cold poached
eggs. These make a refreshing change from hot poached eggs and
can take the place as a salad at brunch or any other meal. The small
selection here will make a perfect addition to your repertoire of
summer, spring, and fall menus, or add them to your next cold
buffet.

## OEUFS AUX CREVETTES (COLD POACHED EGGS WITH SHRIMP)

6 cold poached eggs,
 trimmed
½ pound cooked small
 shrimp, peeled and
 deveined

¾ cup mayonnaise
¾ cup whipped cream
salt and pepper to taste
3 tablespoons minced
 chives or dill

Place the eggs in a serving dish. Surround with the shrimp. Fold
 the mayonnaise into the cream and correct the seasoning with
 salt and pepper. Spoon the sauce over the eggs and sprinkle with
 the chives.
The eggs and sauce can be prepared the day before. Do not
 assemble until just before serving.

Yield: 6 servings

## OEUFS POCHÉS AU CARI MAYONNAISE (POACHED EGGS WITH CURRY MAYONNAISE)

6 cold poached eggs,
   trimmed
curry powder to taste
1 cup mayonnaise

1 hard cooked egg, sieved
   mango chutney
chopped salted cashews
toasted coconut

Arrange the eggs in a serving dish. In a small bowl, mix the curry
   powder and mayonnaise and spoon over the eggs.
Separate the white from the yolk of the hard cooked egg and sieve
   them separately. Place in a small bowl. Place the chutney,
   cashews, and coconut in small bowls.
Serve the eggs and let guests add condiments as they choose.
The ingredients can be prepared the day before, but do not
   assemble until just before serving.

Yield: 6 servings

## OEUFS POCHÉS TARTARE (POACHED EGGS TARTAR)

3 tomatoes, halved
salt and pepper to taste
2 cups cold cooked mixed
   vegetables
1 cup mayonnaise
6 cold poached eggs,
   trimmed

2 tablespoons minced parsley
2 tablespoons minced gherkins
lettuce

Scoop the centers from the tomatoes, discard the seeds, and dice
   the pulp. Season the tomato shells with salt and pepper. Mix the
   pulp with the mixed vegetables and ¼ cup mayonnaise.
Fill the tomato shells with the vegetables and top with the eggs.
   Coat the eggs with the remaining mayonnaise and sprinkle with
   the parsley and gherkins. Serve on a bed of lettuce.
The ingredients can be prepared the day before, but assemble
   shortly before serving.

Yield: 6 servings

Eggs

NOTE

The vegetables are usually carrots, green beans, and potatoes cut into ¼ inch dice, and peas. You can add or substitute beets, fennel, turnip, or peppers.

## OEUFS POCHÉS VIRGINIA CLUB (POACHED EGGS VIRGINIA CLUB)

2 cups cooked corn kernels
⅔ cup mayonnaise
salt and pepper to taste
6 cold poached eggs,
    trimmed

watercress
3 tomatoes, quartered
olive oil
black olives

In a small bowl, mix the corn with ¼ cup mayonnaise and correct seasoning with salt and pepper.

Arrange the corn mixture as a base on a serving platter and chill. Coat the eggs with the remaining mayonnaise and arrange on top of the corn. Garnish the platter with the watercress, and tomatoes seasoned with salt and drizzled with olive oil, and the black olives.

The ingredients can be prepared the day before, but assemble shortly before serving.

Yield: 6 servings

## HARD AND SOFT-COOKED EGGS

Eggs used for soft or hard cooking should be several days old. Air will have had a chance to penetrate the shell, making peeling much easier. If there is a large dent at one end of the egg when you peel it, it was older than desired. Such eggs are not dangerous, they are simply not as pretty.

Because eggs must be treated gently, boiling can be a mistake. If you boil eggs rapidly, they become tough, rubbery, and indigestible. If you treat them gently, you will be rewarded with a firm, but tender white and properly cooked yolk. Besides, overcooking not only makes the eggs tough, but also creates an unsightly but harmless green ring on the yolk.

### To Soft Cook Eggs

Place the eggs in a saucepan large enough to hold them comfortably with 1 inch of water above the top egg. Remove the eggs and place the pan and the water over high heat. Bring to a full rolling boil. Gently lower the eggs into the water, in a basket, or with a slotted spoon. Cover the pan, remove it from the heat, and let stand for 6 to 8 minutes, or until the eggs are cooked to the desired degree of doneness. Immediately run under cold water to stop the cooking and to cool the shell for peeling. If it is necessary to reheat the eggs, put them into a bowl of very hot, but not boiling water until reheated. Use soft-cooked eggs in any poached-egg or any hard-cooked egg recipe requiring the whole egg, for example, Oeufs Dur Tapenade. Instead of cutting the eggs in half before coating with sauce, leave them whole.

### To Hard Cook Eggs

Place the eggs in a pan of cold water with 1 inch of water over the top egg. Place the pan with the eggs and water over high heat and bring it to a full boil. Cover the pan, remove it from the heat and let the eggs stand in the hot water for 12 to 15 minutes. Drain the eggs and run them under cold water to prevent further cooking. The white will be fully cooked and tender and the yolk will be cooked through without any green ring. Reheat as for soft-cooked eggs.

### Cracked Shells

If shells crack when hard- or soft-cooked, it is because the shells were cracked. They may have been cracked when you purchased them, or you may crack them when dropping into the pan. Place the eggs in the pan gently. Eggs taken from the coldest refrigerator and put into boiling water will not crack unless they were cracked beforehand.

### Serving Hard- and Soft-Cooked Eggs

You can eat soft-cooked eggs from the shell set into an egg cup, or you can garnish them elaborately. You can substitute soft-cooked eggs for many recipes that ask for poached or hard-cooked eggs. Interchange the eggs freely for a different effect.

You can prepare soft-cooked eggs the day before and reheat them just before serving. Peeling soft-cooked eggs is tedious and potentially dangerous (too much force and the white will split, allowing the yolk to ooze). Allow plenty of time for the process and cook a few extra eggs, just in case. Cook any unused eggs longer and make egg salad.

We usually serve hard-cooked eggs cold, either plain, or perhaps with some sort of stuffing. Europeans garnish them elaborately and serve them hot or cold depending on the needs of the menu. Again, it is wise to cook them the day before to allow sufficient, unhurried time to peel them. Also if they do not all peel perfectly you can cook a few more. Of course in many recipes, the garnish hides the exterior, so perfectly peeled eggs are not always necessary. Remember, a slightly older egg is easier to peel. If the eggs need to be reheated before being sauced, follow the rules for reheating soft-cooked eggs.

---

## OEUFS DUR À LA BRETONNE
## (HARD-COOKED EGGS BRITTANY)

6 tablespoons butter
½ cup minced onions
½ cup minced leeks
½ cup minced mushrooms

2 cups hot béchamel sauce
6 hard cooked eggs, peeled
  and halved

Preheat the broiler. In a skillet, heat 2 tablespoons of butter and sauté the onions. Set the onions aside. Repeat with the leeks and the mushrooms, sautéing them separately. Mix the cooked vegetables into the béchamel sauce. In the bottom of an 8×11-inch baking dish, spread a layer of sauce and arrange the eggs, cut side down, on top. Coat with the remaining sauce. Glaze under the broiler.

Yield: 6 servings

The dish can be assembled the night before and reheated at 350°F until bubbling and glazed under the broiler if necessary.

### VARIATION

### OEUFS DURS À LA SAUCE MOUTARDE
### (HARD-COOKED EGGS WITH MUSTARD SAUCE)

Add 1 teaspoon dry mustard to 1 cup béchamel sauce. Arrange hard-cooked eggs in a baking dish, coat with sauce, and glaze under the broiler. You can substitute any favorite mustard or use it in addition to the dry mustard.

## OEUFS DUR AURORE (HARD-COOKED EGGS AURORA)

| | |
|---|---|
| 6 hard-cooked eggs, peeled and halved | 1 tablespoon tomato paste |
| 2 tablespoons butter, softened | 1½ cups Sauce Aurore |
| | salt and pepper to taste |

Preheat the oven to 350°F. Remove the yolks from the eggs and force the yolks through a sieve. In a bowl, mix the yolks, 2 tablespoons butter, tomato paste, and ¼ cup Sauce Aurore. Correct seasoning with salt and pepper.

Fit a pastry bag with a #4 open star tip and fill the whites. Arrange in a baking dish and coat with the remaining sauce. Bake until heated and the sauce is bubbling.

Yield: 6 servings

The dish can be assembled the day before and reheated just before serving.

# OEUFS DURS À LA CHIMAY (STUFFED EGGS CHIMAY)

This recipe combines familiar ingredients in an unfamiliar manner to create a delicious, easily prepared dish.

| | |
|---|---|
| ½ cup minced mushrooms | salt to taste |
| 2½ tablespoons butter | 1 tablespoon grated Parmesan cheese |
| 6 hard-cooked eggs, halved | |
| 1 cup Mornay sauce | |

Preheat the broiler. In a small skillet, sauté the mushrooms in 1 tablespoon butter until the liquid evaporates. Remove the yolks from the eggs and force through a sieve. Mix the yolks with the remaining butter, mushrooms, ¼ cup Mornay sauce, and salt. Fit a pastry bag with #4 plain tip and stuff the eggs.

Place a thin layer of Mornay sauce in the bottom of a baking dish and arrange the eggs on top. Coat each egg with the remaining sauce and sprinkle with the cheese. Brown under the broiler.

Yield: 6 serving

Can be prepared the day before and reheated at 350°F until
bubbling hot. Brown the top under the broiler if necessary.

---

## OEUFS DUR À LA HOLLANDAISE
## (HARD-COOKED EGGS WITH HOLLANDAISE
## SAUCE)

¼ pound mushrooms,
   minced
2 tablespoons butter
2 tablespoons grated Parmesan cheese

6 hard-cooked eggs, halved
1 tablespoon tomato paste
2 tablespoons heavy cream
¾ cup hollandaise sauce

Preheat the oven to 350°F. In a 9-inch skillet, sauté the mushrooms
in the butter until the liquid evaporates. Remove the yolks from
the eggs and force through a sieve. Stir into the mushrooms with
the cheese, tomato paste, and cream.
With a pastry bag fitted with a #4 large star tip, pipe into the egg
whites and arrange the whites in a baking dish. Reheat the eggs
in the oven for 10 minutes and coat with hollandaise sauce just
before serving.

Yield: 6 servings

Can be prepared for baking the day before.

---

## OEUFS DURS À LA HONGROISE
## (HARD-COOKED EGGS HUNGARIAN STYLE)

6 hard-cooked eggs, halved
4 tablespoons minced onion
4 tablespoons butter
1 teaspoon paprika
salt and pepper to taste

3 ripe tomatoes, ½ inch
   thick slices
lemon juice to taste
½ cup heavy cream

Remove the yolks from the whites and force the yolks through a
sieve. In a small skillet, sauté the onion in the butter until soft,

but not brown. Stir half the onion into the yolks with ½ teaspoon
paprika. Correct the seasoning with salt and pepper.

With a pastry bag, fitted with a #4 large open star tip, fill the whites.

In the remaining butter-onion mixture sauté the tomato slices until
hot and tender. Place the tomato slices and onions in a baking
dish and arrange the eggs on top.

In the skillet, bring the remaining paprika, lemon juice, and cream
to a boil and pour over the eggs. Serve. If necessary, reheat the
eggs in a 350°F oven.

Yield: 6 servings

Can be prepared the day before and reheated in a 350°F oven.

## MEULEMEESTER EGGS

This is a simple egg casserole. Serve with a salad, and fruit for
dessert.

| | |
|---|---|
| 6 hard-cooked eggs, peeled and chopped | ½ teaspoon Dijon mustard |
| ½ pound medium shrimp, cooked, peeled, and deveined | ½ teaspoon minced chervil |
| | salt and pepper to taste |
| | 3 tablespoons grated Gruyère cheese |
| 1 cup heavy cream | 2 tablespoons butter |
| 1 teaspoon minced parsley | |

Preheat the broiler. In a bowl, mix the eggs, shrimp, cream, parsley,
mustard, chervil, salt, and pepper. Turn into a buttered 8×11-
inch baking dish and sprinkle with the cheese. Dot with butter
and brown under the broiler.

Yield: 6 servings

Can be prepared the day before. If necessary reheat in a 350°F oven.

## OEUFS DUR MISTRAL (HARD-COOKED EGGS MISTRAL)

| | |
|---|---|
| 6 hard-cooked eggs, halved | 1 cup mayonnaise |
| salt and pepper to taste | 6 ½-inch thick tomato slices |

6 pimiento-stuffed olives,           ½ cup imported ripe olives
   halved lengthwise                 2 parsley sprigs

Sprinkle the cut sides of the eggs with salt and pepper. Coat the
   rounded sides with mayonnaise and place the eggs, cut side
   down on tomato slices. Arrange on a serving platter and top
   each egg with an olive half, cut side up. Garnish the platter with
   black olives and parsley sprigs.

Yield: 6 servings

Can be assembled shortly before serving.

## HARD-COOKED EGGS WITH SKORDALIA (GARLIC MAYONNAISE)

6 cold hard-cooked eggs,             salt and pepper
   halved                            lemon juice to taste
3 tomatoes, quartered                ½ cup olive oil
½ cup sun-cured black olives         ½ cup fresh white bread
18 small radishes                       crumbs
4 garlic cloves                      ¼ cup ground almonds
yolk of 1 egg                        minced parsley

Arrange the eggs, tomatoes, olives, and radishes on a serving platter.
   In a processor, purée the garlic. Add the egg yolk, salt, pepper, and
   2 teaspoons lemon juice. Turn the machine on and add the olive
   oil in a slow steady stream. Process until thickened. With the
   machine running, add the bread crumbs, almonds, and parsley.
   Correct the seasoning with salt, pepper and lemon juice. Drizzle
   some sauce over each egg and pass the remainder separately.

Yield: 6 servings

Sauce can be made up to 3 days ahead.

## OEUFS DUR EN TAPENADE (HARD-COOKED EGGS WITH OLIVE ANCHOVY CAPER SAUCE)

The name of this classic sauce comes from tapeno, the Provençal
word for caper.

24 black olives, pitted
8 anchovy fillets
½ cup olive oil
2 ounces tuna fish, in oil
3 tablespoons capers,
    drained

lemon juice to taste
cognac to taste
6 hard-cooked eggs
12 ¼-inch thick tomato
    slices

In a processor, purée the olives, anchovies, olive oil, tuna, and
    capers. Correct the seasoning with lemon juice and cognac.
Arrange the egg halves, cut side down on the tomato slices and
    coat with the sauce.

Yield: 6 servings

The sauce can be prepared 2 to 3 days before. Arrange shortly
    before serving.

## OEUFS DUR AUX CREVETTES
## (HARD-COOKED EGGS WITH SHRIMP)

6 hard-cooked eggs, halved
1 pound shrimp, cooked,
    peeled, and deveined
¾ cup heavy cream,
    whipped

¾ cup mayonnaise
salt and pepper to taste
minced chives or dill

Place the eggs, round side up, in a serving dish and garnish with
    shrimp. Fold the cream into the mayonnaise and correct the
    seasoning with salt and pepper. Coat the eggs with the sauce
    and garnish with the chives.

Yield: 6 servings

Can be prepared the night before, covered and refrigerated.

## OEUFS FARCIS À LA PRINTANIÈRE
## (STUFFED EGGS WITH VEGETABLE AND
## RICE SALAD)

1 cup cold cooked rice
½ cup cooked diced carrots

½ cup cooked diced green
    beans

½ cup seeded, diced cucumber
½ cup tarragon vinaigrette
6 hard-cooked eggs, halved
½ cup peeled, seeded, and
   diced tomato

8 tablespoons butter
4 ounces liver paté
4 ounces cream cheese
2 teaspoons tomato paste
bunch of watercress

In a bowl, toss the rice, carrots, beans, cucumber, and tomato with
   the vinaigrette.
Remove the yolks from the whites and force the yolks through a
   sieve. In a bowl, beat the egg yolks with the butter to form a
   smooth paste. Place half the mixture in another bowl and mash
   in the paté. In the first bowl, beat in the cream cheese and
   tomato paste.
Fill half the egg whites with the liver mixture and the other half
   with the tomato mixture. Arrange the salad on a serving platter
   and surround with the eggs. Garnish with the watercress.

Yield: 6 servings

Can be prepared, covered, and refrigerated overnight. Let come
   almost to room temperature before serving.

## OEUFS À LA PARISIENNE
## (HARD-COOKED EGGS PARISIENNE)

6 hard-cooked eggs, halved
6 tablespoons butter
1 tablespoon minced chives
salt and pepper to taste
6 peeled tomatoes, halved
sugar to taste
½ teaspoon minced garlic

1½ cups mayonnaise collee
   (see page 281)
2 tablespoons anchovy paste
1 teaspoon tomato paste
½ cup light cream
4 radishes, thinly sliced
2 teaspoons minced parsley
lemon slices

Remove the yolks from the eggs and force through a sieve into a
   bowl. Beat in the butter, chives, salt, and pepper. Fill the whites.
   Sprinkle the cut side of the tomatoes with salt, pepper, sugar
   and garlic. Place an egg, cut side down on top of each tomato.
   In a bowl, combine the mayonnaise, anchovy paste, tomato
   paste, and just enough cream to make the mixture flow. Coat
   the eggs and tomatoes and chill until set.

Arrange the tomatoes on a platter and garnish with radish slices, minced parsley, and lemon slices.

Yield: 6 servings

Can be prepared, covered, and refrigerated the day before.


## SHIRRED EGGS

Shirred eggs taste like a cross between a fried egg and a poached egg. They are no longer as popular as they once were. I suspect that this is due to a change in stove design. When stoves had a large flat expanse for a top, the egg dishes could be slid over the surface without fear of breaking. When stoves were designed with individual burners, porcelain dishes could not stand the direct heat. Fortunately, with a little planning you can make the eggs using your oven.

Cook shirred eggs in flat bottomed dishes that are about 5-inches in diameter called *cocottes*. Any small, flat-bottomed, overproof dish would work. To prepare several servings, arrange the cocottes on a baking sheet to make handling easier. For several servings when you do not own cocottes, a baking dish serves nicely. Sometimes the whites flow together and you have to cut the portions into squares but the flavor is still present. Also there is a good chance that you will be the only one to know they are usually done in individual servings.

In the past, the filled dish was placed on the flat stovetop to heat from the bottom and then finished in the oven. With today's stoves, it is better to do it all in the oven. Place the cocotte in the oven with just enough butter to film the bottom. When the dish is hot, add the eggs and bake until the white is fully set and the yolk is still runny. You can bake them longer for a firmer yolk.

Serve them plain with a strip of bacon or a link of sausage or garnish them more elaborately. Although the eggs must be baked just before serving, many garnishes can be prepared ahead. If they are ready, the actual baking time is about ten minutes. The time varies depending on the temperature of the eggs and the garnish.

Break the eggs into a custard cup or saucer before putting into the pan in case the yolk breaks. You can then set that egg aside for another use if the yolk breaks.

# OEUFS SUR LE PLAT AU FROMAGE (SHIRRED EGGS WITH CHEESE)

| | |
|---|---|
| 6 4-inch toast rounds | salt and pepper to taste |
| ¼ cup melted butter | 6 tablespoons grated |
| 6 slices Gruyère cheese | Gruyère cheese |
| 6 eggs | |

Preheat the oven to 350°F.

Dip the toast rounds in butter and arrange in baking dishes. Place a slice of cheese on top and bake for 5 minutes, or until the cheese melts.

Place an egg on top of each toast round and season with salt and pepper. Sprinkle with the grated cheese and bake until the white is set, about 10 minutes.

Yield: 6 servings

## VARIATION

### OEUFS SUR LE PLAT OMAR PACHA (SHIRRED EGGS OMAR PASHA)

Sauté ¾ cup minced onions in 3 tablespoons of butter and use as a base instead of the toast.

# OEUFS SUR LE PLAT AUX HARICOTS DE LIMA (SHIRRED EGGS WITH LIMA BEANS)

The addition of cream to the egg yolk is to keep it tender. I have not found a difference and often omit it.

| | |
|---|---|
| 1 onion, thinly sliced | salt and pepper to taste |
| 2 tablespoons butter | 8 eggs |
| 10 ounces cooked lima | 3 tablespoons heavy cream |
| beans | 2 tablespoons grated Parme- |
| 1 teaspoon minced parsley | san cheese |
| 1 tomato, peeled, seeded, | |
| and diced | |

In a skillet, sauté the onion in the butter until soft. Add the lima beans, parsley, and tomato, and cook until heated. Correct seasoning with salt and pepper. Place in 4 to 8 heated egg dishes and top with eggs.

Spoon cream on top, if using, and sprinkle with Parmesan. Bake until set, about 10 minutes.

Yield: 4 to 8 servings

## OEUFS SUR LE PLAT CATALANE (SHIRRED EGGS, CATALONIAN)

6 thin eggplant slices
salt and pepper to taste
6 tomato slices
¾ cup butter

1 garlic clove, crushed
6 to 12 eggs
minced parsley

Preheat the oven to 350°F.

In a large skillet sauté the eggplant in half the butter until tender. Remove, and put each slice in a heated egg dish. Season with salt and pepper.

Sauté the tomatoes in the remaining butter until they start to soften. Drain and place on top of the eggplant slices. Season with salt and pepper.

In the butter remaining in the skillet, sauté garlic until soft, but not browned. Add 1 to 2 eggs to each dish and spoon garlic butter over yolk. Bake until set, about 10 minutes. Sprinkle with parsley.

Yield: 6 servings

## OEUFS SUR LE PLAT AUX CHAMPIGNONS, DIT À LA POLONAISE (SHIRRED EGGS WITH MUSHROOMS, POLISH STYLE)

¾ pound mushrooms, sliced
4 tablespoons butter
1½ cups béchamel sauce
1 cup light cream

1½ teaspoons lemon juice
6 to 12 large eggs
salt and pepper to taste

Preheat the oven to 350°F. In a skillet, sauté the mushrooms in the butter until the liquid evaporates. Stir in the béchamel sauce and the cream. Simmer for 10 minutes and stir in the lemon juice. Divide the sauce among 6 heated egg dishes. Make indentations in the sauce and slide in the eggs. Season with salt and pepper. Bake until set, about 10 minutes.

Yield: 6 servings

---

## OEUFS SUR LE PLAT É LA PORTUGAISE (SHIRRED EGGS PORTGUESE)

1½ cups tomato fondue
  (see page 280)
6 to 12 eggs

salt and pepper to taste
minced parsley

Preheat the oven to 350°F. Place 1 tablespoon of tomato fondue in 6 heated egg dishes. Add 1 to 2 eggs to each dish and season with salt and pepper. Bake until set, about 10 minutes. Surround each egg with hot tomato fondue and sprinkle with minced parsley.

Yield: 6 servings

---

## OEUFS SUR LE PLAT À LA MEXICAINE (SHIRRED EGGS MEXICAN)

12 slices bacon, diced
12 tomato slices
6 canned chiles, minced

6 to 12 eggs
⅓ to ⅔ cup grated Monterey Jack cheese

Preheat the oven to 350°F. Divide the bacon among 6 heated egg dishes and bake until the bacon is crisp. Drain off the bacon fat. Add the tomato slices to each dish and top with 1 tablespoon of minced chile.

Place 1 to 2 eggs in each dish and sprinkle 1 tablespoon of grated cheese over each egg yolk. Bake until set about 15 to 20 minutes.

Yield: 6 servings

---

## OEUFS SUR LE PLAT FLAMENCO (SHIRRED EGGS FLAMENCO)

2 boiled potatoes, ½-inch
  cubes
4 chorizo sausages, ¼-inch
  slices
6 tablespoons butter
3 tomatoes, peeled, seeded,
  ½-inch dice

3 roasted red peppers, diced
¼ cooked peas
salt and pepper to taste
2 teaspoons minced parsley
6 to 12 eggs
¼ cup heavy cream
cayenne pepper to taste

Preheat the oven to 350°F.

In a skillet, saute the potatoes and sausage in the butter until browned.

Add the tomatoes, roasted peppers, peas, salt, pepper, and parsley. Divide among 6 heated egg dishes and top with 1 to 2 eggs. Season eggs with salt and pepper.

Bake for 8 minutes, spoon the cream over the eggs, and bake until set, about 5 minutes longer. Sprinkle with cayenne.

Yield: 6 servings

---

## EGGS BAKED IN TOMATOES

6 tomatoes
salt and pepper to taste
2 tablespoons minced onion
2 tablespoons minced parsley

6 eggs
½ cup bread crumbs
2 tablespoons grated Parmesan cheese
2 tablespoons olive oil

Preheat the oven to 450°F. Remove the tops from the tomatoes and cut a thin slice from the bottom, if needed to keep them stable. Scoop out the centers and drain, upside down, on paper toweling for 10 minutes. Season the inside with salt and pepper and place in a buttered baking dish.

Place a teaspoon of minced onion and parsley into each tomato and break an egg into each tomato. Sprinkle the egg with crumbs and cheese and drizzle with olive oil. Bake until set, about 15 minutes.

Yield: 6 servings

# CORNED BEEF HASH WITH SHIRRED EGGS

½ cup minced onions
2 tablespoons butter
1½ cups diced cooked
   corned beef

2 cups diced, boiled potatoes
½ cup cream
salt and pepper to taste
6 to 12 eggs

Preheat the oven to 350°F. In a skillet, sauté the onions in the
   butter until soft. Add the corned beef and potatoes and mix well.
   Stir in the cream, salt, and pepper.
Shape the mixture into 6 3-inch patties and place in buttered,
   heated egg dishes. With the back of a spoon make an indentation
   in the hash and slide on one or two eggs. Season the eggs with
   salt and pepper. Bake until set, about 10 minutes.

Yield: 6 servings

NOTE:

For a crisper finish, sauté the corned beef patties in butter until
crisp and brown on both sides before putting in the dishes. You
may spread the hash in an 8 × 11-inch baking dish and bake all
servings at once. Many cooks suggest using poached eggs on top of
the heated hash.

# BAKED EGGS

These are similar to shirred eggs, except to keep the mixture more
delicate, bake them in a water bath in small custard cups or
ramekins. Ramekins are small soufflé dishes. The cup should hold
½ to ¾ cup. The finished dish may served from the cup, or
unmolded.

## Water Bath

The French phrase is *bain marie*. To make a water bath, choose a
baking pan large enough to hold the ramekins with about 1 inch
of space between each. Place the filled ramekins in the pan and
add the boiling water halfway up the sides.

You can prepare most of the recipes for baking several hours
ahead. When baked, serve at once. They require about 20 to 30
minutes to bake.

To use this method for crustless "quiche," bake any of quiche

fillings in buttered ramekins in a water bath until set. To test for
doneness, insert a skewer into the center. It should come out clean.

## GEBAKKEN EIREN MET VIEN EN KAAS (BAKED EGGS WITH WINE AND CHEESE)

½ cup heavy cream
¼ cup grated Gruyère
  cheese
2 tablespoons lemon juice
2 tablespoons dry white
  wine

Dijon or Dusseldorf mus-
  tard to taste
salt and pepper to taste
8 eggs
½ cup buttered bread
  crumbs

Preheat the oven to 350°F. Butter 4 ramekins or custard cups.
  Break 2 eggs into each ramekin. In a bowl, beat the cream,
  cheese, lemon juice, wine mustard, salt, and pepper. Spoon over
  the eggs and sprinkle with the bread crumbs. Bake in a water
  bath until set about 25 minutes.

Yield: 4 servings

## BAKED EGGS BRAYEN

6 eggs
6 tablespoons heavy cream
salt and pepper

6 slices buttered toast
1 cup béchamel sauce
minced parsley

Preheat the oven to 350°F. In a bowl, beat the eggs, cream, salt,
  and pepper. Butter 6 ramekins and fill with the egg mixture.
  Bake in a water bath until set, about 20 minutes. Unmold onto
  the toast slices and coat with the béchamel sauce. Sprinkle with
  the parsley.

Yield: 6 servings

## VARIATIONS

Add a slice of heated ham or bacon to each toast slice.
  Add a slice of smoked salmon to each toast slice.
  Serve with hollandaise sauce, tomato fondue, Sauce Aurore, or
velouté.

Add 2 tablespoons minced lobster, crab, or shrimp to the custard and serve with hollandaise or béarnaise.

## OEUFS EN RAMEKIN LORRAINE (BAKED EGGS LORRAINE)

6 teaspoons minced crisp
  bacon
18 thin slices Gruyère
  cheese

6 tablespoons boiling cream
6 to 12 eggs
salt and pepper to taste

Preheat the oven to 350°F.
Place the bacon in 6 ramekins and cover with cheese slices. Spoon
  1 tablespoon of cream into each cup and add 1 to 2 eggs. Season
  with salt and pepper. Bake in a water bath until set about 20
  minutes.

Yield: 6 servings

## RIGODON DE BASSE BOURGOGNE (HAM AND PORK CUSTARD)

½ pound sliced ham
½ pound cooked sliced pork
3 cups milk
salt and pepper

6 eggs, lightly beaten
⅓ cup flour
1 tablespoon butter

Preheat the oven to 350°F.
Butter a 2-quart soufflé dish well. Arrange the meats in alternating
  layers in the bottom. In a saucepan, bring the milk to a boil and
  season with salt and pepper.
In a large bowl, beat the eggs with the flour and gradually add the
  hot milk, beating constantly. Pour the custard over the meats
  and dot the top with butter.
Place in a water bath and bake until set, about 40 minutes. Serve
  in wedges from the casserole. Serve hot or cold.

Yield: 6 servings

NOTE

Be generous with the pepper in this dish. An Italian version uses
¼ pound each of thinly sliced mortadella, Genoa salami, cappicola,
and Provolone cheese.


# FRIED EGGS

Fried eggs with bacon, ham or sausage, toast, and often hash-
browned potatoes is possibly the quintessential American breakfast of a bygone era. European chefs tend to use fried eggs as a
garnish for something else such as in *Weiner schnitzel à la Holstein*,
a sautéed veal cutlet with a fried egg and anchovy garnish. In
France a fried egg is fried in deep fat, twirling the egg in place to
keep an oval egg shape.

### To Fry Eggs

In a small skillet, melt 1 tablespoon of butter. Break the egg into
a saucer as you would for poached eggs, so that if the yolk breaks
it can be set aside for another use. Slide the egg into the hot butter
and let it cook over medium heat until the white sets. During the
cooking, spoon some hot butter from the pan over the yolk to cook
the top. Keep the heat at medium. You may cover the pan to help
cook the yolk. When cooked, slide the egg yolk onto a serving dish.
A perfectly fried egg has a set, not a tough, white with no browned
edges and a runny yolk. Of course different people like their eggs
differently and would consider a perfectly cooked egg a travesty.
They may prefer to cook at a high heat to obtain a crispy brown
bottom to the egg, or to flip the egg over to cook the yolk more
firmly.

### To Fry Eggs French Style

This method is truly a french fried egg. The result is a crusty
exterior with a runny yolk. Usually it garnishes other dishes.

In an omelet pan, place ¼ cup vegetable oil and heat until very
hot but not smoking. (Many chefs do this in a saucepan but I find
that the shape of the omelet pan helps to keep the egg oval.) Break
an egg into a saucer. Have a dry wooden spoon at hand. Slide the
egg into the oil and immediately tilt the pan by the handle to a 45
degree angle, sliding the egg and oil to one side of the pan. Use
the wooden spoon to turn the egg in the oil to shape it into an oval

like a whole egg. Cook, turning often, until the outside of the egg is golden. Drain on paper towels.

## OEUFS À L'ESPAGNOLE
## (FRIED EGGS SPANISH STYLE)

This is the French version of how Spaniards prepare their eggs.

| | |
|---|---|
| 2 eggs, fried | 4 tablespoons tomato sauce |
| 2 tomato halves, | 1 teaspoon minced pimiento |
|   sautéed in oil | ½ cup fried onion rings |

In the center of a plate, arrange the eggs on the tomatoes. In a saucepan heat the tomato sauce and the pimiento and coat each egg with the sauce, or place the sauce around the edge of the plate. Scatter onion rings over the top. Serve immediately.

Yield: 1 serving

## HUEVOS FRITOS À LA ESPAGNOLA
## (SPANISH FRIED EGGS)

This is the Spanish version of how Spaniards prepare fried eggs.

| | |
|---|---|
| 3 green peppers, chopped | salt and pepper to taste |
| 1 large onion, chopped | 6 fried eggs |
| ¼ cup olive oil | 12 toast points |
| 4 tomatoes, peeled, seeded, | |
|   and chopped | |

In a large skillet, sauté the peppers and onions in the oil until softened. Add the tomatoes and cook until most of the liquid evaporates. Correct the seasoning with salt and pepper. Place the pepper mixture on the serving plates and top with a fried egg and serve with toast points.

Yield: 6 servings

The sauce can be prepared ahead and frozen.

## UOVA ALLA SALSA DI GAMBERO
## (EGGS WITH SHRIMP SAUCE)

2 tablespoons minced on-
  ions
2 tablespoons minced parsley
2 tablespoons butter
6 ounces peeled, deveined
  shrimp

½ pound toasted ground
  pine nuts
salt and pepper to taste
6 tablespoons boiling water
12 large shrimp in their
  shells
1 tablespoon butter
6 fried eggs

In a small skillet, sauté the onion and parsley in the butter until
  soft, but not brown. Add the peeled shrimp and pine nuts and
  cook until the shrimp are just cooked. Season with salt and
  pepper. In a processor purée the mixture, adding the water.
  Return to a saucepan and keep warm.
In a small skillet, sauté the remaining shrimp until just cooked.
  Arrange the eggs on serving plates, surround with sauce, and
  garnish with the sautéed shrimp.

Yield: 3 to 6 servings

NOTE

Traditionally you serve the shrimp unpeeled, but you may peel
them. If the sautéed shrimp are small you may want to serve more
than two per person.


## SCRAMBLED EGGS

The simplest foods are often the most difficult to prepare. A
perfectly roasted chicken or sautéed trout is more difficult to
achieve than many elaborate preparations. This also is true of
scrambled eggs. They seem easy, but require skill and attention to
reach perfection.

Scrambled eggs are made from eggs and seasoning. The eggs
become creamy by careful gentle cooking, not adding milk, cream,
or water. When they are almost cooked, they can have a generous
addition of butter, but only once they have set. To make them takes
time: if you are in a hurry make an omelet, if you have half an hour
make scrambled eggs.

They are best served perhaps only with buttered toast points.

Some of the recipes that follow require other ingredients to be cooked in with the eggs, but remember to cook them gently over low heat. Some guests may despise "loose" scrambled eggs, especially the almost soup-like version popular with French cooks. Plan to cook theirs longer, but still over low heat, until the curds are almost set, then transfer to a plate. The retained heat will cook the eggs as they stand. High heat and fast cooking will cause the eggs to toughen and to ooze water.

## SCRAMBLED EGGS

12 eggs                                    8 tablespoons butter
Salt and pepper to taste

In a bowl, beat the eggs with salt and pepper until well combined. If you wish a creamier finish, strain the eggs through a sieve to remove the chalaza, the white "thread" that holds the yolk in suspension in the white. In a 9-inch skillet, melt 4 tablespoons of butter over low heat. Add the eggs and cook, stirring constantly over low heat until the eggs are creamy and cooked, but not hard. When almost cooked, stir in the remaining 4 tablespoons of butter. Serve the eggs immediately or else the retained heat will cause them to overcook and lose their creamy consistency. Allow 20 to 30 minutes for the eggs to cook. The curd that develops on the bottom of the pan should be scraped up constantly with a wooden or rubber spatula and stirred into the mass of egg.

Yield: 4 to 6 servings

NOTE

For large crowds, prepare the eggs in a large double boiler. If necessary, construct a double boiler by fitting two pots together. The water should never boil. When the eggs are warm, keep stirring from the bottom for even cooking.

## OEUFS BROUILLÉS NIÇOISE
## (SCRAMBLED EGGS NIÇOISE)

1 cup cubed slab bacon              2 cups warm eggplant
                                     Provençal (see page 283)

4 tablespoons butter
1 tablespoon minced parsley
1 teaspoon lemon juice

12 eggs
4 tablespoons butter

In a 9 inch skillet, cook the bacon in its own fat until almost crisp.
   Drain off the excess fat. Add the eggplant to the skillet and heat.
In a bowl, cream the butter with the parsley and lemon juice and
   reserve.
Scramble the eggs in the 4 tablespoons of butter. When the eggs
   are almost set, stir in the parsley butter.
Arrange the eggs on a serving platter and surround with the
   eggplant. Serve immediately.

Yield: 4 to 6 servings

## SAUSAGE CUPS WITH CHIVE SCRAMBLED EGGS

1½ pounds mild sausage
   meat
1 tablespoon minced onion
1 cup uncooked quick-cook-
   ing oats
1 egg

¼ cup milk
12 eggs, scrambled
6 ounces cream cheese with
   chives, cut in ½ inch
   cubes

Preheat the oven to 325 °F. In a bowl, mix the sausage, onion, oats,
   egg, and milk. Press the mixture into 6 muffin or custard cups.
   Press a deep hollow into the center of each. Bake for 30 minutes.
   Drain off the excess fat and place sausage cups on paper towels
   on a rack and keep warm in a turned off oven.
Scramble the eggs and when almost cooked, stir in the cheese in
   place of the final addition of butter.
When the cheese is warmed, but not fully melted, spoon into the
   custard cups and serve.

Yield: 6 servings

## SCRAMBLED EGGS WITH SMOKED SALMON

½ cup minced onions
¼ cup butter

1 pound thinly sliced
   smoked salmon

12 eggs, scrambled until al-  
    most done

coarsely ground black pep-  
    per  
minced parsley

In a small skillet, sauté the onions in the butter until soft, but not brown. Add the salmon and just heat.

When the eggs are almost done, stir in the onion-salmon mixture and cook until just done. Serve garnished with pepper and parsley.

Yield: 4 to 6 servings

---

# LOX AND EGGS

1 onion, minced  
1 green pepper, minced  
2 cups sliced mushrooms  
8 tablespoons butter  
½ pound lox, chopped

8 eggs  
1 tablespoon minced parsley  
¼ tablespoon basil  
Tabasco to taste  
salt and pepper to taste

In a skillet, sauté the onion, pepper, and mushrooms in the butter until soft. Lower the heat and add the lox and cook until just heated.

In a bowl, beat the eggs, parsley, basil, Tabasco, salt, and pepper and add to the salmon mixture. Cook, stirring over low heat until just set. Serve immediately.

Yield: 4 servings

NOTE

Often these are cooked to a drier state than ordinary scrambled eggs. Cook a minute or two longer than usual. Be careful about adding salt since the lox is salty.

---

# OEUFS OFFENBACH (SCRAMBLED EGGS WITH TUNA AND SHRIMP)

2 tomatoes, peeled, and  
    seeded

2 tablespoons butter  
12 eggs, scrambled

3 anchovy fillets, minced
3 ounces tuna, flaked
6 slices buttered toast

12 peeled shrimp, cooked
2 tablespoons minced parsley

Cut the tomatoes into 6 ¼-inch slices and dice the remainder. In
a skillet, sauté the tomato slices in the butter until heated. When
the eggs are almost set, stir in the anchovies and tuna fish. Place
toast on hot plates and top with a tomato slice. Spoon the eggs
over the tomatoes and garnish with the shrimp, diced tomatoes,
and parsley.

Yield: 6 servings

## SCRAMBLED EGGS À LA CARACAS

2 ounces smoked dried
   beef, minced
3 cups peeled, seeded, and
   chopped tomatoes
¾ cup grated Parmesan
   cheese

¼ cup minced onion
pinch of cinnamon
pinch of cayenne
6 tablespoons butter
9 eggs, beaten

In a skillet, sauté the beef, tomatoes, cheese, onion, cinnamon, and
cayenne in the butter until the tomatoes are soft and the liquid
evaporated. Stir in the eggs and scramble until the eggs just set.
Serve immediately.

Yield: 4 to 6 servings

## OMELETS

There is a mystique about making omelets. You must use the right
pan. You can only use it for omelets. You can never wash it. You
must beat the eggs. You must not beat the eggs.

There are people who brag that they have never washed their
omelet pan—all too often you know it! If you make omelets at least
once a week, then wipe the pan with paper toweling and salt. If
you make omelets once a month, or less, then an unwashed pan
may be unpleasant, if not unhealthy. The oil retained in the pan
can turn rancid.

## Omelet Pans

An omelet pan (sauteuse) has a flat bottom with gently sloping sides. Traditionally they are made of steel, which transfers heat immediately to the contents of the pan. These pans rust easily and are prone to sticking unless very well seasoned. The speed with which you can make an omelet may not compensate for the maintenance problems.

Most professional kitchens now use aluminum pans. They can be polished to mirror brightness with steel wool pads and can be seasoned easily. This means you can use the pan for other foods and easily reseason it when you need it for omelets. Often, unless food has stuck to the pan and had to be scrubbed off, the pan retains enough residual oil to allow you to prepare an omelet without reseasoning.

Besides aluminum there are many non-stick pans that require no more than a light swirl of butter before you make an omelet. If storage space is a problem, an aluminum or non-stick pan makes more sense since it is less to store and it is available for other uses.

## To Season an Omelet Pan

Scour a new steel or aluminum pan with steel wool pads. (It is unnecessary to season a non-stick pan.) Rinse well and dry. Place about 1 inch of unflavored vegetable oil into the pan and place over very low heat until the oil is very hot, but not smoking, about one hour. Turn off the heat and cool the oil in the pan. Drain off the oil and wipe the pan with paper toweling. (You can re-use the oil for sauteing or deep frying.) This may seem like a lot of work for one omelet, but makes sense if you are making several. You can prepare the pan several days before you need it.

## To Cook an Omelet

A three-egg, single-serving omelet is the most reasonable size to make. It will cook quickly and easily. If you need to serve several people, you can make this size quickly enough to serve everyone without delay. Larger omelets are extremely difficult to cook properly and take as long to prepare as several smaller ones. And, who wants half an omelet?

Break the eggs into a bowl, season with salt and pepper, and, with a fork, beat about 40 vigorous strokes. Some cooks believe that adding 1 tablespoon of water makes a lighter omelet. I disagree: fast, deft cooking accomplishes that. Practice on yourself before serving others.

Over high heat, heat the pan until very hot. Add 1 tablespoon of butter, which should start to sizzle immediately, bubble up, and begin to smell nut-like. As soon as the butter melts, pour the eggs into the pan and let set for about 5 seconds. Hold a fork with the tines horizontal to the pan and stir the eggs in a circle while shaking the pan back and forth with the other hand. It is similar to rubbing your stomach while patting your head. If you keep both hands close to one another it will be easier. The object is to keep the egg mixture moving so that it does not stick to the pan.

As the omelet begins to set, pull the sides toward the center and lift the edges to let the uncooked egg flow underneath. When the center of the omelet is almost set, but still moist, place the filling in a line across the center. Tilt the pan back toward the handle and use the sloping sides of the pan and a fork to help turn one third of the omelet over the filling. Put the pan on the side of the stove and place the palm of your hand under the handle with your thumb pointing away from you. Grasp the handle firmly. In one fluid movement tilt the pan in the opposite direction, sliding the omelet to the side of the pan opposite the handle and flip the omelet onto a plate shaping it into a perfect oval.

The color should be pale yellow with no browning because browning changes the flavor and toughens the eggs. If your guests demand browned omelets, cook it a few minutes longer. Serve omelets immediately, while they are still light and puffy. The slightly undercooked center will continue to cook from the heat of the omelet and the filling. The whole process takes only 30 to 45 seconds.


### Omelets for a Crowd

Omelets do not hold. They must be served when they are cooked and therefore must be made to order. You can set up a production line for quick service. Practice making a few for yourself before you plan to serve a crowd for brunch. Entertaining can be difficult enough without starting your day cooking under intense pressure.

Allow 3 eggs for each omelet. Break the eggs into a bowl, season with salt and pepper, and beat well. Strain the eggs to remove the chalazae which toughen when heated and to remove any bits of shell. Use a 6-ounce ladle to measure each serving and follow the previous directions. With a little practice you can serve 6 people in less than 5 minutes.

If you are offering a selection of fillings, have your guests make their choices before you start to cook their omelet. No one wants to wait for a guest to decide while you have a cooked omelet in hand.

### Folding and Filling Omelets

There are several ways to fold and fill omelets. The classic method is to put the filling in the center third and fold over the two sides as described. Sometimes the omelet is folded and turned out without any filling, a slit is cut along the length of the omelet, and the filling is put into the slit. On occasions the filling is put on half the omelet and covered with the other half, so that it looks like a large turnover, usually with some filling showing. You also can slide the unfilled omelet onto a plate and spoon the filling on top.

Fillings for omelets are limitless: do not restrict yourself to the few suggestions here. For example, many of the fillings for crêpes, or the meat and fish preparations in other chapters are suitable fillings for omelets. So are many leftovers. Check the refrigerator for likely fillings. Odd bits of cheese, leftover vegetables, or unfinished meats or fish can all be used as fillings for omelets. Remember that omelets began as the thrifty French housewife's answer to the stretching of leftovers. If you want to serve lobster or caviar on a limited budget, using a small amount in an omelet is one way of appearing extravagant while watching your wallet.

### Other Types of Omelets

In addition to the classic folded omelet there are the pancake-like frittata found in areas around the Mediterranean and the omelet soufflé.

The frittata usually has chopped foods mixed with the eggs. Cook it in a large, heated, well-buttered or oiled skillet until set and browned on the bottom. Slide it onto a large plate and flip it over into the pan to finish cooking the other side. Serve frittata cut into wedges. Because they taste good at room temperature, they are especially pleasant for a picnic.

Omelet soufflés are similar to soufflés. Separate the eggs and add the flavoring to the yolks. Beat the whites until stiff and fold into the yolks. They also are similar to omelets. Heat the omelet pan, fill with the egg mixture, and allow it to set for a few minutes over medium heat. Then bake the omelet at 425°F until it is puffed and cooked. You must serve it immediately.

## OMELET AUX FINES HERBES (OMELET WITH HERBS)

3 eggs
salt and pepper to taste

1 tablespoon mixed fresh
    minced parsley, chervil,
    chives, and tarragon
1 tablespoon butter

In a bowl, beat the eggs with the salt, pepper, and herbs about 40 vigorous strokes. In a hot omelet pan, melt the butter. Add the eggs and cook, shaking the pan back and forth and stirring with a fork, until almost set. Tilt the omelet back toward the handle, reverse your hand and tilt out onto a serving plate. Serve at once.

Yield: 1 serving

## OMELETTE À L' ARLESIENNE (OMELET WITH EGGPLANT AND TOMATOES)

1 recipe eggplant Provençal
    (see page 283)

2 3-egg omelets
minced parsley

Have the eggplant mixture prepared and hot. Make the omelets and fill with the eggplant mixture. Turn out and garnish with the parsley.

Yield: 2 omelets

The eggplant mixture can be made several days ahead or frozen.

## OMELETTE SAVOYARD (FOLDED OMELET WITH POTATOES AND CHEESE)

1 cup sliced boiled potatoes
4 tablespoons butter

½ cup grated Gruyère
    cheese

¼ cup heavy cream                    2 3-egg omelets
salt and pepper to taste             minced parsley

In a 7-inch skillet, heat the potatoes in the butter. Stir in the cheese,
   cream, salt, and pepper. Keep warm.
Prepare the omelets and fill with the potato mixture and fold.
   Sprinkle with the minced parsley.

Yield: 2 servings

The potato mixture can be prepared the day before and gently
   reheated.

## OMELETTE AU BROCCIO (OMELET WITH GOAT CHEESE)

6 eggs                               1 cup Broccio or other goat
large pinch fresh mint                  cheese
salt and pepper to taste             mint sprigs
3 tablespoons butter

In a bowl, beat the eggs with the mint, salt, and pepper. Make 2
   omelets. When almost set, crumble the cheese in the center and
   fold. Turn onto a heated platter and garnish with mint sprigs.

Yield: 2 servings

## OMELETTE GARGAMELLE (MUSHROOM AND CHEESE OMELET)

2 cups minced mushrooms              3 3-egg omelets
3 scallions, minced                  1 tablespoon grated Parme-
5 tablespoons dry vermouth              san cheese
¾ cup heavy cream                    3 thin slices Gruyère cheese
salt and pepper to taste             paprika
1 teaspoon cornstarch

Preheat the broiler. In a saucepan, simmer the mushrooms, scallions, vermouth, and ½ cup heavy cream for 5 minutes. Correct
   the seasoning with salt and pepper. In a small bowl, mix the

remaining cream and cornstarch and add to the pan. Cook, stirring until thickened. Prepare the omelets and fill, using only half the mushroom mixture. Arrange the omelets on ovenproof baking dishes and pour on the remaining mushroom mixture. Add the cheeses and sprinkle with paprika. Broil until golden brown. Serve at once.

Yield: 3 servings

The filling can be made a day ahead and reheated.

## OMELETTE À LA BOURGUIGNONNE (OMELET WITH SNAILS)

½ cup minced onions
⅓ cup minced shallots
2 tablespoons minced garlic
2 tablespoons butter
4 tablespoons flour
1 cup whole stewed tomatoes, drained

4½ ounce can snails
¼ cup minced cooked carrots
salt and pepper to taste
2 3-egg omelets

In a skillet, sauté the onion, shallots, and garlic in butter until soft, but not brown. Stir in the flour over low heat until it starts to turn golden. Stir in the tomatoes and ¼ cup liquid from the snails. Cook, stirring, until thickened and smooth. Add the snails, carrots, salt, and pepper to taste. Simmer 10 to 15 minutes.

Prepare the omelets and fill with the snail mixture and fold. Serve immediately.

Yield: 2 servings

The filling can be prepared ahead and frozen.

## L'OMELETTE BARON DU BARANTE (LOBSTER AND MUSHROOM OMELET)

1½ pounds mushrooms sliced

4 tablespoons butter
salt and pepper

½ cup dry port
½ cup heavy cream
1 pound lobster meat, sliced

6 3-egg omelets
grated Parmesan cheese

In a 9-inch skillet, saute the mushrooms in the butter until the liquid evaporates. Season lightly with salt and pepper. Stir in the port and cream and reduce by half. Add the lobster meat and heat gently until hot, without boiling. Prepare the omelets and fill with the lobster mixture. Serve immediately.

Yield: 6 servings

---

# BRAZILIAN OMELET

½ pound lean ground beef
1 pound stewed tomatoes
1 green pepper, julienne
1 tablespoon minced green
  chilis

1 teaspoon chili powder
salt to taste
¼ teaspoon sugar
4 3-egg omelets

In a 9-inch skillet, brown the beef in its own fat. Drain off the excess fat. Stir in the tomatoes, pepper, chilis, chili powder, salt, and sugar. Simmer for 5 minutes.
Prepare the omelets and fill with the mixture. Slit the omelets lengthwise to expose the filling.

Yield: 4 servings

The filling can be prepared ahead and reheated.

---

# OMELETTE AUX PISSENLITS (OMELET WITH DANDELION GREENS)

1 bunch dandelion greens,
  washed, and chopped
¼ inch thick slice country
  ham, diced
1 tablespoon butter

9 eggs
salt and pepper to taste
pinch of ground coriander
3 tablespoons lard

In a 9-inch skillet, sauté the greens and the ham in the butter until heated. Beat the eggs with the salt, pepper, and coriander. Stir

in the greens and ham. Using the lard, prepare 3 omelets, letting them brown lightly before folding.

Yield: 3 servings

## OMELETTE À LA BÉARNAISE (OMELET BEARN STYLE)

| | |
|---|---|
| 5 ounces cornichons, capers, or pickled peppers | 1 tablespoon tomato purée |
| ¼ pound bacon, diced | 9 eggs, lightly beaten |
| 2 tablespoon oil | salt and pepper to taste |
| | 3 tablespoons butter |

Drain the cornichons and mince. In a 7 inch skillet, sauté the bacon in the oil until browned. Drain off the excess fat and discard. Stir in the peppers and tomato purée and simmer 1 minute. Let the mixture cool for 1 minute and stir into the eggs. Correct the seasoning with salt and pepper. Prepare 3 omelets using the butter.

Yield: 3 servings

## OMELETTE NORMANDE (APPLE OMELET)

Not all omelets are savory. You can serve sweet omelets for brunch, or as a winning dessert after a light supper.

| | |
|---|---|
| 1½ pounds apples, peeled, cored, and sliced | 3 tablespoons calvados |
| 3 tablespoons butter | 3 3-egg omelets |
| | sugar |

Preheat the broiler.

In a 9-inch skillet, sauté the apples in the butter with 1 tablespoon of calvados until softened.

Prepare the omelets and fill with the apples, fold and turn onto a heatproof platter. Sprinkle the omelets with sugar and glaze until golden brown. Flame with the remaining calvados (see note.)

Yield: 3 to 6 servings

NOTE

To flame the calvados; in a small saucepan warm the Calvados over low heat. Ignite and pour over the omelet. Substitute almost any fruit for the apples and use a complimentary liqueur. Serve Grand Marnier with Strawberries or oranges; Kirsch with strawberries or raspberries; Anisette with Strawberries or peaches; Rum with peaches or grapes.

## SWEET OMELET SOUFFLÉ

8 eggs, separated
1 cup sugar flavoring (see
   note)

¼ teaspoon salt
2 tablespoons butter

Preheat the oven to 425°F. In a bowl, beat the egg yolks with ½ cup of sugar and the liquid flavoring of your choice until light in color, and smooth and thick enough to form a ribbon.

In a separate bowl, beat the egg whites with the salt until they form soft peaks. Beat in the remaining sugar, 1 tablespoon at a time, beating the whites until stiff and glossy. Fold the whites into the egg yolks and fold in other flavoring as listed in the note, if desired.

In a deep 10-inch skillet, with a heatproof handle, melt the butter over medium heat. Spread ¾ of the batter in the skillet, smoothing the surface. Put the remaining batter into a pastry bag fitted with a large #6 B tip, and pipe rosettes and swirls over the souffle.

Place the pan over medium heat and cook 3 minutes, or until the bottom is set, but not browned.

Transfer the pan to the oven and bake 8 minutes in the upper third of the oven, until the top is puffed, firm and golden brown.

Serve at once.

Yield: 6 to 8 servings

NOTE

For flavorings, use 1 tablespoon of vanilla, or 2 tablespoons of a favorite liqueur to flavor the yolks. You can also fold ½ to ¾ cup toasted ground almonds, walnuts, pecans, or hazelnuts into the batter. For texture and additional flavor, fold in minced fresh fruit. Use about 1 cup of well-drained fruit.

## KAISERSCHMARRN (EMPEROR'S OMELET)

Franz Joseph, the Austro-Hungarian Emperor loved this strange but delicious sweet, which is a cross between and omelet and soufflé.

⅔ cup raisins

2 ounces cognac

4 tablespoons sugar

5 eggs, separated

1 cup heavy cream

1 cup flour

6 tablespoons flour

4 tablespoons sugar

confectioners' sugar

Preheat the oven to 350°F.

Butter a 2-quart soufflé dish. In a small bowl, macerate the raisins in the cognac for 30 minutes. Stir 4 tablespoons sugar into the egg yolks and add the heavy cream, stirring constantly. Add the flour gradually, stirring constantly, until the batter is smooth. Beat the egg whites until stiff, but not dry.

Fold into the batter. Pour into the soufflé dish and bake for 10 to 15 minutes, or until the omelet is puffed and golden.

In a skillet, melt 6 tablespoons of butter. With a fork, tear the omelet into pieces, about 1½ inches square. Put the pieces into the skillet with the cognac-raisin mixture and 4 tablespoons of sugar.

Sauté the chunks until they have a light coating of butter and sugar. Serve sprinkled with the confectioners' sugar.

Yield: 4 to 6 servings

## FRITTATA DI ZUCCHINI (ITALIAN FLAT ZUCCHINI OMELET)

2 small zucchini, thinly sliced

flour

3 tablespoons olive oil

6 eggs, lightly beaten

1 tablespoon grated Parmesan cheese

salt and pepper to taste

pinch of ground thyme

Dredge the zucchini in the flour. Sauté in the olive oil in a 10-inch skillet until golden brown and tender.

In a bowl, mix the eggs, cheese, salt, pepper, and thyme. Pour over
the zucchini, in the skillet, and cook until set and browned on
one side.

Slide the omelet onto a plate and then flip it over into the pan.
Brown the second side. Serve hot or warm, cut into wedges.

Yield: 2 to 4 servings

---

## FRITTATA DI PORRI (LEEK FRITTATA)

5 large leeks, white part
   only, cut into ½ inch-
   thick slices

4 tablespoons olive oil
6 eggs
salt and pepper

In a bowl, soak the leeks in cold water to cover for 20 minutes.
Drain and rinse under cold running water. Dry well.

In a 10-inch skillet, heat 3 tablespoons olive oil. Add the leeks and
sauté until softened. Transfer to a bowl and let cool. Beat the
eggs, salt, and pepper and stir in the leeks.

In a 10-inch skillet, heat the remaining oil until hot. Add the egg
mixture and cook as for Frittata di Zucchini (page 127).

Yield: 2 to 3 servings

---

## SOUTH AMERICAN OMELET

1 large avocado, halved
8 eggs
salt and pepper to taste

1 tablespoons olive oil
2 tablespoons butter

With a melon baller make small balls of half the avocado. Cut the
remaining avocado into ½ inch cubes.

In a bowl beat the eggs with the salt and pepper. Add the diced
avocado. Cook in the oil and butter to make a flat omelet. Turn
out and garnish with avocado balls.

Yield: 3 to 4 servings

## OMELETTE ROPA VIEJA (CUBAN "OLD CLOTHES" OMELET)

2 tomatoes, peeled, seeded, and chopped

2 tablespoons butter

½ cup shredded chicken or ham

4 eggs, lightly beaten

1 tablespoon minced parsley

In a 7-inch skillet, heat the tomatoes in the butter. Add the chicken or ham and cook until slightly thickened. Add the eggs and parsley and cook over low heat until set and lightly browned. Slide the omelet onto a plate and turn over into the pan to cook the second side. Cook until browned. Serve hot or warm.

Yield: 1 to 2 servings

## OMELETTE À LA SAVOYARDE (FLAT SAVOY OMELET)

2 boiled potatoes, thinly sliced

7 tablespoons butter

8 eggs, lightly beaten

¼ cup grated Gruyère cheese

1 teaspoon chervil

salt and pepper to taste

In a 9-inch skillet, sauté the potatoes in 6 tablespoons butter until browned.

In a bowl, mix the eggs, Gruyère cheese, chervil, salt, and pepper. Pour over the potatoes and mix the potatoes so the eggs settle to the bottom of the pan. Cook, undisturbed until golden. Run a flexible spatula under the omelet to loosen and slide out onto a plate. Add the remaining butter to the pan and flip the omelet over into the pan to cook the second side until browned.

Yield: 3 to 4 servings

## LA PIPERADE DU PAYS BASQUE (BASQUE PEPPER OMELET)

1 green pepper, thinly sliced

1 tablespoon olive oil

4 tomatoes, peeled, seeded, and chopped

1 onion, thinly sliced                    salt and pepper
½ clove garlic, crushed                   2 tablespoons butter
¼ cup diced ham                           4 eggs

In a 7-inch skillet, sauté the pepper in the olive oil until soft. Add
    the tomatoes, onion, garlic, and ham and season with salt and
    pepper.
Add the butter and simmer until the tomatoes are a soft puree and
    the mixture thickens slightly.
Beat the eggs and season with salt and pepper. Add to the vegetable
    mixture in the skillet and cook until barely set. Slide out of the
    pan and serve.

Yield: 1 to 2 servings


NOTE

Serve this flat omelet barely set, not browned on both sides like
the other versions.


## SOUFFLÉS

Soufflés, like omelets, strike terror into the hearts of many other-
wise justifiably confident cooks. Soufflés are just another means of
preparing thrifty, delicious meals from simple ingredients. A
soufflé is nothing more than a béchamel (cream) sauce, enriched
with egg yolk flavored with cheese, vegetables, fish, or meat and
leavened with beaten egg whites.

The principal cause of fear in preparing soufflés, is that so many
writers talk of waiting for the soufflé and it not waiting for the
guests. It is true that, once baked, the soufflé must be served within
minutes, if not seconds, of removing from the oven. But, once
assembled, the soufflé will keep, covered, on the counter, or even
in the refrigerator for an hour or two before baking. You can easily
prepare all the ingredients, assemble them and cover the soufflé
with plastic wrap. Let it wait in the refrigerator or on the counter
until you are ready to eat. Remember souffles take a matter of
minutes to cook, usually no more than 25 to 35 minutes. The guests
can enjoy a drink and a snack or perhaps a bowl of fruit while it is
cooking. When cooked, wow them when you bring it into the
dining room in its soaring height.

*Basic Soufflé Mixture*

---

# BÉCHAMEL SAUCE

The béchamel sauce used for soufflés is thicker than that used for sauces. The sauce version is on page 275.

3 tablespoons butter                    1½ cups milk
3 tablespoons flour

In a 1-quart saucepan, melt the butter, stir in the flour, and cook the roux until it starts to turn golden. Stir in the milk and cook, stirring until the mixture is thick and smooth. Simmer, stirring often, until reduced to 1 cup. The sauce should be very thick.

Yield: Enough for a 1-quart soufflé

NOTE

There are versions of soufflés that use beaten egg yolks in a hot purée instead of béchamel as the base.

*Egg Yolks*

Beat the egg yolks, 4 for this quantity of béchamel, into the sauce, one at a time, over heat. Bring the mixture just to the boil to form the liaison between the sauce and the yolks. The base is ready for the flavoring.

*Flavorings*

Puréed, full-flavored vegetables such as cauliflower, broccoli, and spinach will flavor a soufflé delightfully. Foods with a less definite flavor often need to be left in larger pieces, such as coarsely grated cheese, or finely ground, such as chicken or ham, to accent their flavor.

Sometimes the best flavor results from slicing the food, combining it with a cream sauce, and putting it at the bottom of the dish. Top the mixture with a cheese soufflé and bake in the usual manner. The flavor from the sauce mixture perfumes the cheese soufflé and serves as a sauce. (See Soufflé de Homard Plaza Athenée.)

You can prepare the base and add the flavoring and chill until the next day. Reheat the base over moderate heat, stirring until hot but not boiling before folding in the beaten egg whites.

## Egg Whites

Use one or more egg white than yolks. Beat the whites with a pinch of salt until almost stiff, but not dry. If too stiff, you will have trouble folding them into the base mixture, if underbeaten, there will not be enough air to inflate the soufflé.

Gently fold the beaten egg whites into the base. If the base is very stiff, stir about ¼ of the whited into the base. Do not worry if they deflate. Gently fold the remaining whites into the base, taking care that they do not deflate. At this point you can cover the soufflé and hold it for an hour or two before serving.

## Soufflé Dishes

The customary soufflé dish is white porcelain with a flat bottom and straight sides. You can use any flat-bottomed, straight-sided ovenproof container. I have used a saucepan, charlotte molds, and even cake tins. The dish should hold about 1-quart, enough for 4 servings. For larger numbers it is better to use 2 or more dishes than try to bake a 2-quart soufflé. It is difficult for the heat to penetrate larger amounts.

Soufflés cook successfully in individual soufflé dishes, ramekins, or custard cups. Each guest gets an individual serving that holds up better because it does not have to be cut into portions. When cooking individual soufflés, heat a baking sheet in the oven and then place the dishes on the sheet. You can remove them all at once and the hot baking sheet gives added heat, to give greater lift to the soufflé.

Whatever dish you are using, butter the inside generously and sprinkle with fresh bread crumbs, or sugar for a sweet soufflé, if desired. If the soufflé mixture is thick enough to mound, it is not necessary to collar the dish, just run your thumb around the edge of the dish to separate the mixture from the dish. That will help to give the soufflé a top hat. If the mixture is too thin, or you want a very tall soufflé, attach a collar.

### To Collar a Soufflé Dish

Cut a piece of metal foil, parchment paper, or waxed paper, long enough to encircle the dish and overlap the ends by at least 2 inches. Fold the collar in half lengthwise. It should extend as high above the rim of the dish as below it. Tie securely with string. If you are using foil, you only need to crimp the upper edge and press it securely around the base of the dish. Butter the inside upper half of the collar.

### Baking a Soufflé

Put the baking rack in the lowest position possible in the oven. If you use a gas stove, with the heat source under the oven floor, bake the soufflé on the floor of the oven. Preheat the oven to 375 °F for an entree souffle and 425 °F for a dessert soufflé. Bake an entree soufflé about 25 to 35 minutes. Dessert soufflés cook in about 15 to 20 minutes. Individual souffles cook in 12 to 18 minutes. Serve immediately.

Although you can hold a soufflé before baking, once baked, you must serve it immediately. If you try to delay serving it you may well have a sunken pancake.

### When is a Soufflé Cooked?

Generally, the French serve soufflés when the outside is golden brown, and the center is very hot but still slightly fluid. The moisture in the center serves as a sauce. Americans tend to prefer soufflés cooked more fully to an almost cake-like consistency. Try them both ways and cook them to your preference.

### Rolled Soufflé

To serve many guests, it may be easier to make a rolled soufflé, rather than the traditional version. Bake the soufflé mixture in a sponge roll pan and unmold. Place the filling along a long edge and roll the soufflé like a jelly roll and place it on a serving dish. Serve a sauce on the side, or poured over the top. The texture of a rolled soufflé is firmer than a regular soufflé so you can slice it. Serve rolled soufflé as soon as it is filled and rolled. Truly let the guests wait for it. It is worth the wait.

# SOUFFLÉ AU FROMAGE (CHEESE SOUFFLÉ)

| | |
|---|---|
| 3 tablespoons butter | pinch of grated nutmeg |
| 3 tablespoons flour | 4 egg yolks |
| 1½ cups hot milk | ¾ to 1 cup grated Gruyère |
| ½ teaspoon salt | Parmesan, cheddar, or |
| pinch of cayenne pepper | chevre |
| | 5 egg whites |

Preheat the oven to 375°F.

Butter a 1-quart soufflé dish or 4 1-cup ramekins. Sprinkle with bread crumbs. Prepare collars, if desired.

In a 1-quart saucepan, melt the butter, sift in the flour, and cook the roux until the mixture starts to turn golden. Stir in the milk and cook, stirring, until the mixture is thick and smooth. Stir in the salt, cayenne, and nutmeg. Reduce to 1 cup, stirring often. Beat in the egg yolks, one at a time and bring just to boil. Remove from the heat and stir in the cheese until melted.

Beat the egg whites until stiff, but not dry, and fold into the cheese mixture. Pour into the prepared soufflé dish. Bake on the lowest rack of the oven for 12 to 18 minutes for individual soufflés or 25 to 35 minutes for a 1-quart soufflé.

Yield: 4 servings

## VARIATIONS

### SOUFFLÉ AU FROMAGE ET JAMBON

Fold 1 cup very finely diced, or ground ham and 2 tablespoons Dijon mustard into the soufflé base.

### ROLLED CHEESE SOUFFLÉ

Butter an 11 × 17-inch jelly roll pan, line with waxed paper, and butter the paper. Sprinkle with bread crumbs. Spread the cheese soufflé mixture in the bottom of the pan and bake for 12 minutes, or until golden and just barely baked.

Place two sheets of waxed paper, slightly overlapping, on a work surface. Turn the soufflé onto the waxed paper and peel off the bottom paper. Fill, if desired, roll, and serve with a sauce. (Use spinach or chopped, cooked tomatoes for a filling.)

# SOUFFLÉ AU FROMAGE AUX CROÛTONS D'AIL (CHEESE SOUFFLÉ WITH GARLIC CROÛTONS)

The croûtons give a crunchy texture inside the smooth soufflé.

1 recipe cheese soufflé with
  Gruyère cheese
1 cup garlic croûtons

2 cups tomato sauce (see
  page 280)

Fold the croûtons into the soufflé mixture just before folding in the egg whites. Bake. Serve the sauce separately.

Yield: 4 servings

# CROÛTONS D'AIL (GARLIC CROÛTONS)

¼ cup butter
2 to 4 garlic cloves, split

1 cup bread cubes, crusts removed

In a skillet, melt the butter and cook the garlic until golden brown, but not burned. Remove the garlic and discard. Sauté the bread cubes in the butter until golden on all sides.

Yield: about 1 cup

# SOUFFLÉ DE CHOUFLEUR (CAULIFLOWER SOUFFLÉ)

1 head cauliflower
salt and pepper to taste
1 teaspoon onion juice
2 tablespoons grated Parmesan cheese

8 anchovy fillets, minced
1 recipe cheese soufflé without cheese

Preheat the oven to 375°F. Prepare the soufflé dish and set aside. Remove the stems from the cauliflower and break into florets. Steam over boiling salted water until very tender. Purée in a food mill or processor. Season the purée with salt, pepper, onion juice, cheese, and anchovy fillets. Add the purée to the béchamel and egg yolk mixture. Fold in the egg whites and bake.

Yield: 4 servings

NOTE

To remove the juice from an onion, cut in half horizontally. Using a lemon or orange juicer, ream out the juice from each half.

## SOUFFLÉ DE GOURILOS (ESCAROLE SOUFFLÉ)

| | |
|---|---|
| 1 head escarole, shredded | ½ teaspoon Worcestershire |
| 3 scallions, thinly sliced | sauce |
| 3 tablespoons butter | 1 recipe cheese soufflé with |
| | cheddar cheese |

Preheat the oven to 375 °F.
Prepare a soufflé dish and set aside.
In a 3 quart saucepan of boiling salted water, blanch the escarole for 5 minutes. Drain and squeeze dry. In a 9-inch skillet, sauté the scallions in the butter until soft, but not browned. Add the escarole, and cook, stirring, until the liquid evaporates. Fold into the soufflé base with the Worcestershire sauce and the cheese. Fold in the egg whites and finish as a regular soufflé.

Yield: 4 servings

## SOUFFLÉ DE HOMARD PLAZA ATHÉNÉE (LOBSTER SOUFFLÉ)

The brother of Louis Diat, Chef at the Ritz in New York for many years, created this famous dish at the Plaza Athénée in Paris many years ago. To create a lobster soufflé with full flavor, he made a creamed lobster base for the bottom of the dish and then topped that with a cheese soufflé. The server scoops to the bottom of the dish and serves the lobster as a sauce for the soufflé.

| | |
|---|---|
| 1 2-pound lobster | ½ cup dry white wine |
| 1 tablespoon butter | ½ cup heavy cream |
| 1 tablespoon minced carrot | ½ cup cream sauce (see |
| 1 tablespoon minced celery | page 275) |
| 1 tablespoon minced chives | 1½ tablespoons heavy |
| ½ tablespoon minced pars- | cream |
| ley | 1½ tablespoons dry sherry |
| salt and pepper to taste | 1 recipe cheese soufflé |
| ¼ cup vegetable oil | made with half Parmesan |
| ½ teaspoon paprika | and half Gruyère cheese |
| 1 tablespoon cognac | |

Preheat the oven to 375°F.

Prepare a 1-quart soufflé dish with a collar.

While the lobster is still alive, separate the tail and body with a sharp knife. Remove the claws from the lobster and chop each claw into 3 pieces. Chop the tail into 3 pieces. Chop the body in half lengthwise and then each section crosswise into 4 pieces.

In a large skillet, sauté the carrot and celery in the butter until soft. Stir in the chives, parsley, salt, and pepper. Add the oil, chopped lobster, and paprika and cook the lobster, stirring, until the lobster turns red. Stir in the cognac, wine, and ½ cup cream and simmer for 10 minutes. Remove the lobster from the sauce and take the meat from the shells. Discard the shells. Cut the meat into ¼ inch slices.

Reduce the sauce in the pan by half. Stir in the cream sauce, remaining cream, and the sherry and cook 1 minute. Strain. Fold ½ of the sauce into the lobster and place in the bottom of the prepared soufflé dish. Keep remaining sauce warm.

Prepare the soufflé and place it over the lobster and bake as usual for about 35 minutes. Serve the soufflé with the lobster and pass remaining sauce.

Yield: 4 servings

NOTE

The lobster sauce can be prepared several days ahead and re-heated, or frozen. It can be served alone with rice or noodles, or the dish can be prepared as a rolled soufflé.

## SALMON BROCCOLI SOUFFLÉ

1 recipe cheese soufflé
   made with ¼ cup grated
   Parmesan cheese
½ cup cooked flaked salmon
1½ teaspoons tomato paste

1 teaspoon minced dill
10 ounces cooked broccoli,
   puréed
¼ teaspoon nutmeg
2 tablespoon grated Parmesan cheese

Preheat the oven to 375°F.

Prepare a 1-quart soufflé dish. Before folding the egg whites into the soufflé base, divide the base into two parts. Mix the salmon, tomato paste, and dill into one part, and the broccoli and nutmeg into the remaining base. Fold half the egg whites into each mixture.

Place the broccoli in the bottom of the soufflé dish and top with the salmon mixture. Sprinkle the top with the two tablespoons of grated Parmesan.

Bake for 35 to 40 minutes.

Yield: 4 servings

## SOUFFLÉ AUX CREVETTES À L'ESTRAGON (SHRIMP SOUFFLÉ WITH TARRAGON)

4 tablespoons butter
2 tablespoons minced onion
1 tablespoon minced shallot
1 teaspoon minced garlic
2 cups tomatoes, peeled,
   seeded, and chopped
salt and pepper to taste
1½ tablespoons dried tarragon
1 tablespoon minced parsley

⅓ cup dry white wine
1 pound shrimp, peeled,
   and deveined
cayenne pepper to taste
2 tablespoons cognac
1 recipe cheese soufflé
   made with half Parmesan
   and half Gruyère cheese
Parmesan cheese

Preheat the oven to 375°F.

Prepare a 1½ quart soufflé dish. In a 10-inch skillet, sauté the onion, shallot, and garlic in 2 tablespoons butter until soft. Add the tomatoes, salt, pepper, tarragon, and parsley. Simmer 5 minutes. Add the wine and simmer 15 minutes.

In a 9-inch skillet, sauté the shrimp in the remaining butter with the cayenne until they start to turn pink. Add the cognac, and ignite, averting your face. Add the tomato sauce and correct the seasoning with salt and pepper.

Prepare the soufflé mixture. Bake as directed for a cheese soufflé and serve sprinkled with the Parmesan cheese. This can also be made as a rolled soufflé and filled with the sauce mixture.

Yield: 6 servings

The sauce can be prepared ahead and frozen.

---

## ROULADE DE FROMAGE AU COQUILLES ST. JACQUES (ROLLED CHEESE SOUFFLÉ WITH SCALLOP SAUCE)

3 tablespoons butter
2 tablespoons minced garlic
1½ pounds scallops
¼ cup dry white wine
½ cup tomato sauce
1¼ cups heavy cream
1 teaspoon minced basil

½ teaspoon dried oregano
2 egg yolks
salt and pepper to taste
2 tablespoons minced parsley
1 recipe cheese soufflé with
Gruyère cheese

Preheat the oven to 375 °F.

Prepare a jelly roll pan for rolled soufflé (see page 132). In a 9-inch skillet, melt the butter and sauté the garlic for 1 minute, or until soft, but not browned. Add the scallops and cook over high heat for about 1 minute, or until just barely under-cooked. With a slotted spoon, remove the scallops and set aside. Add the wine, tomato sauce, and 1 cup cream to the skillet and simmer for 3 minutes. Add the basil and oregano.

In a bowl, mix the egg yolks with the remaining cream. Stir some hot tomato-cream into the egg yolk mixture to warm it. Add the egg yolk mixture to the remaining tomato-cream and heat until warm and lightly thickened. Do not boil. Correct the seasoning with salt and pepper and set aside.

Prepare the soufflé mixture and bake as for a rolled soufflé. Meanwhile, reheat the scallops in the sauce mixture without boiling. Unmold the soufflé, fill with half the scallop mixture, roll, and place on a platter. Spoon the remaining sauce over the soufflé and serve.

Yield: 6 servings

The sauce and scallops can be prepared ahead. Take care not to overcook the scallops.

---

# ROULADE DE JAMBON
# AU CRÈME DE MOUTARD
# (HAM ROLL WITH MUSTARD CREAM SAUCE)

1 recipe cheese soufflé
1 pound ham, finely ground
Salt and pepper to taste
2 teaspoons dried tarragon
¼ cup dry Madeira

1 cup sour cream
1 tablespoon Dijon mustard
1 teaspoon dried tarragon
2 tablespoons minced parsley

Preheat the oven to 375°F.
Prepare a jelly roll pan for a rolled soufflé.
To the sauce base for the soufflé, add the ham, salt, pepper, 2 teaspoons tarragon, and Madeira. Mix well. Fold in the egg whites and bake as a rolled soufflé for 10 to 12 minutes or until just set. Meanwhile, in a saucepan, heat the cream, mustard, tarragon, and parsley until hot, but not boiling. Unmold and roll the soufflé and serve the sauce on top.

Yield: 4 to 6 servings

---

# ROULADE D'ÉPINARDS AUX CHAMPIGNONS
# (ROLLED SOUFFLÉ WITH SPINACH AND
# MUSHROOMS)

1 recipe basic soufflé
2 pounds spinach, stripped, wilted, squeezed dry, and minced
1½ pounds mushrooms, minced

3 tablespoons butter
nutmeg to taste
salt and pepper to taste
¾ cup heavy cream
1 cup hollandaise sauce

Preheat the oven to 375°F.

Prepare a jelly roll pan for a rolled soufflé. Prepare the soufflé mixture and fold the spinach into the base before adding the egg whites. Bake for 10 to 12 minutes.

Meanwhile in a skillet, sauté the mushrooms in the butter until the liquid evaporates. Season with nutmeg, salt, and pepper. Stir in the cream and simmer until thickened.

Unmold the soufflé, fill with the mushroom mixture, and roll. Serve with the hollandaise sauce over the top.

Yield: 6 servings

---

# DESSERT SOUFFLÉS

Sweet foods are often eaten at breakfast and brunches, and of course you can serve a sweet soufflé after a lunch or dinner. As with entree soufflés, the basic recipe is much the same—a cream base with a flavoring and egg white leavening. The principal difference is that you use more egg whites and less sauce.

---

# SOUFFLÉ À LA VANILLE (BASIC VANILLA SOUFFLÉ)

½ cup milk
1-inch piece vanilla bean
2 tablespoons butter
1½ tablespoons flour

5 egg yolks
3 tablespoons sugar
6 egg whites
1 tablespoon sugar

Preheat the oven to 425°F.

Butter and sugar a 1-quart soufflé dish. Add a collar if desired. In a small saucepan, scald the milk with the vanilla bean and let steep for 10 minutes. In a medium saucepan, melt the butter, stir in the flour, and cook until the roux just starts to turn golden. Stir in the scalded milk and cook, stirring, until the mixture is thick and smooth. Simmer for 5 minutes. (It should be quite thick.) Remove the vanilla bean.

In a small bowl, beat the egg yolks with 3 tablespoons sugar until light in color. Stir into the sauce mixture.

In another bowl, beat the egg whites until stiff, adding the remaining tablespoon of sugar during the final moments of beating. Fold into the base and pour into the prepared soufflé dish. Bake for 15 to 20 minutes.

Yield: 4 servings

### CHOCOLATE SOUFFLÉ

Melt 1½ ounces unsweetened chocolate with the milk and add 2 extra tablespoons of sugar to the egg yolks.

### COFFEE SOUFFLÉ

Beat 2 tablespoons of double-strength coffee into the sauce mixture.

### ORANGE SOUFFLÉ

Omit the vanilla from the milk and add the grated rind of 1 orange, 2 tablespoons orange juice, and 1 tablespoon orange liqueur into the base.

### FRUIT-FLAVORED SOUFFLÉ

Add ½ cup puréed fruit to the sauce mixture with a complementary liqueur, if desired. For example, add orange, raspberry, or kirsch to strawberry purée; rum, cognac, or kirsch to pineapple purée; Framboise or kirsch to a raspberry purée; or Poire William, kirsch, or crème de cacao to pear purée.

CHAPTER

5

*Quiches*

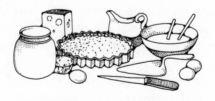

$A$ few years ago, quiche and brunch were synonymous. They went together like ham and cheese. Quiche was one of the first "foreign" foods that Americans accepted without hesitation. We ate eggs, fried and scrambled for breakfast and when we were ill, poached. Omelets were for the effete and almost anything else we looked at askance. Then quiche arrived shortly after the Second World War. It started in homes, moved to brick-walled restaurants with hanging plants, and then into almost every food emporium.

Unlike many fads, especially food fads, quiche held its sway for years instead of months. Even now they have their aficionados. You still find quiche on luncheon and brunch buffet menus, but seldom do you hear of someone going out for quiche as they once did. This is unfortunate, because quiches are delicious, easily prepared, and open to flights of the imagination. Because they are no longer common to every brunch, they are a welcome sight. Guests express enthusiasm combined with long-forgotten pleasure at the sight of quiche.

A quiche is a pie shell filled with flavoring ingredients such as cheese, fish, and meat and held together with a custard. You can prepare a quiche ahead and reheat it, or even freeze it. Of course, like most foods, they are best when served within minutes of baking. You can make them in any size. Some people enjoy the novelty of tiny miniature quiches for hors d'oeuvre. (I do not like these because there is so little room for filling.) Make standard pie shell sizes from 7 inches to 12 inches, or use any sheet pan that will fit in your oven. For hors d'oeuvre, I prefer this method. Cut the sheet of quiche into small squares, to serve lots of filling on a wafer of crust. If you really like lots of filling, you can use a deeper pan. Try making a quiche in a springform pan with 2- to 3-inch sides. Use twice as much filling and allow half again as much time to cook the filling. For those who consider any saving of calories worthwhile, you can even prepare the ingredients in custard cups without a pie shell. Refer to the section on baked eggs (Chapter 4) to learn how to prepare these in a water bath.

### The Pie Shell

Pie recipes are on page 146. If you are short of time, or unskilled at pastry making, try the frozen, unbaked shells in your market. They are suitable.

Bake the pie shell about 15 minutes, or until it just starts to color, before adding the filling. This ensures that the shell will be fully cooked when the filling is baked. Some writers suggest brushing the shell with lightly beaten egg white to seal if before baking.

## The Filling

You can use almost anything in a custard to make a quiche filling. Creative cooks use quiche as another method of changing leftovers into something exciting. Usually the ingredients need to be pre-cooked because they will not cook in the custard. Use cured foods such as ham or smoked salmon as is, but plan to cook any other meat, fish, or vegetables.

## The Custard

There are no strict rules for the custard. Four eggs and 2 cups of milk or cream makes enough filing for a 9-inch shell with about 1½ cups of filling. For a creamier, richer custard, use an extra egg yolk or two and use medium or heavy cream instead of the milk.

## Baking

Bake quiche at 375°F to 400°F for 35 to 55 minutes. For a deeper quiche, lower the temperature to 350°F and bake for 60 minutes or longer. Do not try to rush the cooking by raising the oven temperature. The eggs will harden and you will have a watery, if not "scrambled" quiche instead of the silken creamy quiche you expected. To test for doneness, insert a knife halfway between the edge and the center. The blade should come out clean. If you cook the quiche so that the knife comes out clean in the center, there is a good possibility that the retained heat will overcook the quiche and turn the custard watery. Let the quiche rest for at least 10 minutes before cutting to allow it to finish cooking and to settle. It will not become cold in that short time.

## Freezing

Freshly baked quiche are unequaled, but they do freeze for future use. After the quiche cools, wrap it securely in metal foil or another freezer wrap. Freeze as quickly as possible and keep as cold as possible. Serve the quiche within a month for the best flavor. To serve, unwrap, and let thaw to room temperature. Reheat in a 350°F oven until warm, about 20 minutes. To tell if it is hot enough, insert a metal knife blade or skewer into the center. Leave it for 30 seconds and then touch it with your fingers. Serve the quiche when the skewer is hot.

# QUICHE LORRAINE (BACON AND CHEESE CUSTARD PIE)

This is one version of quiche from Alsace-Lorraine. Some insist that bacon is never used and others add sautéed onions. You can change this and most quiche recipes to suit your needs.

| | |
|---|---|
| 6 slices bacon, cooked | 4 large eggs |
| 5 ounces thinly sliced | salt and pepper to taste |
|   Gruyère cheese | nutmeg to taste |
| 1 9-inch pie shell, half baked | butter, optional |
| 2 cups heavy cream | |

Preheat the oven to 375°F.

Arrange the bacon and cheese in the bottom of the pie shell. In a large bowl, beat the cream, eggs, salt, pepper, and nutmeg until well mixed. Strain into the shell and dot with butter, if desired. Bake for 35 to 40 minutes.

Yield: 6 servings

Can be frozen.

## VARIATIONS:

### CHEESE

Substitute ½ pound grated cheddar, crumbled feta, or other cheese for the bacon and Gruyère cheese.

### MUSHROOM

Substitute ½ pound sliced mushrooms, sautéed in 2 tablespoons butter until the liquid evaporates, for the bacon and cheese.

### ONION

Substitute 2 large, thinly sliced onions sautéed in 3 tablespoons of butter until soft, about 20 minutes, but not brown, for the bacon and cheese.

### SPINACH

Substitute 10 ounces cooked, drained, and chopped spinach for the bacon and cheese.

# QUICHE AU HOMARD (LOBSTER QUICHE)

2 tablespoons minced shallots
1½ tablespoons butter
½ pound lobster meat,
   cooked and diced
2 tablespoons cognac
½ teaspoon dried tarragon

2 cups heavy cream
4 eggs
1 teaspoon minced chives
salt and pepper to taste
Tabasco sauce to taste
1 9-inch pie shell, half baked

Preheat the oven to 375°F.

In a small skillet, sauté the shallots in the butter until soft, but not
   brown. Stir in the lobster and heat. Sprinkle with the cognac and
   tarragon and simmer 1 minute. Remove from the heat.

In a bowl, beat the cream, eggs, chives, salt, pepper, and Tabasco.
   Fold in the lobster mixture and turn into the pie shell. Bake for
   35 to 40 minutes.

Yield: 6 servings

NOTE:

Substitute shrimp, crab, or scallops for the lobster.

---

# SALMON QUICHE

3 tablespoons minced shallots
2 tablespoons butter
1 pound salmon, poached,
   skinned, boned, and
   flaked
3 tablespoons minced dill

salt and pepper to taste
¼ cup liquid from poaching
   the salmon
1 9-inch pie shell, half baked
1 cup heavy cream
4 eggs

Preheat the oven to 375°F.

In a 7-inch skillet, sauté the shallots in the butter. Mix into the
   flaked salmon with the dill, salt, pepper, and poaching liquor.
   Put into the pie shell.

In a bowl, beat the cream and eggs together and season with salt
   and pepper. Pour into the shell and bake for 35 to 40 minutes.

Yield: 6 servings

## MEXICAN CUSTARD TART

1 tablespoon minced scal-
    lions
2 tablespoons butter
4 ounces green chilies,
    minced
1 9-inch pie shell, half baked

2 cups grated cheddar
    cheese
4 large eggs, lightly beaten
1 cup heavy cream
½ teaspoon salt

Preheat the oven to 375°F.
In a small skillet, sauté the scallions in the butter until soft. Stir in
    the chilies and heat.
Place in the pie shell and sprinkle with the cheese. In a bowl, beat
    the eggs, cream, and salt to taste and pour into the pie shell.
    Bake for 35 to 40 minutes.

Yield: 6 servings

NOTE:

Use canned, mild chilies, or for added spice add 1 teaspoon minced
jalapeño.

## QUICHE HONFLEUR (SEAFOOD QUICHE)

3 pounds mussels, scrub-
    bed, and bearded
2 shallots, minced
1 large onion, minced
¾ cup dry white wine
salt and pepper to taste
½ pint oysters

¼ pound shrimp, peeled
    and deveined
1 9-inch pie shell, half baked
1 cup heavy cream
4 eggs
nutmeg to taste

Preheat the oven to 375°F.
In a 3-quart casserole, mix the mussels, shallots, onions, wine, salt,
    and pepper. Cover and bring to a boil. Simmer 5 minutes. Strain
    and reserve the liquid. Remove the mussels from the shells and
    reserve the meat.
In a small saucepan, poach the oysters in their liquor and drain.
    In a small saucepan, poach the shrimp in the strained mussel
    liquor. Place the mussels, oysters, and shrimp in the pie shell.
In a medium bowl, beat the cream, eggs, salt, pepper, and nutmeg.

Add ½ cup mussel liquid and poor into the shell. Bake for 35 to 40 minutes.

Yield: 6 servings

---

# ITALIAN TUNA CUSTARD PIE

6 eggs
¼ cup milk
7 ounces tuna in oil,
  drained and flaked
½ pound grated mozzarella
  cheese

salt and pepper to taste
½ teaspoon dried basil
½ teaspoon dried oregano
1 9-inch pie shell, half baked

Preheat the over to 375°F.
In a bowl, beat the eggs and milk until blended. Stir in the tuna, cheese, salt, pepper, basil, and oregano. Pour into the shell. Bake for 35 to 40 minutes.

Yield: 6 servings

---

# BEEF AND TOMATO QUICHE

1 bunch scallions, thinly
  sliced
2 tablespoons butter
1 pound ground beef
1 large tomato, peeled,
  seeded, and chopped
1½ teaspoons salt

½ teaspoon dried marjoram
½ teaspoon dried thyme
½ teaspoon pepper
1½ cups heavy cream
4 eggs
1 9-inch pie shell, half baked
1 tablespoon minced parsley

Preheat the oven to 375°F.
In a 9-inch skillet, sauté the scallions in the butter until soft. Add the beef and cook, breaking it up, until it loses its color. Add the tomato, salt, marjoram, thyme, and pepper, and simmer 5 minutes. In a bowl, beat the cream and eggs together. Add the meat mixture and pour into the shell. Bake for 35 to 40 minutes.

Yield: 6 servings

# MUSHROOM, ONION AND SAUSAGE QUICHE

½ pound sliced onions
4 tablespoons butter
2 eggs
2 egg yolks
2 teaspoons Dijon mustard
½ cup granted Parmesan
　cheese

1¼ cups light cream
½ pound sliced mushrooms
tablespoon lemon juice
salt and pepper to taste
½ pound sausage meat,
　cooked and crumbled
1 9-inch pie shell, half baked

Preheat the oven to 375 °F.

In a small skillet, sauté the onions in 2 tablespoons butter until soft, but not brown. In a 9-inch skillet sauté the mushrooms in 2 tablespoons butter and lemon juice until soft and the liquid evaporates. Correct the seasoning with salt and pepper.

In a bowl, beat the eggs, egg yolks, mustard, Parmesan, and cream. Stir in the onion and mushroom mixtures. Stir in the sausage and pour into the prepared shell. Bake for 35 to 40 minutes.

Yield: 6 servings

# ZUCCHINI AND HAM QUICHE

¼ cup minced onion
1 garlic clove, minced
2 tablespoons butter
salt and pepper, to taste
1¼ pounds zucchini, thinly
　sliced

¼ pound sliced boiled ham,
　minced
4 eggs
¾ cup milk
½ cup heavy cream
1 9-inch pie shell, half baked
¼ cup grated Parmesan

Preheat the oven to 375 °F.

In a 9-inch skillet, sauté the onion and garlic in the butter until soft, but not brown. Add the salt, pepper, and zucchini and cook until the zucchini is tender. Stir in the ham.

In a bowl, beat the eggs, milk, and cream together. Correct the seasoning with salt and pepper. Stir in the zucchini mixture and pour into the pie shell. Sprinkle the top with the Parmesan cheese and bake for 35 to 40 minutes.

Yield: 6 servings

# Crêpes, Pancakes, and Waffles

*C*rêpes and pancakes are only marginally related. Crêpes are thin sheets of dough used to enclose fillings of various types. Pancakes are quick breads made of leavened batter, cooked on a griddle or skillet, and served with toppings. Crêpes appear as first courses, main courses, and desserts at breakfast, luncheon, and dinner. Pancakes appear at breakfast and possibly for supper, but not usually as a first course or dessert.

## CRÊPES

Like quiche, crêpes are a particular favorite among cooks and party givers. Because they are bland, they make perfect containers for flavorful fillings. Simple to prepare, they freeze beautifully. You can freeze them in flat packets of 6 or 12 to fill as needed. They will thaw quickly at room temperature. Or, for a special event, fill them ahead and thaw overnight in the refrigerator, or thaw and reheat in a Microwave oven.

A definite advantage to serving crêpes for breakfasts and brunches is you can prepare them ahead. Usually you reheat them after filling and before serving. A word to the wise: if you are delayed in serving, it is generally better to let the food cool and reheat it, instead of trying to keep it warm. Keeping food warm dries it out.

Assemble crêpes in different ways for variety. Place the filling on the crêpe and roll it into a tube before reheating. Or, fold them into quarters and place the filling in the folds. Or, stack them like a cake with the filling placed between each crêpe, and serve the cake cut into wedges. You can select the filling method to suit your mood, and sometimes, the filling. Chunky fillings do not stack well.

### Additional Filling for Crêpes

Besides the fillings given in this chapter, you can use many omelet fillings, and some sauced and fish recipes are suitable. Use the creamed lobster mixture from the Lobster Plaza Athénée (see page 136) for a delicious filling.

### Crêpe Pans

Steel is the traditional metal for crêpe pans. The pans have a flat bottom and are sloped but not like the curved sides of an omelet pan. They rust easily and need seasoning before initial use and after any heavy scouring. Many cooks wipe the pans with coarse salt and a towel to remove any stuck bits of batter and only use the pans for crêpes. If space is at a premium, plan to use your omelet pan for crêpes. Follow the directions for seasoning the pan in Chapter 4 (page 117).

### To Cook Crêpes

Use a steel crêpe pan with a 7-inch bottom, or an aluminum or non-stick omelet pan to cook crêpes. Put about 2 teaspoons of butter into the bottom of the pan. Melt the butter over medium heat until it begins to smell nutty. Pour the excess butter into the crêpe batter. With a ladle, scoop about 3 tablespoons of batter into the pan and swirl the crêpe pan to cover the bottom evenly, and pour any excess batter back into the bowl. The crêpe will stay in place unless the pan has too much butter. Place the pan over the heat and cook the crêpe until golden brown on the bottom. With a supple metal spatula, loosen the edges and carefully lift the crêpe, flip it over, and cook the second side until golden. Turn out onto a sheet of foil or waxed paper. Continue with the remaining batter. The first couple of crêpes may fail because the pan is not at the right temperature or you have applied too much butter. Keep going—the third or fourth is almost always a surety. You should not need to butter the pan more than once or twice during the cooking. With practice you should be able to work two or more pans at once to complete the job quickly.

## ENTRÉE CRÊPES

The batter should be the consistency of heavy cream. Make a sample crêpe and add more milk if it is too thick.

| | |
|---|---|
| ¾ cup sifted flour | 4 tablespoons melted butter |
| 3 eggs | ½ teaspoon salt |
| 1 cup milk | |

In a bowl, mix the flour and eggs together to form a paste. Gradually beat in the milk, stirring constantly to make a mixture about the consistency of heavy cream. Add the butter and salt. Strain through a fine sieve and let stand for 2 hours. Cook the crêpes as described above.

Yield: 18 to 24 crepes

NOTE:

To prepare the batter in a blender or a food processor, combine all the ingredients and process until smooth. It does not need to rest before using.

---

# DESSERT CRÊPES

Dessert crêpe batter is thinner than entree crêpes and makes a more delicate product. It is more difficult to cook. For your first attempts, use 1 cup of milk and add additional milk when you are ready to cook them, adding about ¼ cup at a time. Ideally the crêpes should be almost lace-like.

⅔ cups flour
1 tablespoon sugar
pinch of salt
2 eggs

2 egg yolks
1¾ cups milk
2 tablespoons melted butter
1 tablespoon rum or cognac

In a bowl, combine the flour, sugar, and salt. Make a well in the center and add the eggs, and egg yolks, and mix into a thick paste. Very gradually work in the milk to make a smooth batter and add the butter and the liqueur. Let stand for 2 hours. Strain before using.

Can be prepared in a blender or a processor.

Yield: about 24 crepes

---

# GATEAU DE CRÊPES AUX CHAMPIGNONS (CAKE OF MUSHROOM-FILLED CRÊPES)

12 entree crêpes
1½ cups duxelles (see page 283)
2 cups grated Gruyère cheese

2½ cups hot béchamel sauce (see page 275)
½ cup heavy cream

Preheat the oven to 425°F.

On a heatproof platter, place a crêpe and spread it with a layer of duxelles. Cover with another crêpe.

In a saucepan, mix the cheese and béchamel and heat until hot but not boiling. Spoon 1 tablespoon on the crêpe, keep layering the crêpes alternating the mushroom and béchamel fillings. The final layer should be a crêpe.

Add the cream to the remaining béchamel and pour over the top of the cake.

Bake for 10 minutes, or until lightly browned and sizzling hot around the edges. If any the ingredients were refrigerated overnight, reheat them before assembling.

Yield: 6 servings

The crêpes, duxelles, and béchamel can be prepared ahead and frozen.

# MUSHROOM AND WATERCRESS OR SPINACH CRÊPES

2 pounds mushrooms,
  thinly sliced
½ cup butter
½ cup minced onion
½ teaspoon salt
2 tablespoons salt
½ cup dry white wine

2 cups sour cream
3 cups watercress leaves, or
  a 10-ounce package spinach, cooked
½ teaspoon Worcestershire
  sauce
16 entree crêpes

In a 12-inch skillet, sauté the mushrooms in the butter with the onion and salt until soft, but not brown. Stir in the flour and cook, stirring for 5 minutes. Add the wine and cook until thickened. Remove from the heat and stir in the sour cream, watercress, and Worcestershire sauce. Correct the seasoning with salt and pepper. Fill the crêpes and arrange on a buttered baking dish and reheat in a 350°F oven.

Yield: 6 to 8 servings

Prepare the filling the day before and fill the crêpes. Reheat before serving.

## VARIATION

If desired, substitute sweet cream for the sour cream and simmer until thickened before folding in 1 pound wilted and finely chopped spinach.

---

# SPINACH AND DILL CRÊPES

½ cup minced scallion
¾ cup butter
2 pounds spinach, cooked
   and finely chopped
salt and pepper to taste
2 tablespoons minced dill
1 garlic clove, crushed

1 cup sour cream
16 entree crêpes flavored
   with 1 tablespoon
   minced dill
3 tablespoons grated Parmesan cheese
1 cup sour cream

Preheat the oven to 325°F.

In a 9-inch skillet, sauté the scallion in 4 tablespoons butter until soft. Add the spinach and cook until heated. Correct the seasoning with salt and pepper and stir in the dill, garlic, and 3 tablespoons sour cream. Cook, stirring, until the liquid evaporates. Remove from the heat and fold in the remaining sour cream.

Melt the remaining butter. Fill and roll the crêpes and arrange in a baking dish. Pour the melted butter over the top and dust with the Parmesan. Heat until hot, about 10 minutes. Serve the sour cream on the side.

Yield: 6 to 8 servings

Can be prepared the day before and reheated, covered, in the oven until hot.

---

# CRESPOLINI (ITALIAN SPINACH AND CHEESE CRÊPES)

1 pound spinach, cooked
   and minced
1 cup ricotta cheese

2 eggs, lightly beaten
2 teaspoons grated Parme-
   san cheese

16 entree crêpes
1 cup thin cream sauce (see
   page 275)

1 cup grated Italian Fontina
   cheese

Preheat the oven to 325°F.

In a bowl, mix the spinach, ricotta, eggs, and Parmesan cheese. Fill
the crêpes and place in an ovenproof baking dish. Cover with
the cream sauce and sprinkle with the grated Fontina. Bake until
bubbling and lightly browned.

Yield: 6 to 8 servings

Can be prepared for baking the day before.

## CRÊPES FARCIS À LA MONEGASQUE (STUFFED CRÊPES MONACO-STYLE)

¾ cup butter
4 anchovy fillets, minced
½ cup minced onions
2 garlic cloves, minced
3 tablespoons olive oil
5 tomatoes, peeled, seeded,
   and chopped

1 teaspoon oregano
salt and pepper to taste
6 stuffed olives, thinly sliced
1 cup minced pimiento
¾ pound cooked shrimp,
   diced
16 entree crêpes

Preheat the oven to 325°F.

In a small saucepan, heat the butter and the anchovies, stirring,
until the anchovies dissolve.

In a 9-inch skillet, sauté the onion and garlic in the oil until lightly
browned, but not burned. Add the tomatoes, oregano, salt, and
pepper and simmer until thickened, about 20 minutes. Add the
olives, pimiento, and shrimp and heat. Correct the seasoning
with salt and pepper.

Fill the crêpes and arrange in an ovenproof baking dish and drizzle
with the anchovy butter. Bake until hot.

Yield: 6 to 8 servings

Can be prepared the night before and reheated.

## CRÊPES HRH PRINCE BERTIL

1 pound cooked medium
   shrimp
¼ cup minced dill
¾ cup hollandaise sauce,
   (see page 277)

salt and pepper to taste
16 entree crêpes
8 tablespoons butter
4 tablespoons grated Parmesan cheese

Preheat the oven to 350°F.

In a bowl, mix the shrimp, dill, and hollandaise. Correct the
seasoning with salt and pepper. Fill the crêpes and arrange in
an ovenproof serving dish. Drizzle the melted butter over the
crêpes and sprinkle with the cheese. Bake until hot and broil
until golden brown.

Yield: 6 to 8 servings

Assemble and reheat shortly before serving to prevent the hollandaise from separating.

## SEAFOOD CRÊPES, BRANDY'S

2 cups dry white wine
2 cups water
½ cup chopped mushroom
   stems
¼ cup minced onion
1 bay leaf
2 teaspoons cognac
½ pound shrimp, peeled,
   and deveined

½ pound scallops
½ pound King crab, bite-
   size pieces
3 tablespoons butter
3 tablespoons flour
salt and pepper to taste
1 cup heavy cream
16 entree crêpes

Preheat the broiler.

In a 2-quart saucepan, combine the wine, water, mushrooms,
   onion, bay leaf, and cognac. Simmer until reduced to 2 cups.
   Strain. (This is a white wine court bouillon.) Poach the shrimp
   and scallops, separately, in the poaching liquor. Set the fish aside
   and strain the stock. Add the crabmeat to the fish.

In a 1-quart saucepan, melt the butter, stir in the flour, and cook
   until the mixture starts to turn golden. Add the poaching liquor
   and cook, stirring, until thickened and smooth. Correct the

seasoning with salt and pepper. Add the cream, and simmer until reduced by one third. Set aside half the sauce and fold the remainder into the fish.

Fill the crêpes and place in an ovenproof serving dish. Pour the remaining sauce over the crêpes. Glaze under the broiler.

Yield: 6 to 8 servings

Can be prepared for baking the day before. Reheat at 350°F until bubbling hot, and glaze if needed.

# CRÊPES PAULINE (CRÊPES WITH TARRAGON SEAFOOD FILLING)

2 1-pound lobsters
1½ cups water
1½ cups dry white wine
1 tablespoon crushed tarragon
stems from ½ pound mushrooms, diced
½ pound scallops
½ pound shrimp, diced
2 tablespoons butter

2 tablespoons flour
1 tablespoon crushed tarragon
salt and pepper to taste
caps from ½ pound mushrooms, chopped
2 tablespoons butter
1 cup heavy cream
18 crêpes

Preheat the oven to 375°F.

In a kettle, steam the lobsters in the water, wine, tarragon, and mushroom stems for 12 minutes. Remove lobsters and let cool. Add the scallops to the lobster liquor and cook until just barely done, about 1 minute. Drain, and place into a bowl. Add the shrimp and cook until just barely cooked, about 1 minute. Drain, and place into the bowl with the scallops. Strain the poaching liqour and discard the solids.

In a saucepan, melt the butter, stir in the flour, and cook the roux until it starts to turn golden. Add the reserved liquid and cook, stirring, until thickened and smooth. Add the tarragon and simmer 20 minutes. Correct seasoning with salt and pepper. Strain.

In a large skillet, cook the chopped mushroom caps in the butter over high heat until the liquid evaporates. Remove the mushroom caps to the bowl and deglaze the skillet, with the sauce. Strain into another bowl and stir in the heavy cream.

Shell the lobster and cut the meat into bite-sized pieces. Place the
meat into a bowl with the scallops, shrimp, and mushrooms.
Add just enough of the sauce to bind the fish and mushrooms.
Correct the seasonings with salt and pepper.

Fill the crêpes with the seafood mixture and place in an
ovenproof serving dish and coat with the remaining sauce.
Bake for 20 minutes, or until bubbly and lightly flecked with
brown.

Yield: 6 to 9 servings

## CRÊPES WITH SALMON AND PEA FILLING

1 pound salmon steak
½ cup peas
2 cups fish-flavored
   Suprême sauce

12 entree crêpes
¼ cup heavy cream,
   whipped

Preheat the oven to 350°F.

Poach the salmon in lightly salted water until just cooked, about 4
minutes. Let cool in the liquid. Remove and discard the skin and
bones from the salmon, and flake the fish.

In a bowl, combine the salmon, peas, and 1 cup of supreme sauce.
Fill the crêpes with the salmon mixture and arrange in a lightly
buttered gratin pan.

Fold the cream into the remaining sauce and coat the crepes. Bake
until bubbly and golden brown. If desired run under a broiler
to darken the top.

Yield: 6 servings

Can be prepared the day before and heated just before serving.

## CRÊPES DE VOLAILLE VERSAILLAISE
## (CHICKEN CRÊPES VERSAILLES)

5 tablespoons butter
5 tablespoons flour
1 cup hot milk

1 cup hot chicken stock
4 tablespoons chopped
   mushrooms

1 tablespoon butter
3 shallots, chopped
2 cups cooked diced chicken
3 tablespoons dry sherry
1 egg yolk

4 tablespoons heavy cream
12 crêpes
2 tablespoons heavy cream,
   whipped

Preheat the broiler.

In a saucepan, melt the butter, stir in the flour, and cook until it starts to turn golden. Stir in the milk and stock and cook until thickened and smooth. Let simmer for 25 minutes, stirring often.

In a small skillet sauté the mushrooms in 1 tablespoon butter until lightly browned. Add the shallots and cook 1 minute longer. Add the chicken, sherry, and ¾ of the sauce.

To the remaining sauce add the egg yolk and cream, and stir over low heat until thickened, but do not boil.

Spread the crêpes with the chicken mixture, roll, and place in an ovenproof serving dish. Fold the whipped cream into the reserved sauce and coat the crêpes. Glaze under the broiler and serve.

Yield: 6 servings

Can be prepared for reheating the day before.

## CURRIED CHICKEN FILLED CRÊPES WITH CHUTNEY

¾ cup butter
2 cups minced onions
½ cup minced carrots
½ cup minced celery
1 apple, chopped
3 to 4 tablespoons curry
   powder
3 tablespoons flour

2 cups chicken stock
1 cup light cream
1 cup unsweetened coconut
   milk
2 cups poached chicken,
   cubed
¼ cup minced mango chutney
16 entree crêpes

Preheat the oven to 350°F.

In a 2-quart saucepan, melt the butter and sauté the onions, carrots, celery, and apple until soft, but not brown. Stir in the curry powder and flour and cook 2 minutes, stirring. Stir in the chicken stock and simmer 15 minutes. Add the cream and coconut milk and simmer 5 minutes.

Force the mixture through a sieve or purée in a processor. Fold half the sauce into the chicken with the chutney. Fill the crêpes with the chicken mixture and arrange on an ovenproof serving dish. Spoon the remaining sauce over the top.

Heat until piping hot.

Yield: 6 to 8 servings

Can be prepared the night before.

# CRÊPES NIÇOISE (CRÊPES NICE-STYLE)

1 cup ground lean veal
1 cup ground lean pork
¼ cup minced shallots
1 tablespoon minced parsley
dash of cayenne pepper
salt and pepper to taste
3 tablespoons butter
1 tablespoon flour

¾ cup heavy cream
12 entree crêpes
1 cup thinly sliced mushrooms
juice of 1 lemon
2 cups warm béchamel sauce
grated Parmesan or Gruyère cheese

Preheat the broiler.

In a 12-inch skillet, sauté the veal, pork, shallots, parsley, cayenne, salt, and pepper in the butter until the meats lose their color and start to brown.

Sprinkle with flour and cook, stirring, for 3 minutes. Add the cream and cook, stirring until lightly thickened. Fill the crêpes and arrange in an ovenproof serving dish.

In a 1-quart saucepan, mix the mushrooms and lemon juice with water to cover. Simmer 10 minutes. Strain and fold the mushrooms into the béchamel sauce and pour over the crêpes. Sprinkle with the cheese. Glaze under the broiler.

Yield: 6 servings

Can be prepared the night before and reheated at 350°F.

# CRÊPES WITH HAM AND MUSHROOM STUFFING

| | |
|---|---|
| 4 shallots, minced | 1½ cups béchamel sauce |
| 3 tablespoons butter | 3 tablespoons heavy cream |
| ⅓ pound mushrooms | 8 entree crêpes |
| chopped | 4 thin slices ham, halved |
| salt and cayenne pepper to | ⅔ cup heavy cream |
| taste | ½ cup grated Gruyère |
| grated nutmeg to taste | cheese |

In a small skillet, sauté the shallots in 2 tablespoons of butter over medium heat until soft, but not brown. Stir in the béchamel sauce and cream.

Place the crêpes on a counter and spread with a little of the mushroom sauce and top with a ham slice, add more sauce, and roll. Place in a buttered baking dish.

In a bowl, mix the remaining ⅔ cup cream, Gruyère cheese, and 1 tablespoon butter and pour over the rolls. Brown under a broiler.

Yield: 4 to 8 servings

Can be prepared the day before and reheated.


# CRÊPES FAVORITES (CRÊPES WITH RED PEPPER AND SWEETBREADS)

| | |
|---|---|
| 2 sweet red peppers, diced | salt and pepper to taste |
| 1 pound sweetbreads, | lemon juice to taste |
| blanched and diced | 16 entree crêpes |
| ½ cup diced ham | ½ cup melted butter |
| 4 tablespoons butter | grated Parmesan cheese |
| 2 cups chicken velouté (see | |
| page 276) | |

Preheat the oven to 350°F.

In a 9-inch skillet, sauté the peppers, sweetbreads, and ham in 2 tablespoons of butter. Add the velouté and simmer 5 minutes. Correct the seasoning with salt, pepper, and lemon juice. Fill the crêpes and arrange in an ovenproof serving dish. Pour the remaining butter over the top and sprinkle with the cheese. Heat in the oven.

Yield: 6 to 8 servings

Can be prepared the night before. Cover with foil to reheat.

## CREPAZE (CAKE OF HAM, CHEESE, AND CRÊPES)

1 cup heavy cream
salt and pepper to taste
10 entree crêpes
6 ounces thinly sliced prosciutto or Westphalian
  ham

6 ounces thinly sliced Vir-
  ginia ham
2 ounces grated Gruyère
  cheese

Preheat the oven to 350°F.

In a small saucepan, heat the cream with the salt and pepper until hot, but not boiling. Lightly butter a charlotte mold, or a ¾-quart soufflé dish. Cut the crêpes to fit the dish.

Place a crêpe in the bottom of the dish and top it with a slice of prosciutto and a tablespoon of cream. Keep layering, alternating the ham slices as you proceed, and finish with a crêpe.

Heat in the oven until very hot. Unmold onto a heatproof platter and sprinkle with the cheese. Place under the broiler until the cheese melts and is lightly browned. Serve cut into wedges.

Yield: 6 to 8 servings

Can be prepared ahead and heated before serving.

## CRÊPES FARCIS PROVENÇALE (CRÊPES PROVENCE STYLE)

¾ cup olive oil
1 eggplant, cubed
2 zucchini, diced
3 onions, thinly sliced

1 green pepper, thinly sliced
1 red pepper, thinly sliced
4 tomatoes, peeled, seeded,
  and chopped

1 teaspoon dried basil
½ teaspoon dried oregano
2 tablespoons minced parsley
2 cloves garlic, minced

salt and pepper to taste
16 entree crêpes
16 slices prosciutto
¾ cup melted butter
½ cup grated Parmesan cheese

Preheat the oven to 350°F.

In a large skillet, sauté the eggplant in one half cup olive oil until browned. Remove to a bowl. Sauté the zucchini in the remaining oil until browned. Add the onions, peppers, and tomatoes to the skillet and simmer until the juices evaporate. Season with basil, oregano, parsley, garlic, salt, and pepper. Return the eggplant to the skillet and cook 5 minutes or until tender.

Line each crêpe with a slice of prosciutto, and fill with the vegetable mixture. Arrange on an ovenproof baking dish and drizzle with butter. Sprinkle with the cheese. Reheat.

Yield: 6 to 8 servings

Can be prepared for baking the day before.

---

# GATEAU DE CRÊPES À LA NORMANDE (NORMANDY APPLE CAKE)

4-5 cups sliced Cortland apples
⅓ cup sugar
8 tablespoons butter, melted

12 dessert crêpes
6-8 stale macaroons, crushed
calvados

Preheat the oven to 350°F.

Spread the apples in 9 × 13 inch baking pan and sprinkle with ⅓ cup sugar and 4 tablespoons melted butter. Bake about 15 minutes or until tender.

Place a crêpe in the center of a buttered ovenproof serving dish and spread with a layer of apples, sprinkle with macaroons, melted butter, and calvados. Continue to layer the ingredients ending with a crêpe, a sprinkle of sugar, macaroons, and calvados.

About 30 minutes before serving, preheat the oven to 375°F and bake until heated.

Yield: 6 servings

Can be prepared for baking the day before.

## CRÊPES AUX POMMES (CRÊPES FILLED WITH APPLES AND CREAM)

3 apples, peeled and cored
6 tablespoons butter
juice of ½ lemon
5 tablespoons apricot jam
5 tablespoons almonds

½ cup heavy cream, whipped
4 tablespoons calvados
12 to 16 dessert crêpes
½ cup crushed macaroons
2 to 3 tablespoons sugar

Preheat the broiler.
In a 9-inch skillet, sauté the apples in 5 tablespoons butter and the lemon juice until soft. Stir in the apricot jam and almonds. Cool and fold in the whipped cream and the calvados. Fill the crepes and fold into quarters. Arrange on an ovenproof serving dish and sprinkle with the macaroons and sugar. Sprinkle with the remaining butter. Glaze under the broiler.

Yield: 6 to 8 servings

Assemble and bake shortly before serving.

## CRÊPES AUX FRAISES (STRAWBERRY CRÊPES)

½ pint strawberries, sliced
¼ cup sugar
3 tablespoons butter
2 tablespoons orange liqueur

½ cup heavy cream
12 dessert crêpes
3 tablespoons sugar

Preheat the broiler.

In a bowl, mix the berries with ¼ cup sugar and let macerate for
    5 minutes.
In a skillet, melt the butter and sauté the strawberries over high
    heat until the sugar begins to caramelize. Add the liqueur and
    cream and cook over high heat until reduced by one-fourth. Fill
    the crêpes and pour the remaining juices over the top. Sprinkle
    with the sugar and glaze under the broiler.

Yield: 4 to 12 servings

Prepare just before serving. If desired, pass whipped cream sepa-
    rately.

---

## CUSTARD AND BERRY FILLED CRÊPES

8 dessert crêpes                        2 cups fresh berries
2 tablespoons heavy cream               ½ cup berry jam
2 egg yolks                             ⅔ cup red wine
2 tablespoons sugar                     ½ cup fresh berries, op-
4 ounces cream cheese                       tional

Preheat the oven to 325°F.
In a food processor, cream the heavy cream, egg yolks, sugar, and
    cream cheese.
If berries (such as strawberries) are large, cut into quarters. In a
    bowl, fold the berries into the cheese mixture. Fill the crêpes
    and arrange the crêpes in ovenproof baking dish.
In a saucepan simmer the jam and wine for 5 minutes and spoon
    over the crêpes. Bake until heated, about 15 minutes. Serve
    garnished with sauce and fresh berries.

Yield: 4 to 8 servings

Can be prepared for baking several hours ahead.

---

## BANANA CRÊPES WITH RUM SAUCE

4 bananas sliced                        2 teaspoons grated orange
9 tablespoons butter                        rind
¼ cup packed brown sugar                ¼ teaspoon ginger

pinch of nutmeg                    ½ cup orange juice
12 dessert crêpes                  ⅓ cup dark rum
½ cup sugar                        vanilla ice cream, optional

Preheat the oven to 325°F.

In a skillet, sauté the bananas in 3 tablespoons of butter with the brown sugar until the sugar melts and coats the bananas. Add 1 teaspoon orange rind, ginger, and nutmeg. Fill the crêpes with the banana mixture and arrange in a buttered ovenproof serving dish.

In the skillet cook the remaining butter and sugar until the mixture turns light brown and the sugar just starts to caramelize. Add the orange juice and bring to a boil. Add the remaining orange rind and rum, and pour over the crêpes. Bake until heated through. Serve with ice cream on the side, if desired.

Yield: 6 to 12 servings

NOTE

This dessert recipe is very rich. For brunch, I omit the rum and pass a pitcher of heavy cream instead of serving ice cream.

---

## CRÊPES AU MOCHA

2 cups flour                       2 egg yolks
2 tablespoons sugar                2 cups milk
pinch of salt                      2 tablespoons melted butter
2 tablespoons grated choco-        1 cup cream, whipped
   late                            1 tablespoon rum
2 tablespoons instant coffee       sugar
2 eggs                             12 dessert crêpes

In a bowl, mix the flour, sugar, salt, chocolate, and coffee. Stir well. Beat in the eggs and egg yolks and add the milk gradually to form a smooth mixture as thick as heavy cream. Add the butter. Allow to rest for 2 hours. Strain the custard if at all lumpy.

Whip the cream and flavor with rum and sugar to taste. Fold into the custard and fill the crêpes. Serve.

Yield: 6 servings

# CRÊPES SOUFFLÉES AU COINTREAU (CRÊPES SOUFFLÉES WITH COINTREAU)

Although crêpes soufflés are usually sweet, there is no reason that the filling cannot be a savory such as a cheese or spinach filling in an entree crêpe.

1 recipe dessert crêpes  
1 recipe orange soufflé  
(page 141)  
granulated sugar

3 tablespoons Cointreau, or other orange-flavored liqueur

Preheat the oven to 400°F.

Prepare the crêpes ahead. Make the orange soufflé and fill the crêpes, folding them into quarters. Place on a buttered ovenproof serving dish. Sprinkle with sugar and bake for 10 minutes or until puffed and golden.

Warm the Cointreau and ignite. Pour over the crêpes and serve flaming.

Yield: 6 to 8 servings

Cannot be prepared more than an hour before baking.

NOTE:

Entree crêpes soufflés do not need the flaming finish.

## PANCAKES, WAFFLES, AND FRENCH TOAST

Make crêpes as thin as possible. They should be just a wisp of dough holding a portion of filling. Make pancakes as thick or thin as you like. Some people prefer very thin, crispy pancakes, while others want thick, large, round discs with a flannel-like texture. These are even called flannel cakes. Pancakes can be garnished during the cooking by sprinkling the uncooked side with berries, sliced fruits, or served with a variety of syrups. Pancakes also may be made with grains other than wheat flour, such as oats or corn. Crêpes are also sometimes made with buckwheat flour.

Pancakes need a leavening. Baking powder is most common, perhaps, but many cooks use baking soda with another acid such as buttermilk or even yeast. Plan to hold back some liquid until you cook the first pancake. If it is too thick, you can always add more liquid.

## *Cooking Pancakes*

A griddle supplies the perfect surface for cooking pancakes: it is a large flat area on which you can make several pancakes at once. Skillets do just as well but limit the number you can cook at one time. Rub the griddle or skillet with a small amount of fat so the pancakes do not stick and are not greasy. A piece of waxed paper rubbed over a stick of butter, or dipped into a small bowl of oil is sufficient. Some people prefer about ⅛ of an inch of fat in the pan to give a crisper finish to the edges of the pancake. The choice is yours.

During the cooking the pancake's upper surface starts to develop small bubbles that open into small holes. When the holes appear it is time to turn the cake and brown the other side. Keep the heat at medium. If it is too high, the first side will darken too much before the holes appear, and if it is too low, it will be too pale. Again, it is your choice. Some people like dark pancakes, while others prefer lighter colored pancakes. Adjust the heat on your stove to suit your preferences. Serve pancakes, like any other quickbread, as soon after cooking as possible. If you try to hold them in the oven until they are all cooked, some people will get soggy pancakes, at best.

## TOPPINGS FOR PANCAKES

### Butter

There is no substitute for real butter, preferably unsalted, with its fresh, creamy flavor and particular melting character. If butter is not within your diet, then consider doing without, and using just a fruit topping. Different, admittedly, but a lot better than the imitations. Butter accompanies different toppings and seldom is it served alone.

### Flavored Butters

Flavor butter with a fruit purée such as strawberry or cherry, or beat in a tablespoon of jam such as raspberry or apricot to give the butter flavor. Flavored butters may be enough topping and also can be served with muffins and other breakfast breads.

### Sugar

Granulated, confectioner's, or brown sugar are appropriate. Serve with butter.

## Cinnamon Sugar

Mix 1 tablespoon of cinnamon with ½ cup granulated sugar, or to taste. You can add ⅛ to ¼ teaspoon grated nutmeg. Serve with butter.

## Maple Syrup

This is the real thing from maple trees, not maple-flavored sugar syrup. It is expensive, but the flavor is unmatched. For New Englanders, there is no substitute. Read the label on container to ensure that you are buying real maple syrup. If you are in New Hampshire or Vermont, you can sometimes select the grade of syrup according to color from dark to light amber. Serve with butter.

## Honey

Try different types of honey to give variety. Clover is the standard, but there are other honeys. The flavor comes from the type of flower most available to the bees. Serve with butter.

## Molasses

Not as popular as it once was, molasses is a delicious topping. Serve with butter the same as maple syrup.

## Other Syrups

In some areas of the United States other syrups are well-liked such as sorghum or Golden Syrup. They are usually served with butter.

## Fruit Toppings

### Cherry

Pit 1 pound cherries and chop coarsely. Mix in sugar to taste and season with a pinch of cinnamon, or 1 tablespoon of anise-flavored liqueur. Let macerate for at least 30 minutes before serving.

### Blueberry

In a saucepan, bring 1 pint of fresh blueberries and ½ cup sugar to a simmer. Add 1 tablespoon grated lemon rind if desired. Serve warm.

### Cranberry

Simmer 2 cups cranberries in ½- to ¾-cup sugar until the berries "pop" and the sugar dissolves. Taste for sweetness and add more sugar, if desired. Flavor with 1 tablespoon grated orange and ¼ cup orange juice, 1 tablespoon minced gingerroot, or ½ teaspoon cinnamon.

*Raspberry*
Simmer 1 pint of raspberries with 2 tablespoons of honey, or to taste for 5 minutes. Stir in 1 pint fresh raspberries and serve warm.

*Strawberry*
Mix 1 pint sliced strawberries with sugar to taste and let stand for at least 30 minutes before serving. For added flavor, add 2 table-spoons grated rind and ¼ cup orange juice.

*Apple*
Use warmed apple sauce, or sauté 1 pound peeled sliced apples in 3 tablespoons of butter and sugar to taste until tender. For added flavor, season with cinnamon, nutmeg, and/or allspice. Serve warm.

*Pear*
Sauté 1 pound peeled, sliced pears in 3 tablespoons of butter and sugar to taste. Flavor with a pinch of cinnamon or ginger. Or, add 1 teaspoon grated lemon rind or 1 tablespoon of grated orange rind. Or, sauté the pears, cut in dice, with 1 cup cranberries and sugar to taste until the pears are tender and the cranberries "pop." Serve warm.

*Pineapple*
Cut off the frond and base of a pineapple and peel the sides, removing the eyes. Cut in half vertically and remove the core. Chop one half and purée in a processor with ½ cup sugar. Simmer in a saucepan for 5 minutes. Chop the remaining pineapple into bite-size pieces and heat in the pineapple syrup until hot. Serve warm.

## BASIC PANCAKES

| | |
|---|---|
| 2 cups flour | 2 eggs |
| 2 teaspoons baking powder | 1½ cups milk |
| 1 teaspoon salt | 2 tablespoon melted butter |
| 3 tablespoons sugar | |

In a 1-quart bowl, mix the flour, baking powder, salt, and sugar. In a small bowl, beat the eggs and milk, and stir into the dry ingredients. Stir in the melted butter. Let stand 4 minutes. Heat a griddle or skillet and brush with melted butter. Ladle out the batter into several small or one large pancake. Cook until the bubbles on top open and the underside browns. Turn and cook the second side until golden. Serve hot with your choice of topping.

Yield: 4 to 6 servings

Pancake batter is forgiving, and although part of the baking powder action takes effect immediately, the second action happens only when heated. Therefore you can prepare the batter a day or more ahead and use it when needed. Many people prepare the batter in advance and keep it in a covered pitcher, ready to pour and cook.

## VARIATIONS

### THINNER

Add more liquid for a thinner pancake.

### THICKER

Use 1 cup of milk or a little more for thicker pancakes.

### SOUR MILK

You can use sour, or soured milk for added tang to the batter (buttermilk provides a similar tang). To sour milk, add 1 tablespoon of vinegar or lemon juice to the milk. It will sour immediately.

### BLUEBERRY OR RASPBERRY

Toss 1 cup of blueberries with ½ cup flour and stir into the batter.

### CHERRY OR STRAWBERRY PANCAKES

Pit the cherries. Slice the cherries or strawberries. Ladle the pancake batter onto the griddle and put 1 to 2 tablespoons of fruit in the center of each pancake before it sets.

### APPLE PANCAKES

Sauté 2 peeled, sliced apples in 1 tablespoon butter until tender. Sprinkle with sugar, cinnamon, and/or nutmeg to taste. Ladle the batter onto the griddle and put a tablespoon or more of apple mixture in the center of each pancake before it sets.

## PEACH, PEAR, NECTARINE OR APRICOT

Follow the directions for apple pancakes.

## GRAIN PANCAKES

Substitute 1 cup of whole wheat, rolled oats, cornmeal, rye buck-wheat, or bran for 1 cup of flour.

---

# FUNNEL CAKES

There is some questions whether these are pancakes or doughnuts. To me they are pancakes cooked in deep fat and a delicious change from the usual breakfast fare.

| | |
|---|---|
| 2 cups flour | 2 eggs, lightly beaten |
| 1 tablespoon sugar | 1¼ cups milk |
| 1 teaspoon baking powder | oil for deep frying |
| ¼ teaspoon salt | |

In a bowl, mix the flour, sugar, baking powder, and salt. Make a well in the center and stir in the eggs and milk to make a smooth batter.

In a 12 inch skillet, heat 1½ inches of oil until very hot, but not smoking (375°F).

To shape the cakes use a funnel a half inch opening. Place an index finger under the tip of the funnel and pour in ½ cup of batter. Hold the funnel over the hot fat, remove your index finger, and rotate the funnel to form spiraling, interconnecting rings. You can cook 2 or 3 cakes at a time.

Fry the rings until golden, turn, and fry the second side. Keep warm on paper towel-lined baking sheet in a 250°F oven while cooking the remaining batter. If the batter becomes too stiff, add more milk, 1 tablespoon at a time. Serve the warm cakes with molasses, honey, or maple syrup.

Yield: about 12 cakes

## NOTE

An alternate shaping method is to insert the handle of a wooden spoon into the center hole of the funnel. Pour in the batter and swirl the funnel over the hot fat to make the connecting rings. Lift the spoon handle to control the flow of batter.

## WAFFLES

1½ cups flour
1 teaspoon baking powder
½ teaspoon salt
½ teaspoon baking soda

2 eggs, separated
1 cup sour cream
2 tablespoons melted butter

In a 1 quart bowl, mix the flour, baking powder, salt, and soda.
In a small bowl, beat egg yolks with the sour cream and stir into the dry ingredients until well mixed. Stir in the butter. Shortly before cooking, beat the egg whites until they are stiff but not dry, and fold into the batter. Cook in the waffle iron according to instructions.

Yield: 6 servings

NOTE:

Serve with the toppings suggested for pancakes. Pass a bowl of whipped cream, if desired, with the fruit toppings.

## PAIN PERDU (LOST BREAD OR FRENCH TOAST)

This is another example of the frugal French housewife using leftovers. Best made from old bread, not rock hard, but several days old. Traditionally the bread soaked in the egg mixture overnight so the bread could absorb all the liquid. Long soaking makes the best French toast.

6 double thick slices bread
6 eggs, lightly beaten
¾ cup milk

1 tablespoon sugar
pinch of nutmeg

The bread slices should be 1½ to 2 inches thick, but standard American bread slices will suit. Place the bread in one layer in a baking dish.

In a bowl, beat the eggs, milk, sugar, and nutmeg. Pour over the
bread and let stand for at least 10 minutes or up to 24 hours.
The longer the bread soaks, the more liquid it will absorb. But
the slices will be more difficult to move.

In a skillet, heat the butter and transfer the bread slices on a spatula
to the hot butter. Sauté until golden brown. Turn and cook the
second side. Serve immediately.

Yield: 6 servings

Serve with butter and any of the pancake toppings.

NOTE

During cooking the slices puff up, and then deflate when removed
from the heat.

## VARIATIONS

Use Challah, brioche, or whole grained breads.

### PAIN PERDU À L'ORANGE, ORANGE FRENCH TOAST

Add 1½ teaspoons rum and ¾ teaspoon orange liqueur to the egg
mixture before soaking the bread. Serve with orange butter.

CHAPTER

*Appetizers*

$A$ppetizers in the sense of deli foods equal brunch. You can visit a good delicatessen or gourmet shop and buy everything you need for a splendid and pleasing brunch that is ready to serve at almost a moment's notice. These shops have large assortments of bagels, challah, rye, pumpernickel, and whole-grain breads. They have smoked salmon, whitefish, sable, and other smoked and pickled fish. They have tuna, herring, and other fish salads. They have cream cheese, flavored cream cheeses, and various other spreads. Not to mention all sorts of cold meats and cheeses. And, very probably, coffee cakes. They usually have an assortment of coffee so you can prepare all one bean and roast, or mix several to create your blend. Canned or bottled herring salad and herring in cream sauce or wine sauce sit next to sardines in mustard, tomato, or plain. Additionally they have an assortment of pickles and pickled foods to accompany all this. All it takes is a few dollars and the ability to limit yourself. I find that let loose in such a shop, I buy far more than I could ever eat for one meal. But then there is always tomorrow.

For many, "appetizers" really means hors d'oeuvre. These nibbles, noshes, snacks serve a welcome accompaniment to mixed drinks, they assuage the appetite before the main event, and occupy your guests while they wait for the remaining guests to arrive. And they give the cook needed time to get the rest of the meal on the table. The type of breakfast or brunch you plan determines whether appetizers as such are needed at all. If it is an early morning brunch, a glass of orange or tomato juice is sufficient. As the day wears on, more socializing before the main course is the norm, and therefore there is a greater need for something on which to nibble.

Appetizers can be a selection of smoked fish, or more elaborate preparations including chicken livers in bacon, cheese pastries, or small puffs with a savory filling. Many people prefer to start with fruit (see Chapter 11). Do not overdo: remember it is supposed to be a light meal. This is not the time to demonstrate all your skills with hors d'oeuvre. Tempt your guests with two, three, or perhaps four hors d'oeuvre, concentrating on those that require little work, like dips and spreads. A large selection, like a big display of bagels, cream cheese, smoked fish, several hot hors d'oeuvre, and some dips is apt to make them mistakenly believe that that *is* the brunch, not just the appetizer. Unless of course it is.

# RAW VEGETABLES

These have become a standard at almost every gathering. Fortunately with their growing presence, a growing appreciation exists. Do not plan to serve these for an early breakfast, but when there will be socializing before the meal, vegetables and a dip should be first on your menu. Guests can choose to dip the vegetables, or not, and of course the bright cheerful colors are a bonus. Select vegetables that are not only colorful, but also different. Search out fennel, snow peas, and royal beans, and try to avoid cucumbers, carrots, and celery. Select dips with a light flavor and texture instead of highly-spiced offerings.

---

# SALSA COLORADO (SPANISH PEPPER AND ALMOND SAUCE)

3 garlic cloves
1 teaspoon salt
½ cup blanched almonds,
   lightly toasted
2 red peppers, peeled

2 tomatoes peeled and
   seeded
2 hard-cooked egg yolks
1 cup olive oil
¼ cup sherry vinegar
¼ teaspoon cayenne

In a food processor with the machine running, add the garlic, salt, and the almonds. Chop with on/off turns to the consistency of coarse meal. Add the tomatoes and peppers, and process until almost smooth. Blend in the vinegar and cayenne.
Add the egg yolks and, with the machine running, pour in olive oil in a slow steady stream.
Serve with vegetables, thin slices of garlic toast, or toasted pita bread.

Yield: 2 cups

Can be prepared several days ahead.

---

# CRISPY SHALLOT DIP

⅔ cup olive oil
2 pounds shallots, thinly
   sliced

2 sprigs thyme
8 ounces cream cheese, softened

1 pint sour cream                    salt and pepper

In a large skillet, heat the olive oil over moderately high heat. Lower the heat to low and cook the shallots and thyme, stirring occasionally, until the shallots are brown and crisp, about 30 minutes. Drain on paper toweling. Discard the thyme. In a bowl, mash the cream cheese and sour cream and stir in the shallots. Season with salt and pepper.

Yield: $3\frac{1}{2}$ cups

Can be prepared the day before.

## SPINACH VEGETABLE DIP

$\frac{1}{2}$ cup cooked spinach, minced

3 ounces cream cheese, softened

$\frac{2}{3}$ cup yogurt or sour cream

$\frac{2}{3}$ cup minced scallion

nutmeg to taste

salt and pepper to taste

Squeeze the excess moisture from the spinach. In a bowl, mix the spinach with the cream cheese, yogurt, scallion, nutmeg, salt, and pepper. Mix well and let rest 1 hour. Serve with vegetables.

Yield: 2 cups

Keeps 4 days in the refrigerator.

## VEGETABLE DIP

1 cup sour cream

$\frac{1}{2}$ cup tomatoes, peeled, seeded, and chopped

2 tablespoons minced scallions

2 tablespoons minced parsley

2 tablespoons minced celery

1 tablespoon minced green pepper

salt and pepper to taste

Tabasco to taste

In a bowl, mix the sour cream, tomatoes, scallions, parsley, celery, green pepper, salt, pepper, and Tabasco. Serve with vegetables, tortilla chips, or crackers.

Yield: 2 cups

Can be prepared the day before.

---

# TARAMASALATA

⅓ 8-ounce jar *tarama* (carp roe)
1 small onion, grated
1½ cups olive oil

4-5 slices white bread, crusts removed
¼ to ½ cup lemon juice

In a food processor, combine the tarama and onion. Turn on the machine, add 3 tablespoons olive oil and process until smooth.
Soak the bread in ½ cup water for 3 minutes, squeeze out excess liquid. With the machine running, add the bread, olive oil, and lemon juice alternately using all the ingredients until the mixture is the consistency of mayonnaise. Serve with vegetables, toasted pita, or as a filling for puffs.
If desired, thin any leftover tarama with olive oil and use as a salad dressing.

Yield: 2½ cups

Can be prepared several days ahead.

---

# SMOKED SALMON DIP

4 ounces smoked salmon, shredded
⅓ cup heavy cream

pepper to taste
1 teaspoon capers

In a processor, purée the salmon, cream, pepper, and capers. Put into a bowl and grind black pepper over the top.

Yield: 1 cup

Keeps 24 hours in the refrigerator.

## CHIPPED BEEF DIP

8 ounces cream cheese, softened
8 ounces sour cream
½ cup minced chipped beef

2 tablespoons horseradish,
  or to taste
salt and pepper to taste

In a food processor, purée the cream cheese and sour cream. Add
  the beef with on/off turns and season with the horseradish, salt,
  and pepper. The meat should not be puréed.

Yield: about 2½ cups

Keeps 3 days in the refrigerator.

## SPREADS

Spreads are the host's delight. You can usually make them the day
before and place them in their serving bowl. Surround with
crackers or breads and let people prepare their serving. Whenever
hors d'oeuvre are called for, spreads should be on the top of the
list. Many spreads are mostly cheese and replace the hackneyed
display of a wedge of brie and cubes of Swiss. The spreads are often
more economical to make and much more interesting than the
usual chunk of cheddar.

## CERVELLE DE CANUT (SILKWORKER'S BRAINS, FRESH CHEESE WITH SHALLOTS AND HERBS)

6 ounces cream cheese
½ cup heavy cream
1 tablespoon dry white wine
2 teaspoons olive oil

1 shallot, minced
1 tablespoon minced parsley
1 tablespoon minced chives
salt and pepper to taste

In a food processor, mix the cheese, cream, wine, oil, and shallot.
  Transfer to a bowl and mix in the parsley, chives, salt, and
  pepper.

Yield: about 1½ cups

Can be prepared several days ahead.

# GEFULLTER CAMEMBERTKASE (CAMEMBERT FARCI–STUFFED CAMEMBERT)

This is one of my favorite cheese presentations. Pipe the cheese into the shell to resemble a little mountain.

1 Camembert, approxi-
   mately 12 ounces
½ cup butter
salt to taste
paprika to taste

½ cup heavy cream
¼ cup seedless grapes
½ cup toasted, slivered almonds

Carefully cut the center out of the camembert, leaving the bottom and sides about ¼ inch thick. In a food processor, purée the removed cheese, butter, salt, and paprika to taste with the cream.

Put into a pastry bag with a #4 large open star tip and pipe into the shell. Before serving, decorate the cheese with grapes and almonds. Serve with dark bread.

Yield: 1½ cups

Can be prepared a day or two ahead.

NOTE

Pipe the whipped cheese into the case by holding the pastry bag straight up and piping a ½ inch mound all over the surface of the case. The next layer starts one row in and you keep mounding the cheese to create a little mountain of cheese.

# BASIL AND PROVOLONE LOAF

This is another favorite. Simple ingredients create delicious flavors. Use this idea to create your versions. For example: smoked salmon with grated creamy havarti and lots of chives, or ham with grated Gruyère and Dijon mustard. Cream cheese is usually the base, but mascarpone provides a richer and softer cheese.

12 ounces cream cheese,
   softened
¼ cup grated Parmesan

1 tablespoon minced garlic
1½ tablespoons minced
   fresh basil

½ teaspoon salt                      6 slices provolone, grated
¼ teaspoon pepper                    ½ cup pine nuts
1 teaspoon olive oil                 12 ounces mozzarella,
                                       grated

Place the cream cheese in a bowl and beat until light and fluffy.
    Add the Parmesan, garlic, basil, salt, and pepper. Brush a 7 × 4
    × 2 loaf pan with ½ teaspoon oil, line with plastic wrap and
    brush again. Spread ⅓ cup of basil-cheese mixture in bottom of
    the pan, and sprinkle provolone over the cheese. Spread with
    ¼ cup basil cheese mixture and sprinkle on ¼ cup pine nuts,
    pressing in gently.
Spread with 2 tablespoons of basil cheese mixture and arrange
    ½ of mozzarella on top. Cover with basil cheese mixture and
    more provolone and spread with basil cheese. Make a layer of
    nuts and another layer of cheese spread, place remaining moz-
    zarella on top. Spread with basil cheese and top with remaining
    provolone and remaining basil cheese.
Chill 12 hours. Unmold to serve. If desired sprinkle the top with
    minced basil leaves or pine nuts.

Yield: 15 servings

Can be prepared several days ahead.

---

# WALNUT ORANGE CHEESE SPREAD

1 cup cream cheese                   4 ounces bitter orange mar-
½ cup heavy cream                      malade
½ cup chopped walnuts                1 teaspoon dry mustard
salt and paprika to taste

In a bowl blend the cheese, cream, walnuts, salt, and paprika.
    Shape into a flat cake on a serving dish.
In a bowl, mix the marmalade and mustard together. Spread over
    the cheese. Serve with cocktail breads.

Yield: 2 cups

Can be prepared several days ahead.

# SMOKED BLUEFISH SPREAD

1½ cups smoked bluefish
½ cup sour cream
1 tablespoon lemon juice

¼ cup minced scallions
pepper

Skin and bone the fish and mash it in a bowl. Stir in the sour cream, lemon juice, and scallions to make a smooth paste. Season with black pepper and pack into a crock.

Yield: about 2 cups

Can be prepared several days ahead.

# BIRD'S NEST

This traditional Scandinavian specialty is not only attractive to look at but also delicious to eat.

1 tablespoon capers, drained
1 medium onion, minced
1¼ cups minced herring

3 tablespoons minced parsley
½ cup cooked beets, minced
1 raw egg yolk

On a 9-inch platter, arrange the ingredients as follows. Place the capers in the center and surround with a ring of onions, herring, parsley, and beets. Place the egg yolk in half its shell in an egg cup at the side of the platter. When ready to serve, pour the egg yolk into the center of the platter and mix all the ingredients together. Serve with Swedish flat bread or rye bread.

Yield: 2 cups

Can be prepared the day before.

## NOTE

The egg yolk is not necessary. For a prettier presentation, leave the nest as arranged and let guests spread the bread with their favorite items.

## SALMON SPREAD

2 cups cooked flaked
  salmon
⅓ cup mayonnaise
¼ cup minced onion
2 tablespoons dry
  sherry
2 tablespoons minced
  parsley

1 teaspoon Dijon
  mustard
½ teaspoon mashed
  garlic
pepper to taste
lime juice to taste
salt to taste

In a bowl, mix the salmon, mayonnaise, onion, sherry, parsley, mustard, garlic, and pepper. Mix well and correct the seasoning with lime juice and salt.

Yield: 2½ cups

Can be prepared several days ahead.

## SHRIMP LEEK AND DILL SPREAD

½ cup butter
3 leeks, minced
¼ cup minced shallots
1½ pounds shrimp, peeled,
  and deveined
½ cup sour cream

1¼ teaspoons salt
½ teaspoon pepper
2 tablespoons minced
  dill
crackers or toast

In a skillet, melt ¼ cup butter and cook the leeks and shallots, covered until soft. In another skillet, heat remaining butter and sauté the shrimp until just cooked. Coarsely chop ⅓ of the shrimp and set aside.

In a food processor, purée remaining shrimp with pan juices, leeks, sour cream, salt, and pepper. Turn into a bowl and stir in the chopped shrimp and minced dill. Chill. Serve with crackers.

Yield: 2½ cups

Can be prepared several days ahead.

# CAPUNATINA CON TONNO (SICILIAN EGGPLANT RELISH WITH TUNA)

½ cup olive oil
1 eggplant, diced
1 onion, diced
2 stalks celery, diced
3 tomatoes, peeled and
   diced
⅓ cup Calamata olives,
   chopped
⅓ green olives,
   chopped

3 tablespoons raisins,
   soaked in warm water,
   drained
1½ tablespoons capers
2 tablespoons red wine vinegar
2 tablespoons pine nuts,
   toasted
salt and pepper
6½ ounce can tuna
   in oil

In a large skillet, heat 2 tablespoons oil. In batches, sauté the eggplant until browned. Transfer the eggplant to a medium bowl as it cooks and set aside.

Heat remaining 2 tablespoons oil in a skillet and sauté onion and celery until soft, but not brown. Add the reserved eggplant, tomatoes, olives, raisins, capers, and vinegar. Simmer 20 minutes and stir in the pine nuts and salt and pepper to taste. Cool. Fold in tuna shortly before serving.

Yield: 4 cups

# CURRIED CHICKEN ALMOND SPREAD

1¼ cups minced cooked
   chicken
¼ cup chopped toasted al-
   monds
2 teaspoons minced onion

½ teaspoon salt
¼ teaspoon curry powder,
   or to taste
pepper to taste
⅓ cup mayonnaise

In a bowl, mix the chicken, almonds, onion, salt, curry powder, and pepper. Add just enough mayonnaise to bind. Serve with crackers, bread, or use to fill pastries.

Yield: 1½ cups

This is best if prepared the day before.

## HOT HORS D'OEUVRE

There are many hot hors d'oeuvre suitable for serving at a brunch. This limited list provides some suggestions and I hope encourages you to use your imagination to expand on the ideas here. Many fillings for omelets and crêpes also can be used to fill phyllo dough, or bread cases.

## DIABLOTIN (CHEESE TOAST)

6 ounces grated
  Gruyère
2 eggs, lightly beaten

dash of paprika and
  cayenne
4 slices white bread,
  toasted

Preheat the oven to 400°F. In a bowl, mix the cheese, eggs, and seasonings. Spread the mixture on the toast about ¼ inch thick. Bake 15 minutes or until bubbly. Trim the crusts from the bread and cut into triangles. Serve.

Yield: 16 toasts

The mixture can be prepared the day before. Make the toast and spread with the topping shortly before serving.

## HOT LOBSTER CANAPÉS

1 cup minced, cooked lob-
  ster
1 tablespoon horseradish
2 tablespoons minced black
  olives

salt to taste
mayonnaise to bind
36 bread rounds
¼ cup grated Parmesan
  cheese

Preheat the oven to 375°F.
In a small bowl, mix the lobster, horseradish, olives, salt, and mayonnaise together. Spread the mixture on the bread rounds and sprinkle with Parmesan cheese. Bake for 10 minutes or until bread is lightly golden around the edges. Serve hot.

Yield: 36 servings

The mixture can be prepared the day before, but do not spread on the bread until just before serving. Use the mixture to fill phyllo if desired.

# FINNAN HADDIE TOASTS

2 tablespoons butter
2 tablespoons flour
⅔ cup light cream
1 cup cooked, flaked, finnan haddie

½ teaspoon lemon juice
salt and pepper to taste
6 slices bread, toasted
6 tablespoons bread crumbs
2 tablespoons melted butter

Preheat the broiler.
In a saucepan, melt the butter, stir in the flour, and cook until bubbly. Stir in the cream and cook until thickened and smooth. Fold in the finnan haddie, lemon juice, salt, and pepper.
Spread the mixture on the toast and cut into 4 triangles. In a small bowl, mix the bread crumbs with the melted butter and sprinkle over the toasts. Broil until golden.

Yield: 24 servings

The mixture can be made ahead. Make the toast and spread with the topping shortly before serving.

# SCALLOPS AND PROSCIUTTO

1½ pounds sea scallops
1 tablespoon minced garlic
juice of 2 limes
2 teaspoons salt
pepper to taste

½ teaspoon minced basil
½ pound thinly sliced prosciutto
melted butter

Cut scallops in half. In a bowl, mix the garlic and lime juice and stir in the scallops. Cover and marinate for several hours.
When ready to serve, season with salt, pepper, and basil.
Preheat the oven to 450°F.
Wrap the scallops in the prosciutto and skewer, brush with butter,

and bake 10 minutes or until just cooked. Serve these without baking, if desired.

Yield: about 12 servings

Do not marinate more than 4 hours if baking. If serving raw, marinate overnight.

# GAMBAS AL AJILLO (SHRIMP WITH GARLIC)

1½ pounds medium shrimp, peeled and deveined
¾ cup olive oil

3 garlic cloves, thinly sliced
1 tablespoon minced parsley
salt and pepper to taste

Preheat the oven to 450°F.
In a baking dish, mix the shrimp, olive oil, garlic, parsley, salt, and pepper and marinate for 1 hour. Bake the shrimp for about 5 minutes, or until just done. Serve hot or at room temperature.

Yield: about 10 servings

Can be prepared for baking the day before.

# TONDINI DI PATATE (POTATO ROUNDS)

1 pound large potatoes, peeled and sliced
½ teaspoon salt
1 tablespoon butter
½ cup grated Parmesan cheese
1 egg

pepper to taste
pinch of nutmeg
¼ pound Fontina cheese, thinly sliced
¼ pound prosciutto, thinly sliced

Preheat the oven to 350°F.
Boil the potatoes in salted water for 10 minutes or until done. Drain and mash or force through a ricer. Beat in the butter, Parmesan cheese, egg, pepper, and nutmeg, until the butter melts. Shape heaping tablespoons of the mixture into little balls

and place on a buttered baking sheet and flatten the top. Bake for 15 minutes.

With a cookie cutter, cut the Fontina and the prosciutto into rounds the size of the potatoes. Top each round with a slice of cheese and a slice of prosciutto. Bake until the cheese melts, about 4 minutes.

Yield: about 20 rounds

Potatoes can be prepared for baking the day before.

---

# SPINACH AND HAM TOASTS

| | |
|---|---|
| ¼ cup minced shallots | 4 ounces cream cheese |
| 1 garlic clove, minced | ¼ cup minced ham |
| 2 tablespoons butter | 1 teaspoon Dijon mustard |
| 10 ounces spinach, thawed | 12 slices bread |
| ½ teaspoon rosemary | ½ cup grated Gruyère |
| nutmeg to taste |    cheese |
| salt and pepper to taste | butter |

In a skillet, sauté the shallots and garlic in the butter until soft but not brown. Squeeze the spinach dry and mince. Add to the skillet with the rosemary, nutmeg, salt, and pepper and cook, stirring until heated. Stir in the cream cheese, ham, and mustard and cook until thickened and the cheese melts.

Toast the bread on both sides, trim the crusts, and butter each slice. Spread with a layer of spinach mixture and sprinkle with the Gruyère. Broil until the mixture is bubbly. Cut into quarters and serve.

Yield: 48 servings

The spinach mixture can be prepared the day before. Do not make the toast and finish until almost ready to serve.

---

# SAUSAGE TOASTS

| | |
|---|---|
| ¼ pound sausage meat | 1 tablespoon minced parsley |
| 1 large egg | ½ teaspoon anchovy paste |

Oil for deep frying                    minced parsley
4 slices white bread, crusts
    removed

In a bowl, mix the sausage meat, egg, parsley, and anchovy paste.
Heat vegetable oil to 375°F.
Spread the bread slices with the sausage mixture, mounding in the
    center. Cut into triangles and fry until golden, about 2 minutes.
    Sprinkle with parsley and serve.

Yield: 16 triangles

Can be prepared for frying the day before.

## LAMB SAUSAGE SKEWERS

1½ pounds ground lean            ¾ teaspoon rosemary,
    lamb                             crushed
⅓ cup minced parsley             ⅓ cup olive oil,
3 tablespoons toasted pine       salt and pepper to taste
    nuts                         olive oil
3 garlic cloves, minced

Preheat the broiler. In a bowl, mix the lamb, parsley, pine nuts,
    garlic, rosemary, olive oil, salt, and pepper. Chill 1 hour. Shape
    into small sausages and skewer. Broil, brushing with olive oil.

Yield: about 20 skewers

Can be prepared to broiling the day before.

## STRUDEL OR PHYLLO APPETIZERS

Although you can serve many pastries at brunch, phyllo seems
most appropriate. The light, delicate layers provide a taste of pastry
without being too filling. Remember that many fillings for omelets,
crêpes, and spreads for other hors d'oeuvre suit phyllo pastry.
    The prepared, frozen pastry is available in many supermarkets,
if there is not a Middle Eastern food store nearby. The pastry is
easy to handle if you follow a few simple steps. When ready to
work, unwrap the pastry onto a counter and cover with waxed

paper and a towel wrung out in cold water. Remove one sheet of pastry, leaving the others covered with the waxed paper and the damp towel so it does not dry out. Brush the sheet with butter, (use a delicate brush, preferably goose feather) and if the pastry is very thin, cover with a second sheet and butter it before filling and shaping.

## SHAPING PHYLLO DOUGH

### Rolls

Spread the filling in a row along one edge of the pastry. Fold in the sides about 2 inches and roll to make it into a log. Place on a baking sheet and brush with melted butter. Make crosswise cuts half way through the pastry, about an inch part before baking.

### Small Logs

Brush 1 sheet of pastry with butter and cut into 3-inch wide strips. Put a generous teaspoon of filling at one end and fold in the edges, one half-inch on each side. Roll the length of the pastry to make a small log. Place on a baking sheet and brush with melted butter.

### Triangles

Brush 1 sheet of phyllo with butter and cut into 3-inch wide strips. Place a teaspoon of filling at one end of a pastry strip. Pick up one corner and fold it over the filling so the short edge aligns with one long edge to form a triangle. Pick up the uppermost point and fold it straight down to keep the triangular shape. Continue until you reach the end of the strip. Place the pastry seam side down on a baking sheet, and brush with melted butter. (The method is the same as folding the American flag. Good scouts know how.)

### Main Course Pastries

Most fillings can be used in larger quantities to make individual main course portions. Prepare the pastry as a single large log, to be cut into slices after baking, or make large logs or triangles. Use 2 sheets cut in half for each individual portion.

### Baking

Unless another temperature is specified, bake phyllo at 400°F. Small pastries take about 25 to 30 minutes, and larger pastries take 45 to 60 minutes. The pastry is cooked when it is golden brown.

**Preparing Ahead**

Phyllo freezes well. Fill and shape the pastries, brush with butter, and place on a baking sheet. Freeze until firm and store in plastic bags. Let thaw for 30 minutes at room temperature and bake until golden.

   Baked pastries also may be frozen, but handle carefully because they break easily.

# CRAB FILLING FOR PHYLLO

1 cup minced mushrooms
1 tablespoon butter
½ pound crabmeat

½ to ¾ cup béchamel
   sauce
salt and pepper to taste

Preheat the oven to 400°F. In a small skillet, sauté the mushrooms in the butter until the liquid evaporates. Stir in the crabmeat and enough béchamel sauce to bind. Correct the seasoning with salt and pepper. Fill pastry and bake.

Yield: enough filling for 24 individual pastries

Can be prepared ahead and frozen.

# SAUSAGE MUSHROOM STRUDEL

2 pounds Italian sweet sausage, peeled
2 pounds mushrooms,
   minced
¼ cup minced shallots

6 tablespoons butter
salt and pepper to taste
1 pound ricotta cheese
1 pound phyllo
1½ cups melted butter

Preheat the oven to 400°F.

In a large skillet, crumble the sausage meat and cook, stirring, breaking it into bits until it loses its color. Remove to a bowl.

In the skillet, sauté the mushrooms and shallots in the 6 tablespoons butter until the liquid evaporates. Correct the seasoning with salt and pepper. Add to the sausage and stir in the ricotta cheese. Correct the seasoning. Fill the pastry and bake.

Yield: enough for about 100 individual pastries, or 2 large logs to
serve as main course for 6 to 8

## VARIATIONS

Substitute cream cheese, cottage cheese, or chèvre (goat cheese)
for the ricotta.

Use a mixture of ½ blue cheese and ½ ricotta.

Substitute hot sausage for sweet, or use chopped kielbasa or
chorizo.

CHAPTER

8

*Fish*

*F*or many, fish is brunch: their day starts with great platters of smoked salmon or lox, bowls of white fish salad, and selections of smoked white fish and sable. Match these with garden-fresh tomatoes, cream cheese, sliced onion, and gratings of black pepper and you need nothing else. For others, breakfast fish means fried fillets or deep fried codfish balls and a generous pot of baked beans. Sautéed fish fillets, especially if there is a fisherman in the family, is a perfect beginning. Lake trout or perch caught that morning by a willing angler can start any morning memorably.

There are many other fish preparations, such as stews, pies, and fish cakes, that are suitable for breakfast and brunch and that keep for several hours or overnight. Make these the day before, knowing that you can heat them the next day. Do remember that they will reheat best if allowed to sit at room temperature for an hour or so before heating. Often you can reheat in a microwave oven. Others taste best if heated in a standard oven just before serving.

Other fish preparations, such as baked or sautéed fish take a very brief time to cook, so wait until you are ready to serve before cooking it. As always, attempting to keep food warm, while waiting to serve it, too often means that it will be dry and flavorless. If it is necessary to hold the food after you have prepared it, let it cool and reheat in the microwave or oven until just hot. Do not cook it any more.

## BASIC SAUTÉED FISH

For breakfast or brunch, select small fish such as trout, lake fish, smelts, or fillets of larger fish such as salmon, haddock, cod, or sole.

1 cup flour
1 teaspoon salt
⅛ teaspoon pepper
1 to 2 pounds fish
4 to 6 tablespoons clarified butter

4 tablespoons butter, optional
1 to 2 tablespoons lemon juice
1 tablespoon minced parsley

In a plastic bag, mix the flour, salt, and pepper. Add the fish and shake in the flour to coat lightly. Shake off any excess flour.

In a large skillet, heat just enough clarified butter to coat the bottom of the pan until hot, but not smoking. Sauté the fish until golden on both sides and just cooked. Remove to a serving platter. If the butter burns, pour it off and replace with fresh butter. Stir in the lemon juice and parsley and cook 30 seconds. Pour over the fish and serve immediately.

Yield: 4 to 8 servings

NOTE

Allow about ¼ pound fish fillet per person, or ½ pound of whole fish or fish steak. A good rule of thumb is to cook the fish 10 minutes per inch of thickness. A 1-inch steak cooks in 10 minutes, a ½-inch steak in 5 minutes.

## VARIATION

For a crisper coating to the fish, mix ½ cup flour and ½ cup cornmeal with the salt and pepper.

## DEEP FRIED FISH

Select small whole fish such as smelts, or cut fillets of fish into strips about ½ inch × ½ inch × 3 inches.

| | |
|---|---|
| 1 quart oil for deep frying | ⅛ teaspoon pepper |
| 1 cup flour | 1 pound fish |
| 1 teaspoon salt | lemon wedges |

In a 2-quart saucepan, heat the oil to 375°F. In a plastic bag, mix flour, salt, and pepper. Toss the fish in the flour to coat lightly and shake off the excess flour. Deep fry until golden. Drain on paper toweling. Serve immediately with the lemon wedges on the side.

Yield: 4 servings

## CLAM PIE

This is an old New England dish. Substitute scallops, shrimp, crab, or oysters for the clams if clams are not readily available.

Pastry for a 2-crust 9-inch
  pie
1 tablespoon minced
  parsley
¼ cup minced onions
3 tablespoons butter
3 tablespoons flour

1 cup heavy cream
½ cup clam juice
3 cups minced clams
1 egg yolk
1 tablespoon heavy
  cream

Preheat the oven to 425°F.

Line a 9-inch pie plate with pastry and sprinkle with the parsley.

In a 1-quart saucepan, sauté the onions in the butter until soft, but not brown. Add the flour and cook the roux until it starts to turn golden. Stir in the cream and clam juice and cook, stirring until the sauce comes to a boil and is thick and smooth. Stir in the clams and turn into the pie shell.

Roll the remaining pastry and cover the top of the pie. Make an air vent.

In a small bowl, mix the egg yolk and cream and brush over the pastry. Bake for 40 minutes, or until the pastry is golden brown.

Yield: 6 to 8 servings

Can be frozen and baked, or reheated after freezing.

---

## CODFISH BALLS OR CAKES

1 cup salt cod
2 cups diced, peeled potatoes
pinch of white pepper
1 egg

½ tablespoon butter
oil for deep frying
tomato sauce, optional (see
  page 280)

Rinse the fish in cold water, place in a bowl, and soak in cold water for 1 hour. Rinse again. (Some salt cod is saltier than others, taste the water. If it is very salty, let it soak longer.)

In a 3-quart saucepan, cover the fish and potatoes with water and simmer until the potatoes are cooked.

Drain and mash the potatoes and fish in a bowl with a wooden spoon or potato masher. Beat in the pepper, egg, and butter. Cool. Shape into 1-inch balls and deep fry at 375°F until golden.

Serve with tomato sauce if desired. Many cooks prefer to serve them with cocktail sauce.

Yield: about 48 small balls

The balls freeze well before or after cooking.

**CODFISH CAKES**

Shape the mixture into flat cakes, about the size of a hamburger. Sauté in melted butter until golden on both sides.

Yield: about 6 cakes

---

# BAKED COD WITH TOMATOES AND POTATOES

2 tablespoons olive oil
1 pound new potatoes,
   thinly sliced
1 onion, thinly sliced
1 garlic clove, minced
1 teaspoon ground cumin
1 tablespoon ginger,
   grated
1 green pepper, cubed
2 tablespoons tomato paste

2 tablespoons balsamic vinegar
salt to taste
1 pound scrod fillets
4 plum tomatoes, thinly
   sliced
1 tablespoon minced pars-
   ley mixed with 1 tablespoon minced savory

In a large skillet, heat the olive oil and brown the potatoes on both sides. Add the onions, garlic, and savory and sauté for 3 to 5 minutes or until the onions begin to soften. Add the green pepper and cook until it starts to soften. Add the tomato paste, vinegar, and salt and bring to a simmer.

Place the fish on top and cover with the tomato slices. Cover the pan and cook, until the fish is just done, ten minutes per inch of thickness. Arrange on a plate and sprinkle with parsley and savory. Boil the juices in the pan until syrupy and pour over the fish and vegetables.

Yield: 4 to 6 servings

If desired, prepare to the point of adding the fish the day before.

## CABILLAUD FECAMPOISE
## (BREADED SAUTÉED COD WITH APPLES)

1½ pounds cod fillets
salt and pepper to taste
2-3 eggs
1 cup fine dry bread crumbs
1 cup flour
8 tablespoons butter

1 lemon quartered
4 cooking apples, peeled,
  cored, and diced into ½
  inch cubes
1 tablespoon Benedictine

Cut the cod into 4 to 6 serving pieces and season with salt and
   pepper.
Place the eggs in one pie plate and whisk until blended. Place the
   bread crumbs in a second pie plate, and the flour, seasoned with
   salt and pepper, in a third pie plate.
Dredge the cod in the flour, roll in the eggs and then in the crumbs
   to coat completely. Press crumbs into the fish to help adhere.
   Let stand on a wire rack for 20 minutes.
In a skillet, melt 4 tablespoons of butter and add the cod. Cook over
   medium heat for 3 to 4 minutes on each side until golden and just
   cooked. Arrange on a platter and sprinkle with lemon juice.
Meanwhile, in another skillet, melt the remaining butter and sauté
   the apples until softened. Add the Benedictine and swirl to mix
   with the apples and pour over the cod.

Yield: 4 to 6 servings

Store the cod on a rack, in the refrigerator if preparing the day
   before.


## FISKEPUDDING
## (NORWEGIAN FISH PUDDING)

This is a favorite recipe. The simplest ingredients of fresh fish and
cream combine to make a delicious dish. With a food processor
the recipe assembles quickly and will wait overnight for cooking.
In addition, you can vary it with the sauce suggestions listed below,
or substitute salmon, sole, or other fish for the cod.

1 tablespoon butter
½ cup light cream

2 tablespoons dry bread
  crumbs

Yield: about 6 large cakes or 48 hors d'oeuvre

Cover the shaped cakes with waxed paper and refrigerate overnight if desired.

---

# DEVILED CRABS

The recipe suggests serving these in scallop or clam shells in
individual servings. You may place the crab in a casserole for to
serve more easily.

| | |
|---|---|
| 1½ cups crab meat, picked over | pinch nutmeg |
| 2 tablespoons butter, melted | 1 garlic clove, minced |
| 2 tablespoons flour | ½ onion, minced |
| 1 cup clam broth | 2 mushrooms, minced |
| 2 egg yolks, beaten | 1 teaspoon Worcestershire sauce |
| 1½ teaspoons dry mustard | cracker crumbs |
| dash of Tabasco | melted butter |

Preheat the oven to 400°F.
In a skillet, sauté the onions, mushrooms, and garlic in the butter
until tender. Stir in the flour, salt, pepper, mustard, and nutmeg.
Add the clam stock and cook, stirring until thickened. Stir in the
egg yolks and fold in the crab.
Turn into scallop or clam shells and sprinkle with cracker crumbs.
Drizzle with butter and bake for 8 to 10 minutes, or until browned.

Yield: 6 servings

Can be prepared the day before.

---

# BAKED HADDOCK COTTAGE STYLE

| | |
|---|---|
| 3 pounds haddock fillets | 6 mushrooms, minced |
| salt and pepper to taste | 2 tablespoons minced parsley |
| juice of 1 lemon | |
| 12 common crackers, crushed | ½ cup butter |
| 6 scallions, thinly sliced | 16 slices bacon |

Preheat the oven to 400°F. Sandwich the fish fillets in pairs and place in a buttered baking dish. Season with salt, pepper, and lemon juice. In a bowl, mix the crackers, scallions, mushrooms, parsley, and butter. Spread over the fish and lay the bacon slices on top. Bake until the fish is cooked, about 20 minutes, depending on the thickness of the fish sandwiches. Allow about 10 minutes per inch of thickness.

Yield: 6 to 8 servings

Can be prepared for baking the night before.

## LOBSTER NOODLE CASSEROLE

2 tablespoons butter, melted
2 tablespoons flour
2 cups milk
3 tablespoons dry white
  wine
½ teaspoon dry mustard
¼ teaspoon Worcestershire
  sauce

1 teaspoon minced garlic
Tabasco to taste
¾ pound cooked lobster
  meat, diced
4 ounces thin noodles,
  cooked and drained
¼ pound grated Cheddar
  or Gruyère

Preheat the oven to 375°F.

In a saucepan, melt the butter, stir in the flour, and cook until it starts to turn golden. Add the milk, stirring until thickened and smooth. Stir in the wine, mustard, Worcestershire sauce, garlic, and Tabasco. Fold in the lobster meat and noodles.

Spoon half the mixture into a buttered casserole and add half the cheese. Fill with remaining mixture and top with the remaining cheese. Bake for 20 minutes.

Yield: 4 servings

Can be prepared the day before and baked just before serving.

## BAKED FRESH MACKEREL OR BLUEFISH

½ pound bacon, cut in julienne

1 bunch scallions, thinly
  sliced

| 4 mackerel or bluefish fillets | 4 tomatoes, peeled and |
| salt and pepper to taste | diced |
| juice of 1 lemon | 4 bay leaves |
| 1 pound mushrooms, thinly | minced parsley |
| sliced | 12 littleneck clams, |
| | optional |

Preheat the oven to 400°F.

In a small skillet, sauté the bacon until almost crisp. Add the scallions and cook until soft but not brown. Pour off the bacon fat. In a baking pan, arrange the fillets in one layer and season with salt, pepper, and lemon juice. Scatter the mushrooms-scallion-bacon mixture, tomatoes, bay leaves, and parsley over the fish. Rinse the clams and arrange around the fish. Cover the pan with foil and bake for 20 minutes.

Yield: 4 to 6 servings

Can be prepared for baking the night before.

---

# SCALLOPED OYSTERS

| ½ cup cracker crumbs | salt and pepper to taste |
| 1 cup fresh bread | pinch of nutmeg |
| crumbs | 4 tablespoons oyster |
| ½ cup melted butter | liquor |
| 1 pint oysters | 2 tablespoons heavy |
| | cream |

Preheat the oven to 400°F.

In a bowl, mix the cracker and bread crumbs with the butter. Place a thin layer in the bottom of an 8 × 11 inch ovenproof dish. Cover with a layer of oysters and season with salt, pepper, and nutmeg. Sprinkle on half the oyster liquor and the cream. Make another layer of crumbs, oysters, seasonings, and liquid. Make a final layer of crumbs. Do not make more than 2 layers of oysters, or they will not cook properly. Bake for 30 minutes.

Yield: 4 servings

Can be prepared for baking the night before.

## SALMON AND CHIVE CAKES WITH CHIVE BUTTER

Since this recipe uses raw salmon, make sure the cakes are fully cooked, but not overcooked before removing from the heat.

| | |
|---|---|
| ¼ cup mayonnaise | 1½ pounds salmon fillet, |
| 1 tablespoon lemon juice | minced |
| 2 teaspoons dry mustard | 1¼ cups bread crumbs |
| dash Tabasco | 4 ounces butter |
| 2 teaspoons salt | 1 cup dry white wine |
| 1 teaspoon pepper | 1 tablespoon lemon juice |
| ½ cup minced chives | ½ cup minced chives |

In a bowl, mix the mayonnaise, lemon juice, mustard, Tabasco, salt, pepper, and chives. Add the salmon and 1 cup bread crumbs and mix lightly.

Shape into 4 cakes, about 1 inch thick and dust with the remaining bread crumbs. Place on a rack, cover with waxed paper and chill 1 hour.

In a skillet, melt 4 tablespoons butter, and sauté the salmon cakes until browned, about 5 minutes on each side. Transfer to a plate and keep warm.

Discard the butter and wipe the skillet clean. Add the wine and lime juice to the skillet and reduce to half. Lower the heat and whisk in the remaining butter. Stir in the coriander and season with salt and pepper.

Yield: 4 servings

Can be prepared for cooking the day before.

NOTE

For a change in flavor and texture use crushed crackers instead of bread crumbs.

## SCANDINAVIAN SALMON CAKES

The cooked salmon and rye bread crumbs give this recipe a different personality from the previous recipe. Serve with a dill-flavored mayonnaise or a mixture of chopped fresh tomato and minced dill.

12 ounces salmon fillet
½ cup rye bread crumbs
1 onion, minced
2 tablespoons minced dill

2 teaspoons capers
2 teaspoons horseradish
1 egg white

Preheat the broiler.
Broil salmon until just cooked.
In a bowl, mix the bread crumbs, onion, dill, capers, horseradish, and egg white. Flake the salmon, mix into the bread crumbs, and shape into 4 patties. Sauté in butter or broil until golden.

Yield: 4 servings

## CREAMED SALMON WITH PEAS

2 cups cream sauce (see page 275)
1 pound salmon fillet, poached and flaked

1 cup cooked peas
salt and pepper to taste
6 slices buttered toast, optional

In a saucepan, heat the cream sauce and gently fold in the salmon and peas. Correct the seasoning with salt and pepper. Heat until hot. Serve on slices of buttered toast.

Yield: 6 servings

The creamed salmon mixture can be prepared the day before and reheated.

### NOTE

Although traditionally served on toast, you can serve this over a bed of rice, or fold into freshly cooked pasta. Thin the sauce with more milk, or cream, if serving with pasta.

## MOUSSE DE SAUMON (SALMON MOUSSE)

1¼ pounds salmon fillets
2 large egg whites

1¾ cup heavy cream
1 teaspoon salt

cayenne pepper to taste  
1½ cups hollandaise sauce

2 cups sautéed mushroom  
caps  
minced parsley

Preheat the oven to 350°F.

Butter a 1½ quart mold and set aside.

In a food processor, purée the salmon. With the machine running, add the egg whites and process for 1 minute. Slowly pour in the cream and process until absorbed. Season with salt and cayenne pepper. Turn into the prepared mold and place in a baking pan and fill with 1 inch of hot water.

Bake for 35 to 40 minutes, or until a knife inserted in the center comes out clean. Remove from the water bath and let stand for 10 minutes. Unmold onto a serving platter.

Coat with the Hollandaise sauce and arrange the mushroom caps around the outside edge. Sprinkle with the parsley.

Yield: 6 servings

Can be prepared for baking the night before.

---

## SCALLOP CAKES

6 slices stale white bread  
¾ cup evaporated milk  
6 tablespoons unsalted butter  
¼ cup plus 2 tablespoons vegetable oil  
1 cup minced onion  
1 cup minced celery  
1 cup dry white wine  
1 large bay leaf

1 garlic clove, minced  
1½ pounds sea scallops  
2 eggs  
½ cup minced scallion  
¼ cup minced parsley  
1¾ teaspoons salt  
¾ teaspoons pepper  
3 dashes Tabasco sauce  
3½ cups bread crumbs

In a bowl, soak the bread, broken into small bits, in the evaporated milk until the milk is absorbed. Mash with a fork.

In a skillet, melt 4 tablespoons butter and cook the onion and celery until softened. Set aside.

In a saucepan, simmer the wine, bay leaf, garlic, and 1 cup of water for 1 minute. Add the scallops and poach until just done. Drain and chop the scallops coarsely.

Stir in the soaked bread, onion mixture, eggs, scallion, parsley, salt, and pepper. Cover and refrigerate for 1 hour. Stir 2 cups of bread crumbs into the mixture.

Place 1½ cups bread crumbs on a piece of waxed paper and shape the scallop mixture into cakes 3 inches in diameter and about 1 inch thick. Set on baking sheet, cover with waxed paper, and refrigerate for 1 hour.

*To Pan Fry*  In a skillet heat 1 tablespoon of butter and 1 tablespoon of oil and cook the cakes in a single layer until golden. Turn, and cook the second side about 10 minutes.

*To Bake*, preheat the oven to 500°F. On baking sheets place 1 tablespoon butter and melt in the oven. Arrange cakes on sheet. Bake 5 minutes, turn over, and bake 5–7 minutes longer.

Yield: 6 servings

---

# SCALLOPS PROVENÇALE
# WITH SPINACH NOODLES

1½ pounds tomatoes, peeled, seeded, and chopped
1 bay leaf
salt and pepper to taste
¾ cup flour
1 pound scallops

½ cup olive oil
1 tablespoon minced garlic
3 tablespoons butter
½ pound spinach noodles, cooked
2 tablespoons butter

In a 9-inch skillet, bring the tomatoes to a boil. Set a sieve over a bowl and pour in the tomatoes. Drain for 5 minutes. Put the drained juice into a saucepan and reduce by half. Add the tomato pulp, bay leaf, salt, and pepper and simmer 3 minutes.

Season the flour with salt and pepper and dredge the scallops. Heat the oil in a 9-inch skillet until very hot. Add the scallops and sauté until golden. It is more important not to overcook them than to brown them. Add the scallops to the tomato sauce.

Add the garlic and butter to the skillet and sauté until the garlic turns golden but does not burn. In a serving platter, toss the noodles, scallops, and tomato sauce. Pour the garlic butter and parsley over the top.

Yield: 4 to 6 servings

The tomato sauce and garlic butter can be prepared the night
   before.

## MOUSSE DE COQUILLES ST. JACQUES (SCALLOP MOUSSE)

2 pounds scallops
2 tablespoons butter
1 tablespoon minced shal-
   lots
salt and pepper to taste
½ cup dry white wine
2 egg yolks

2 cups heavy cream
nutmeg to taste
Tomato Mushroom Cream
   sauce (see below)
2 tablespoons minced parsley

Preheat the oven to 375°F.
Butter a 2 quart mold.
Cut 1 cup of scallops into ½ inch cubes and set aside. In a 9-inch
   skillet, sauté the shallots in 1 tablespoon of butter until soft, but
   not brown. Add the diced scallops, season with salt and pepper,
   and cook until barely firm. Add the wine and cook 1 minute.
   Remove the scallops with a slotted spoon and reserve. Reserve
   the liquid in the skillet to use in the sauce.
In a food processor purée the remaining scallops. Add the egg yolk
   and process until blended, scraping down the sides as needed.
   When puréed, add the cream in a steady stream until absorbed.
   Season with salt, pepper, and nutmeg to taste. Turn into a bowl
   and fold in the reserved scallops.
Fill the mold with the mousse and smooth the top. Cover with a
   sheet of buttered waxed paper, buttered side down.
Place the mold in a baking pan with 1 inch of hot water and bake
   for 45 minutes, or until a knife inserted in the center comes out
   clean. Meanwhile prepare the tomato sauce as directed.
Remove the waxed paper and pull off the brown skin on the surface
   of the mousse. Unmold onto a serving platter.
Drain any liquid that accumulates and add to the sauce. Pour the
   sauce over the mousse and sprinkle with parsley.

Yield: 6 servings.

The mousse can be prepared the night before.

# TOMATO MUSHROOM CREAM SAUCE FOR SCALLOP MOUSSE

3 tablespoons butter
3 tablespoons flour
poaching liquor from scallops
1 cup thinly sliced mush-
  rooms
1 tablespoon butter

3 tomatoes, peeled, seeded
  and chopped
1 tablespoon butter
1 cup heavy cream
salt, pepper, and nutmeg to
  taste

In a 1-quart saucepan, melt the butter, stir in the flour, and cook
  the roux until it just starts to turn golden. Stir in the poaching
  liquor and cook, stirring until thickened and smooth.
In a small skillet, sauté the mushrooms in 1 tablespoon butter until
  tender. Add the mushrooms and their liquid to the sauce.
In the same skillet, sauté the tomatoes in the remaining butter for
  10 minutes. Add to the sauce with the heavy cream. Heat the
  sauce, stirring, until hot. Correct the seasoning with the salt,
  pepper, and nutmeg.

Yield: 3 cups

Can be prepared the day before.

# SHRIMP MAQUE CHOUX

4 tablespoons butter
1 onion, chopped
1 green pepper, chopped
1 jalapeño pepper, minced
1 pound shrimp, peeled
  and deveined

10 ounces corn kernels
1 cup heavy cream
1 teaspoon salt
½ teaspoon pepper
dash Tabasco

In a skillet, melt the butter over moderate high heat. Add the
  onion, green pepper, and jalapeño pepper and sauté until soft,
  but not brown. Stir in the shrimp and cook until opaque. Add
  the corn and cream and cook 5 minutes longer, or until heated.
  Season with salt, pepper, and Tabasco.

Yield: 4 servings

Do not prepare ahead.

## UMIDO DI GAMBERI AL POMODORO PICCANTE (SHRIMP WITH TOMATOES AND HOT PEPPER)

1½ pounds shrimp, shelled
   and deveined
3 tablespoons minced onion
⅓ cup olive oil
2 teaspoons minced garlic
pinch hot red pepper

3 tablespoons minced parsley
1½ cups canned Italian tomatoes, chopped with
   their juice
salt to taste

Rinse shrimp and drain.

In a skillet, cook the onion in the olive oil until soft, but not brown.
   Add the garlic and hot pepper and cook, stirring until the garlic
   just starts to turn golden. Do not burn.

Add the parsley, tomatoes, and their juice and season with salt.
   Simmer until thickened, about 20 minutes.

Add the shrimp and mix into the sauce. Cover and cook 2 to 3
   minutes or until just done.

Yield: 4 to 6 servings

Do not prepare ahead.

NOTE:

Serve with rice, or over pasta.

## SAUTÉED SHRIMP WITH TOMATOES, MUSHROOMS AND FETA CHEESE

¼ cup olive oil
1 pound large shrimp,
   deveined
8 scallions, minced
1½ cups diced tomatoes

1 cup diced mushrooms
¾ cup crumbled feta cheese
2 tablespoons dry white
   wine

In a skillet, heat the oil and sauté the shrimp for 1 minute or until
   they just start to turn pink.

Add the scallions, tomatoes, and mushrooms and stir until well
   mixed. Add the cheese and mix well. Cook 1 minute longer,

add the wine, and simmer 1 minute longer. Serve with cooked rice.

Yield: 4 to 6 servings

Do not prepare ahead

---

# SCAMPI ALLA BARESE (SHRIMP WITH SWEET PEPPERS)

Scampi are large shrimp. To be authentic, use shrimp sized U-12 to U-15 (under 12 or 15 to the pound).

1 cup flour
salt and pepper to taste
1 pound large shrimp,
   peeled and deveined
¾ cup olive oil
1 tablespoon minced garlic
1 green pepper, chopped

1 yellow pepper, chopped
½ cup dry white wine
1½ cups thinly sliced mushrooms
½ teaspoon dried oregano
⅓ cup fish stock or clam
   broth

Season the flour with salt and pepper and dredge the shrimp. Shake off any excess flour.

Heat ¾ cup olive oil in a large skillet and cook the shrimp over high heat until golden, about 1½ minutes. Drain. Remove and discard ½ the olive oil.

In the remaining oil in the skillet sauté the garlic and peppers for 3 minutes or until the peppers start to soften. Add the wine and mushrooms and season with oregano, salt and pepper. Cook 1 minute. Add the shrimp to the skillet with the stock and cook, 1 minute longer. Serve.

Yield: 4 to 6 servings

Cannot be prepared ahead.

CHAPTER

9

*Meats*

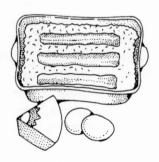

*T*he first meat, if not the only meat we think of when we think of breakfast is pork, either as rashers of bacon, sausage links or patties, or thick slices of ham. The aromas of frying bacon permeate the house and our mouths start to water. Years ago these were made from well-fattened hogs and consequently contained quantities of fat, much of which remained in the pan, to be saved as a cooking fat for other foods, and the rest of which we ate. Today, hogs are on a diet and pork has much less fat than in the past, but it still has fat, and sausages and bacon have an enormous percentage of fat. Many meat packers produce "imitation" bacon, sausages, and ham from turkey or other poultry. Some products are relatively good and serve as a substitute for the person who needs to have these flavors regularly. My samplings suggest that spicier preparations come closer in flavor to the real thing, so sausages from chicken or turkey taste more like breakfast pork sausages, than say, turkey bacon tastes like bacon. Most though are a poor imitation indeed. I prefer to restrict my consumption and enjoy real bacon and eggs a few times a year.

In some areas, starting the day with a small steak is still common. A good friend who is also a fashion model has started her day with a 3 ounce steak for years. The steak is lean to begin with, and it is broiled so that as much fat drains off as possible. Her sleek figure is proof that there is nothing wrong with eating meat: the problem is eating too much meat. Many hosts still feel that they must provide 8 or 12 ounce servings per person. Today, we know that that much meat is not needed. For most of us, it is simply too much. Still there is no need to completely avoid the luscious flavor of meat.

For brunch you can offer a variety of meat dishes. Depending on the weather and location, you can offer substantial meat dishes like stews, or have just a few slivers of chicken in a salad. Ski weekends sometimes call for substantial fare for those just off, or those going onto, the slopes. Summer brunches often mean only the lightest of fare so we can loll around the lawn, pool, or deck and enjoy a lazy afternoon.

One of the appealing qualities of most breakfast and brunch meat dishes is that you can prepare them ahead and reheat them without loss of quality.


## CHICKEN

For brunch, I prefer to have dishes that you can prepare ahead and only need to reheat, or finish the cooking. This is not the time to stand over a hot stove. There are always exceptions. For a summer brunch with everyone on the porch watching the sailboats race I am happy to prepare grilled chicken or other meats because I can also be with the guests.

When preparing broiled chicken, allow a quarter of a chicken per person. Serve both breasts and legs so guests can select their favorite piece. Broil the chicken with only salt and pepper, or try one of the marinades suggested below.

---

# BASIC BROILED CHICKEN

2 2- to 3-pound chickens,                    salt and pepper to taste
   cut into quarters

Preheat the grill or broiler.
Season the chickens with the salt and pepper and place on the grill
   or in the broiler with the skin closest to the heat. Cook 15
   minutes, moving the chicken to make sure it does not burn.
   Turn and cook the unskinned side for 10 minutes longer, or
   until the chicken is cooked. Again move to make sure the meat
   does not burn.
Let stand for 5 minutes before serving.

Yield: 8 servings

Serve hot or cold. If prepared ahead and refrigerated, bring to
   room temperature before serving for the best flavor.

## VARIATIONS

### ROSEMARY GARLIC MARINADE

Marinate the chicken in ½ cup olive oil mixed with 1 tablespoon minced rosemary and 2 crushed garlic cloves for up to 24 hours before broiling.

### CURRIED MARMALADE MUSTARD CHICKEN

In a heavy saucepan simmer 1 cup orange marmalade, ½ cup Dijon mustard, ¼ cup honey, 1 tablespoon curry powder, and 1 tablespoon lemon juice for 5 minutes. Brush over the chickens and marinate for 1 hour before broiling.

# CHICKEN BROCCOLI AND NOODLE CASSEROLE

3 cups poached, diced
    chicken
4 cups Sauce Suprême (see
    page 277)
1 bunch broccoli, cut into
    florets and cooked

salt and pepper to taste
nutmeg to taste
¼ pound fine or medium
    noodles, cooked
4 tablespoons butter
¼ cup grated Gruyère or
    Parmesan cheese

Preheat the oven to 350°F.
Butter an ovenproof baking dish, about 11 × 13 inches.
In a large bowl, mix the chicken, 2 cups of sauce, and the broccoli.
    Season with salt, pepper, and nutmeg.
Toss the noodles with the butter and arrange in the baking dish.
    Place the chicken-broccoli on top of the noodles and pour over
    the remaining sauce. Sprinkle with the cheese and bake until
    bubbling hot.

Yield: 6 servings

Can be prepared for baking and frozen.

# CIORBA (RUMANIAN CHICKEN STEW)

1 chicken, quartered
2 cups chicken stock
1 teaspoon salt
½ teaspoon pepper
2 carrots, julienne
1 green pepper, julienne
1 red pepper, julienne
8 scallions, chopped
2 tomatoes, chopped

¼ pound green beans, cut
    in 2 inch lengths
1 cup cauliflower florets
½ cup minced dill
½ cup minced parsley
4 ounces egg vermicelli
2 egg yolks
⅔ cup sour cream
¼ cup lemon juice

Remove any pieces of fat from the chicken pieces.
In a saucepan, combine the chicken the stock, salt, pepper, and 3
    cups water and bring to a full boil. Lower the heat to a simmer
    and add the carrots, green pepper, red pepper, scallions, toma-
    toes, green beans, and cauliflower. Partially cover and simmer
    until the chicken is tender, skimming as needed.

Add the dill, parsley, and vermicelli. Cook until noodles are tender. Remove from heat and let stand for 5 minutes. Remove any fat from the surface.

In a small bowl, beat the egg yolks and sour cream. Gradually whisk in some hot liquid and stir back into the stew. Stir in lemon juice, salt, and pepper and serve hot.

Yield: 4 servings

For easier eating, let the chicken cool after it is tender and remove and discard the skin and bones. Remove the fat from the liquid. Return the chicken meat and continue. To prepare ahead, cook chicken and vegetables and let chill overnight: remove any fat and reheat. Cook the noodles and finish the sauce shortly before serving.

---

# CHICKEN AND VEGETABLE STEW

Using toasted bread as a base for soups and stews is common in France and Italy.

| | |
|---|---|
| 1 3-pound chicken | 1 tablespoon minced tarra- |
| 8 cups chicken stock | gon |
| salt and pepper to taste | ½ cup soup pasta |
| 3 carrots, thickly sliced | 3 tablespoons butter |
| 5 celery stalks, thickly sliced | 1 tablespoon lemon juice |
| 3 leeks, thickly sliced | 4 slices Italian bread |
| bouquet of bay leaf, parsley, | olive oil |
| and thyme | ½ cup grated Parmesan |
| 4 garlic cloves, crushed | cheese |
| | 4 springs parsley |

In a 4-quart casserole, bring the chicken and stock to a boil skimming any scum. Add 2 teaspoons salt, the carrots, celery, leeks, bouquet garni, and garlic. Cover and poach for 40 minutes or until the chicken is tender. Remove the chicken.

Strain the stock, reserving the vegetables. Discard the bouquet and garlic. Skim any fat and reduce the poaching liquid by two-thirds. Remove and discard the skin and bones from the chicken and cut into large pieces.

Cook the pasta in boiling salted water until al dente, and drain.

Preheat the broiler.

Brush the bread with the olive oil and broil until golden. Sprinkle
with the cheese and place in deep soup dishes.

Whisk the butter into the chicken stock and add the lemon juice
and tarragon and correct seasoning with salt and pepper. Add
the chicken, vegetables, and pasta and reheat. Spoon the stew
over the bread slices and sprinkle with parsley.

Yield: 4 servings

The stew can be prepared ahead. Do not add the pasta until shortly
before serving.

## CHICKEN AND LEEK PIE

| | |
|---|---|
| 2¼ cups flour | 1 large onion, sliced |
| pinch of salt | 1 teaspoon dried thyme |
| ½ cup butter | salt and pepper to taste |
| ¼ cup iced water | ½ teaspoon grated nutmeg |
| 3 pound chicken | ¼ to ½ cup cream |
| 1 pound piece Canadian | 3 tablespoons cooking liq- |
| bacon | uid from chicken |
| 2 pounds leeks, thinly sliced | ¼ cup minced parsley |

In a bowl, mix the flour and salt and work in the butter until the
mixture resembles cornmeal. With a spoon add the ice water
and form into a dough. Press the dough into a flat cake, wrap
in plastic, and refrigerate for 30 minutes.

On a lightly floured board, roll the pastry into a 9½-inch circle. Place
the circle on a baking sheet and refrigerate until ready to use.

In a 3-quart casserole, place the chicken and bacon, with water to
cover. Bring to a boil, skim the surface, and lower the heat. Add
the leeks, onion, thyme, salt, pepper, and nutmeg. Cover and
simmer gently for 1 to 1½ hours or until the chicken is very
tender. Turn off the heat and let the chicken stand for 1 hour.

Preheat the oven to 400°F. Remove chicken and bacon from casserole. Discard chicken skin, bones and any fat on chicken or
bacon. Cut meats into strips. Strain cooking liquid and set aside.

Select a deep 9-inch baking dish such as a 2-quart soufflé dish. In
the baking dish, layer chicken, bacon, leeks, and onion until all
are used. Pour in enough heavy cream to cover meat and

vegetables, then add 3 tablespoons chicken cooking liquid. Moisten the rim of the dish with cold water. Place the pastry on the dish and press around the edges. Trim the excess. Crimp the edges with a fork and brush with any extra cream. Make several slits in the pastry. Set in a baking pan to catch any overflow and bake for 20 to 25 minutes or until golden.

Yield: 4 to 6 servings

Can be prepared for baking the night before.

## CHICKEN LIVERS IN RED WINE

Chicken livers are a favorite breakfast meet. You can sautée them just in butter with a sprinkling of minced thyme or savory, and a splash of Madeira, or you can prepare them a little more elaborately with this recipe.

| | |
|---|---|
| ½ pound mushroom caps | ½ cup red wine |
| 2 green peppers, minced | 1 bay leaf |
| 3 tablespoons butter | salt and pepper to taste |
| 1½ pounds chicken livers | hot buttered toast |
| 4 tablespoons butter | |

In a 10-inch skillet, sauté the mushrooms and peppers in 2 tablespoons butter until soft.

In a separate skillet, sauté the chiken livers in the remaining butter until browned, but still medium-rare. Add to the mushroom mixture with the wine, bay leaf, salt, and pepper and simmer for 2 minutes. Serve on toast.

Yield: 6 servings

Can be prepared the day before and reheated.

## CHICKEN AND HERB SAUSAGE

| | |
|---|---|
| 1 pound boneless chicken breasts skinned | 1½ teaspoons butter |
| | 1 onion, minced |
| ¼ pound pork butt, cubed | ¼ cup heavy cream |
| ¼ pound fatback, cubed | 1½ teaspoons salt |

white pepper
1 egg
2 tablespoons minced herbs,
   thyme, chervil, marjoram,
   parsley, or chives

3 feet lamb, or 1½ feet hog
   casings
2 cups chicken stock, op-
   tional

In a grinder with a ¼- to ⅜-holed plate, grind the chicken and pork
   butt. Chill for 30 minutes.
Add the fatback to the chicken, grind again, and put into a bowl.
In a skillet, sauté the onion in the butter until soft.
Beat the onion, egg, cream, salt, and pepper into the meat and stir
   in the herbs.
In a small skillet, poach or panfry a small portion to taste for
   seasoning.
Stuff into casings and chill 1 hour.
Poach the sausages in simmering stock until firm, about 6 to 8
   minutes, or grill.

Yield: 6 Servings

# BEEF

Stews, ragouts, daubes, and casseroles are the most common use
of meat for brunch. The exceptions are roast tenderloin—it seems
that people will eat this at anytime—and of course, small steaks, for
the steak-and-egg crowd.

---

## BEEF STROGANOFF

1 pound lean beef fillet,
   ¼ inch strips
1 tablespoon paprika
3 tablespoons vegetable oil
¼ pound mushrooms,
   thinly sliced
¼ cup dry sherry

½ cup beef stock
1 cup sour cream
1 teaspoon lemon juice
salt to taste
½ pound fine noodles,
   cooked

Sprinkle the beef strips with the paprika. In a large skillet, sauté
   the beef in the oil until browned, but still rare. Do not crowd
   the pan: prepare in batches, if necessary. Set cooked beef
   aside.

Add the mushrooms to the skillet and sauté until tender and set aside. Add the sherry to the pan and reduce by half. Add the beef stock and simmer 5 minutes. Remove from the heat and stir in the sour cream, lemon juice, and salt. Return the mushrooms and meat and reheat without boiling. Serve over the noodles.

Yield: 6 servings

Can be prepared ahead and reheated gently.

## BOEUF EN CASSEROLE PROVENÇALE (BRAISED BEEF PROVENÇALE)

2½ pounds eye round or chuck, cut in 1½ inch cubes
3 tablespoons butter
2 tablespoons cognac
3 onions, cut in eighths
1 large garlic clove, minced
4 tomatoes, peeled and chopped
½ cup stuffed olives
2 teaspoons tomato paste
2 teaspoons cornstarch
1 teaspoon meat glaze, optional
½ cup red wine
1 cup chicken stock
¼ cup dry sherry
1 teaspoon currant jelly
1 bay leaf
2 tablespoons minced parsley

In a large skillet, sauté the meat in batches in 2 tablespoons butter until browned. Set meat aside. Add the cognac to the pan, ignite and cook, stirring up the browned bits. Add the remaining butter, onion, and garlic to the pan and sauté for 5 minutes, or until lightly glazed. Add the tomatoes and olives and cook 2 minutes. Remove from the heat.

In a small bowl, mix the tomato paste, flour and meat glaze, if using. Stir into the pan and add the wine, stock, and sherry. Return the pan to the heat and cook until the sauce comes to a boil. Add the beef, jelly, and bay leaf. Cover and simmer over low heat for 60 minutes or longer until very tender. Serve garnished with the parsley.

Yield: 6 servings

Can be made ahead and frozen.

## CREAMED CHIPPED BEEF ON TOAST

This dish gets poor press because so many of us remember it from the military or school cafeterias. Properly and carefully prepared, it is worth more credit.

| | |
|---|---|
| ¼ pound chipped beef | 1 cup heavy cream |
| 4 tablespoons butter | salt and pepper to taste |
| 3 tablespoons flour | buttered toast points or En- |
| 1 cup milk | glish muffins |

Soak the beef in cold water for 30 seconds, drain, and taste the beef. If still too salty, repeat.

Cut the beef into shreds. In a 9-inch skillet, heat the beef in the butter until the edges start to curl. Sprinkle with the flour and cook 1 minute, stirring. Stir in the milk and cream and cook, stirring until the mixture thickens. Correct the seasoning with salt and pepper. Serve on the toast points.

Yield: 4 servings

Can be prepared ahead and reheated.

NOTE

There are several versions of this dish. You can add ½ pound thinly sliced mushrooms, sautéed in 2 tablespoons butter, or stir in 2 ounces sliced pimientos, or 2 cups of grated Cheddar cheese. Or you can add all these ingredients.

## KÖNIGSBERGER KLOPSE (KONIGSBERG MEATBALLS)

| | |
|---|---|
| ¾ cup minced onion | 4 tablespoons butter |
| 1 tablespoon butter | ½ cup flour |
| ¾ pound ground beef | 1 quart chicken stock |
| ¾ pound ground pork | ½ large sardine, drained |
| ¾ cup milk | and sliced |
| 2 slices white bread, crusts | ⅓ cup capers, rinsed and |
| discarded | drained |
| 1 large sardine, drained and | ¼ cup white wine vinegar |
| chopped | salt and pepper to taste |
| salt and pepper to taste | |

In a skillet, sauté the onion in the butter until soft, but not brown. Cool.

In a bowl, mix the beef, pork, and onions.

In a saucepan, heat the milk, add the bread slices, and let them absorb the milk. Add to the meat mixture with the eggs, sardine, salt, and pepper and mix well.

Shape into 24 2-inch balls. They will be soft. Chill to firm.

In a saucepan, over medium heat, melt the butter and stir in the flour. Add the chicken stock and bring to a boil. Add the sardine, capers, vinegar, salt, and pepper.

Simmer the meatballs in the sauce for 15 minutes. Correct seasoning. If too thick, add more stock. Serve with peeled and poached potatoes.

Yield: 6 to 12 servings

Can be prepared ahead and reheated.

## TUNISIAN BEEF SAUSAGES

| | |
|---|---|
| 2 feet sausage casing | 2 teaspoons ground |
| 2 pounds beef, coarsely | pepper |
| ground | 2 teaspoons ground anise |
| 1 tablespoons olive oil | 1 teaspoon dried mint, |
| 1 tablespoon paprika | crushed |
| | 1 teaspoon salt |

Rinse the sausage casing in cold water, place one end over the faucet, and let cold water run through the middle. Slip the casing onto the sausage tube of the mixer.

In a bowl, mix the beef, olive oil, paprika, pepper, anise, mint, and salt. Place the mixture into the feed tube of the mixer and fill the casings. Tie into 3 inch sections, or make one large round coil.

Sauté in a skillet in olive oil until golden brown and cooked.

Yield: 6 to 8 servings

Sausages can be prepared several days in advance and cooked shortly before serving. Can be frozen.

## CORNED BEEF HASH

1 onion, minced
4 tablespoons butter
2 pounds corned beef, diced

1 pound boiled potatoes,
 diced
salt and pepper to taste

In a large skillet, sauté the onion in the butter until soft, but not
 brown. Add the corned beef and potatoes and cook, stirring
 until well mixed and heated.
For a browned crust, flatten the hash in the pan and cook over
 medium heat until a crust forms on the bottom. Place a large
 plate on top of the skillet and flip the hash onto the plate. Place
 another 2 tablespoons of butter in the skillet and when melted,
 slide the hash into the pan and brown the second side.

Yield: 6 to 8 servings

Can be prepared ahead and reheated.

### VARIATIONS

### PATTIES

In a bowl, mix the sautéed onion into the corned beef and
potatoes, shape into patties the size of hamburgers, and sauté them
in additional butter until golden on both sides.

### RED FLANNEL HASH

Add ½ pound diced beets to the hash and mix well.

### CORNED BEEF HASH WITH EGGS

Prepare the hash and serve portions on plates, or make into patties,
and top with fried or poached eggs. You can place the hash in a
cocotte and heat in the oven until hot. Make an indentation in the
center and break one or two eggs into the indentation. Bake as for
shirred eggs.

## TENDRONS DE VEAU À L'ESTRAGON
## (BREAST OF VEAL WITH TARRAGON)

2 pounds boneless breast of
 veal

6 tablespoons clarified butter

½ cup water                             2 teaspoons dried tarragon
3 tablespoons flour                     salt and pepper to taste
½ cup white wine

Preheat the oven to 300°F.

Cut the veal into 1 × 3-inch strips. In a large skillet, sauté the veal
   in the butter until golden. Sprinkle with the flour and cook until
   the flour is golden. Stir in the wine and water and cook, stirring,
   until the sauce thickens.

Transfer to a flame-proof casserole and bring to a boil on top of
   the stove. Season with salt and pepper and 1 teaspoon of
   tarragon. Bake for 1½ hours. Ten minutes before the cooking
   period ends, add the remaining tarragon.

Yield: 4 servings

Can be prepared ahead and reheated, or frozen.

## VEAL AND SAUSAGE RAGOÛT

3 onions, thinly sliced                 2 tomatoes, quartered
2 tablespoons butter                    1 green pepper, sliced
1 pound veal shoulder,                  ½ pound kielbasa, thinly
   ¾-inch cubes                            sliced
2 tablespoons paprika                   1 cup sour cream

In a large skillet, sauté the onions in the butter until soft, but not
   brown. Add the veal and paprika and sauté for 10 minutes. Add
   the tomatoes, pepper, and sausage and simmer until tender,
   about 35 minutes.

Remove from the heat and stir in the sour cream. Reheat, without
   boiling, if necessary.

Yield: 4 to 6 servings

Can be prepared ahead and reheated, or frozen.

## VEAL SAUSAGE

1 pound lean veal, cut into             fatback), or pancetta,
   chunks                                  cubed
2 ounces pork belly (lean               ¼ pound pork butt, cubed

¼ pound pork fat, cubed
3 tablespoons heavy cream
3 tablespoons bread crumbs
1½ teaspoons salt
pinch of nutmeg
1 tablespoon Parmesan
  cheese

¼ pound caul fat or ½ feet
  hog casing
¼ cup olive oil
thick-sliced red onion and
  red pepper for grilling,
  optional

In a meat grinder, with a ¼- or ⅜-inch holed plate, grind the
  veal, pork belly, and pork butt. Add the pork fat and grind
  again.
Heat the cream to warm, and soak the bread crumbs. Mix into the
  meats and season with salt, nutmeg, and Parmesan.
Panfry a small portion of meat to taste for seasoning. Shape into
  3- to 4-ounce patties and wrap in caul fat, or stuff into hog
  casings.
Grill the sausages or sauté until just cooked and serve with grilled
  red onion and pepper, if desired.

Yield: 6 servings

Can be prepared several days ahead or frozen before cooking.

# ROGHAN JOSH (CURRIED LAMB)

2 pounds lamb in 1½-inch
  cubes
½ teaspoon cayenne pepper
1 teaspoon salt
1 cup plain yogurt
1 tablespoon minced
  gingerroot
¼ cup clarified butter

pepper to taste
½ teaspoon turmeric
2 tablespoons minced coriander
1 cup water
½ teaspoon garam masala
  (see note)
pinch of ground nutmeg

In a 2-quart bowl, mix the lamb, cayenne, and salt. Add the yogurt,
  and ginger, and mix again. Cover and marinate at room temperature for 1 hour.
In a skillet, heat the butter until hot and stir in the pepper and
  turmeric. Add the lamb and its marinade, and heat, stirring
  constantly, until it comes to a simmer. Simmer uncovered for 1
  hour.

Sprinkle with the coriander and pour ½ cup water down the side of the pan. Cover and simmer 15 minutes. Stir in ¼ cup water, cover and simmer 15 minutes longer. Stir in the remaining water and cook 10 minutes longer. Pour into a serving bowl and sprinkle with the garam masala and nutmeg.

Yield: 4 to 6 servings

Can be prepared ahead and reheated, or frozen.

NOTE:

Garam masala is a mixture of spices available in Asian markets.

# HAM HASH

| | |
|---|---|
| 3 tablespoons butter | 1 cup sour cream |
| 2 cups finely chopped ham | salt and pepper to taste |
| 2 cups sliced cooked potato | 2 tablespoons minced chives |

In a 10-inch skillet, melt the butter, add the ham and potatoes, and heat. When hot, stir in the sour cream, salt, and pepper and heat until hot, without boiling. Serve sprinkled with chives.

Yield: 4 to 6 servings

Prepare just before serving.

# SAUCISSES À LA CAMPAGNARDE (COUNTRY SAUSAGES)

| | |
|---|---|
| 3 tomatoes, chopped | ½ pound mushrooms, thinly sliced |
| salt and pepper to taste | 2 green peppers, peeled and sliced |
| ¼ cup olive oil | ½ teaspoon paprika |
| 6 sweet Italian sausages | ¼ teaspoon cayenne pepper |
| 2 tablespoons dry white wine | ¼ teaspoon dried thyme |
| 1 large onion, thinly sliced | ¼ teaspoon dried rosemary |
| 1 teaspoon minced garlic | |

½ cup roasted red peppers, diced

2 tablespoons minced garlic

2 tablespoons minced parsley

Place the tomatoes in a colander. Sprinkle with salt and drain for 30 minutes.

In a 9-inch skillet, heat 2 tablespoons of oil and add the sausages and wine. Cook over low heat until browned. Remove to a plate and discard the fat.

Add the remaining oil to a large skillet and sauté the onion and 1 teaspoon garlic until soft, but not brown. Add the mushrooms, peppers, salt, and pepper. Cook until the peppers soften. Stir in the paprika, cayenne pepper, thyme, rosemary, and tomatoes. Add the sausages and cook over medium heat until the tomato juices evaporate. Correct the seasoning with salt and pepper.

Arrange on a platter and sprinkle with the roasted peppers, garlic, and parsley.

Yield: 4 to 6 servings

Can be prepared ahead and reheated, or frozen.

## SAUSAGES AND APPLES

1 pound pork sausage links
1 cup maple syrup
½ cup white vinegar

4 medium apples, cored and cut into ½-inch thick slices

In a 9-inch skillet, sauté the sausages until brown and drain. In a 1-quart saucepan, bring the maple syrup and vinegar to a boil. Add the apples and simmer until tender crisp. Drain. Arrange the sausages on a platter and surround with apples.

Yield: 4 servings

Can be prepared the night before and reheated.

CHAPTER 10

# Vegetables and Pasta

*T*he first vegetable that comes to mind at breakfast is the potato: hash browned potatoes—made from last night's leftovers, mixed with some chopped onion, and cooked until crispy and yet still moist, seasoned with a load of black pepper and a judicious amount of salt. The potato mixes so well with the egg yolk from a fried egg or accompanies scrambled eggs perfectly. Some people prefer tomatoes raw or cooked as a breakfast vegetable, but breakfast is usually a high protein, high carbohydrate meal, with the carbohydrates appearing in various breads.

Brunch opens culinary doors. Many vegetable preparations suit the occasion and this is the time to think of casseroles and salads. These are preparations that hold well and require little last minute preparation. You can make many casseroles the day before, or even prepare and freeze them for later use. "Salads" really means composed salads of various chopped, diced or sliced vegetables in a riot of colors and flavors, enhanced by a tasty but not overwhelming dressing. Unless your guests are seated at a table, lettuce salads are awkward and messy to eat. Thick sauces such as Roquefort, Thousand Island, and other dressings often hide the flavors instead of bringing out their best qualities.

Brunch is also the occasion to star a vegetable preparation like an asparagus or carrot pie. You can serve it with a few slices of broiled ham, a salad, and some fruit and the meal is complete. These dishes as part of other meals are overwhelming but fit into the brunch menu perfectly.

Pasta has become a brunch favorite, equalling, if not overtaking, quiche and crêpes. It can be as richly sauced with loads of cream and cheese or as sparse as a sauce of simple chopped tomato salad. Or it can be a combination of creamy sauce tossed with a grand assortment of fresh vegetables. Pasta serves as a side dish, salad, main course, or starter for the meal. Wherever you place it, it is going to be a favorite. Selecting a favorite pasta dish for a pasta lover is nearly impossible.

## ASPARAGUS PIE

| | |
|---|---|
| 2 cups heavy cream | 4 thin slices onion |
| 1 bay leaf | pinch of thyme |
| 4 sprigs parsley | pinch of marjoram |

6 whole peppercorns
3 tablespoons minced lean
    ham
1 tablespoon butter
1 9-inch pie shell, fully
    baked

1 pound asparagus,
    cooked
½ cup grated Gruyère
    cheese
¾ cup fresh bread crumbs
butter

Preheat the broiler.

In a 1½-quart saucepan, simmer the cream, bay leaf, parsley, onion, thyme, marjoram, and peppercorns for 15 minutes. Strain.

In a 1 quart saucepan, heat the ham in the 1 tablespoon of butter and add the cream. Reduce, over high heat, to 1 cup. Line the pie shell with the asparagus spears and pour on just enough of the sauce to cover the asparagus.

Stir the cheese into the remaining sauce and pour on top. Sprinkle with the bread crumbs and dot generously with the butter. Glaze under the broiler.

Yield: 6 servings

Assemble and glaze shortly before serving.

## VARIATION

Substitute fennel, spinach, broccoli, or snow peas for the asparagus.

## CARROT TART

2 pounds carrots, sliced
½ teaspoon sugar
½ teaspoon salt
⅓ cup butter

pepper to taste
¼ teaspoon lemon juice
1 9-inch pie shell, fully
    baked
3 scallions, minced

Preheat the oven to 350°F.

In a 2-quart saucepan, simmer the carrots in enough water to cover, with the sugar and salt, until the carrots absorb the water and are tender. Set aside 1½ cups carrots.

In a food processor, or food mill, purée the remaining carrots and beat in the butter, pepper, and lemon juice. Spread in the bottom of the pie. Arrange the reserved carrots in a decorative design on top and sprinkle with the scallions. Bake for about 20 minutes, or until hot.

Yield: 6 servings

The carrots and shell can be prepared the day before or frozen. Assemble shortly before serving.

## VARIATION

Substitute parsnips, turnips, or potatoes for the carrots.

---

# CAULIFLOWER PURÉE

This can be a fun presentation. Puréed cauliflower tastes remarkably like mashed potatoes. Serve the purée without saying anything and listen to people rave.

| | |
|---|---|
| 1 head cauliflower | 2 tablespoons butter |
| salt and pepper to taste | 2-4 tablespoons heavy |
| 1 clove garlic, peeled | cream |

In a saucepan, simmer the cauliflower, salt, pepper, and garlic in water to cover until tender. Drain and purée the cauliflower and garlic in a food processor until smooth. Add the butter and 2 tablespoons of cream. Process to combine. Return the purée to the saucepan and reheat, correcting the seasoning with salt and pepper and the consistency, if needed, with more cream.

Yield: 6 servings

Can be prepared ahead and reheated.

---

# TOURTEAUX (CORN CAKES GASCONY)

This Gascogne version of corn cakes is savory instead of sweet. If you want a sweet version, omit the salt and pepper and add sugar to taste.

| | |
|---|---|
| ¾ cup corn kernels | ¼ cup milk |
| 2 tablespoons butter | ¾ teaspoon salt |

¼ teaspoon pepper
pinch of grated nutmeg
1 egg

1 egg separated
1 cup flour
1 tablespoon butter

In a food processor, chop the corn. Add the milk, salt, pepper,
    nutmeg, egg, and egg yolk and process until combined. Turn
    into a bowl and let stand for 1 hour.
Beat the egg white until stiff and fold into the corn mixture. In a
    large skillet, heat the butter and cook like pancakes until
    browned on both sides. Drain on paper towels.

Yield: 6 servings

Can be prepared ahead and cooked just before serving.

NOTE:

If serving sweet cakes, accompany with maple syrup if desired.

---

# CORN AND TOMATO CASSEROLE

4 tablespoons butter
2 cups corn
5 tomatoes, peeled, seeded,
    and chopped
1 egg, lightly beaten

1 teaspoon light brown
    sugar
1½ teaspoons salt
black pepper
1 cup soft bread
    crumbs

Preheat the oven to 325°F.
Butter the bottom and sides of a 1½-quart baking dish with 1
    tablespoon of butter.
In a bowl, mix the corn, tomatoes, egg, sugar, salt, and a few
    grindings of pepper. Toss gently and turn into the buttered
    baking dish. Sprinkle with the crumbs and dot with the
    remaining butter. Bake for 1 hour or until crumbs are
    golden.

Yield: 6 servings

Can be prepared the day before and baked when needed.

## CHAMPIGNONS FARCIS PROVENÇALE (STUFFED MUSHROOMS)

Serve these as a side dish. As with most hot stuffed mushroom preparations, they are too messy for an hors d'oeuvre unless served with plates and forks.

1 pound large mushrooms
2 tablespoons olive oil
2 thin slices bread
2 tablespoons milk
2 tablespoons minced parsley

2 garlic cloves, minced
1 egg beaten
¼ cup minced ham
pepper to taste
1 tablespoons fresh bread crumbs

Preheat the oven to 350°F.

Remove mushroom stems and season the 12 largest caps with salt and 1 tablespoon of olive oil. Mince remaining mushrooms and stems.

Remove crusts from bread, soak in milk, and squeeze out the excess moisture.

In a skillet, in 1 tablespoon of oil, sauté the minced mushrooms until the liquid evaporates. Add the parsley, garlic, bread, egg, ham, salt, and pepper. Taste for seasoning.

Fill the caps and sprinkle with remaining bread crumbs and 1 tablespoon of olive oil. Place on a baking sheet and bake for 20 minutes then put under the broiler to brown.

Yield: 12 cups

Can be prepared for the final baking the day before.

## GRATIN OF WILD MUSHROOMS

3 tablespoons bread crumbs
2 tablespoons grated Parmesan
3 tablespoons grated Gruyère
1 tablespoon minced parsley
2 teaspoons minced basil

½ teaspoon minced thyme
2 tablespoons butter
2 tablespoons minced shallots
½ teaspoon minced garlic
½ pound mushrooms, quartered

½ pound assorted wild
   mushrooms, quartered
1½ tablespoons dry
   Madeira

2½ tablespoons medium
   dry sherry
¾ cup heavy cream
salt and pepper to taste

In a small bowl, mix the bread crumbs, grated Parmesan, Gruyère, parsley, basil, and thyme. Set aside.

In a skillet, heat the butter and sauté the shallots and garlic until soft, but not brown. Add the mushrooms and cook, stirring, until the liquid evaporates, and turn into a bowl. Add the Madeira, sherry, cream, salt, and pepper to the skillet and reduce to ½ cup.

Preheat the broiler, add the mushrooms to the sauce, and blend. Turn into a heat proof serving dish and sprinkle with the crumb mixture. Brown under the broiler and garnish with the parsley.

Yield: 4 servings

Can be prepared the day before for the final baking.

# GRATIN D'OIGNONS (ONION GRATIN)

4 pounds onions, minced
2 tablespoons butter
2 tablespoons oil
salt and pepper to taste

nutmeg to taste
3 tablespoons heavy cream
4 tablespoons grated
   Gruyère
1 tablespoon butter

Preheat the oven to 350°F.

Butter a 9 × 13-inch baking dish.

In a skillet, cook the onions slowly in butter and oil until soft, about 10 minutes, stirring as needed. Add the salt, pepper, nutmeg, and cream. Check the seasonings and pour the mixture into the prepared baking dish. Sprinkle with cheese, dot with butter, and bake for 30 minutes, or until golden.

Yield: 6 servings

Can be prepared for the final baking the day before.

# TIAN ROUGE (RED PEPPER AND TOMATO GRATIN)

For the best flavor, serve this dish at room temperature.

½ cup minced parsley
⅓ cup minced basil
1 tablespoon dried thyme
2–3 red peppers
2 tablespoons olive oil

6 tomatoes, thickly sliced
salt and pepper to taste
1 tablespoon capers
2 tablespoons fresh bread
   crumbs

Preheat the broiler.
Mix the parsley, basil, and thyme together. Brush the peppers with
   the oil and broil, turning often, until blistered all over. Place in
   a paper bag, seal and let stand for 15 minutes.
Lower the oven to 400°F.
Peel the peppers discarding the skin and cut into 1 inch strips.
Oil a gratin pan or baking dish and cover with a third of the tomato
   slices, sprinkle with ¼ of the herbs and cover with a layer of half
   the pepper strips. Repeat using the remaining ingredients.
Sprinkle the top with the capers and bread crumbs and drizzle with
   olive oil and bake for 20 minutes. Let cool to room temperature
   before serving.

Yield: 6 servings

Can be prepared the day before and allowed to come up to room
   temperature.

# LA RÂPÉE MORVANDELLE (GRATED POTATO AND CHEESE GRATIN)

This is a particularly rich version of potatoes au gratin.

3 tablespoons butter or walnut oil
2 pounds potatoes
4 ounces cream cheese
½ cup heavy cream

3 eggs
1½ cups grated Gruyère
1 tablespoon cognac
salt and pepper to taste

Preheat the oven to 400°F.
Spread the butter or walnut oil in a gratin and set aside.

In a bowl or processor mix the cheese, cream, eggs, Gruyère, and
    Cognac. Season with salt and pepper.
Grate the potatoes, drain squeezing gently, and pat dry. Immediately
    mix in the cheese and eggs. Spread the mixture in the gratin and
    bake for 45 minutes or until golden brown and crisp on the top.

Yield: 4 to 6 servings

Bake when assembled. This is best if served immediately and not
    reheated.

---

# PATATE AL FORNO (POTATOES WITH ROSEMARY AND GARLIC)

1¾ pounds new potatoes          5 tablespoons olive oil
salt and pepper to taste         2 sprigs rosemary
3-4 cloves garlic, crushed

Preheat the oven to 400°F.
Scrub and wash the potatoes well and boil in salted water until
    tender. Drain, and cut potatoes in half if large, and put into a
    baking dish with the garlic, olive oil, rosemary, salt, and pepper.
    Bake for 20 minutes or until golden.

Yield: 4 to 6 servings

Prepare just before serving.

## VARIATIONS

There are several variations of this theme. Omit the rosemary.
Peel the potatoes, cut into chunks, and boil for 10 minutes. Add
to a casserole with 3 whole unpeeled cloves of garlic for each
person. Bake in ½ cup butter until golden and crisp, about 1 hour.
Prepare as above and flavor butter with 1 tablespoon of curry.

---

# HASSELBACK POTATOES

6 baking potatoes                ½ cup heavy cream
¼ cup butter, melted             2 tablespoons shredded
                                     Gruyère

Preheat the oven to 325 °F.

Scrub the potatoes and place one at a time on a counter between two chopsticks, or pencils. With a sharp knife cut ⅛ inch slices, down to the chopsticks without cutting all the way through the potato.

Place in a bowl of cold water while cutting the remaining potatoes. Drain the potatoes and place in a shallow baking pan and press to open the slices slightly.

Brush with butter and bake until tender, basting occasionally with the cream and pan drippings, about 1½ hours. Press the potato apart gently before each basting.

Sprinkle with cheese and spoon over hot pan drippings and bake until the cheese melts.

Yield: 6 servings

Serve immediately.

---

# LATKES (POTATO PANCAKES)

There are many versions of potato pancakes. See the suggestions after the recipe.

| | |
|---|---|
| 2 large baking potatoes | 1 tablespoon matzo meal |
| 1 small onion, grated | 1 egg, lightly beaten |
| ½ teaspoon salt | 4 tablespoons vegetable oil |
| black pepper | 1 cup apple-sauce or sour cream, optional |

Set a sieve over a mixing bowl.

Grate the potatoes into a sieve and press out excess liquid. Discard the liquid and transfer the potatoes and onions to a large bowl. Season with salt and pepper, and stir in matzo meal and egg, and beat until well combined.

In a large skillet, heat the oil over high heat until hot. Spoon in potatoes in 2–2½-inch cakes and fry for about 2 minutes on each side, or until golden and crisp.

Transfer to a paper towel lined baking sheet If necessary keep warm in a 250 °F oven. Arrange pancakes on a platter and serve with apple sauce and or sour cream.

Yield: about 6 servings

Cannot be prepared ahead.

NOTE

Once grated, the potatoes will darken almost immediately. You must cook them immediately after grating and assembling.

Make a simpler pancake by adding an egg to the potato and seasoning with salt and pepper. For added zest add 1 tablespoon of grated ginger, or 2 tablespoons minced jalapeño pepper.

For a change, mix the potato with grated zucchini, carrot, or asparagus.

## TARTE AUX POMMES DE TERRES (POTATO PIE)

2½ pounds Idaho potatoes, peeled
5 garlic cloves, crushed
3 tablespoons butter
3 tablespoons olive oil

½ teaspoon salt
black pepper
1 tablespoons minced parsley

In a saucepan of boiling salted water, cook the potatoes and 2 garlic cloves until tender. Drain, and when cool slice into ¼ inch rounds. Preheat the oven to 450°F.

In a 9-inch skillet, melt the butter, add two more garlic cloves, and cook until golden, about 5 minutes. Discard the garlic.

In batches, add the potatoes to the skillet over moderately high heat until lightly browned. Season with salt and pepper.

Return all the slices to the skillet and press down firmly. Bake until potatoes are golden and crisp, 20 to 25 minutes.

Turn out onto a platter and sprinkle with parsley and remaining clove of crushed garlic minced together.

Yield: 6 servings

Can be prepared for final baking the day before.

## HASHED BROWN POTATOES

1 onion, chopped
6 tablespoons butter

3 cups cold, sliced boiled potatoes

salt and pepper to taste                    1 tablespoon minced parsley

In a 10-inch skillet, sauté the onions in the butter until soft, but
    not brown. Add the potatoes and cook, stirring occasionally
    until browned on the edges. Season with salt and pepper and
    serve sprinkled with minced parsley.

Yield: 6 servings

Can be prepared ahead and reheated.

## ROESTI (SWISS-STYLE POTATO PANCAKE)

2 pounds baking potatoes,                    8 tablespoons butter
    peeled                                   salt and pepper to taste

Just before cooking, grate the potatoes, rinse under cold running
    water, and drain. Press out the excess moisture.
In a 9-inch skillet, melt 4 tablespoons of butter and add the
    potatoes. Press the potatoes into a flat cake. Over medium heat,
    cook for about 15 minutes. Check to make sure the potatoes are
    not burning. Season the top with salt and pepper.
With a spatula, loosen the cake and slide it onto a dinner plate.
    Add the remaining butter to the pan and flip the potato cake
    into the pan. Season with salt and pepper and cook the second
    side until golden. Slide onto a serving platter and cut into
    wedges.

Yield: 6 servings

Cannot be made ahead.

## CANDIED SWEET POTATOES

This is usually served as a dinner vegetable, but if the main course
for brunch is a whole ham, this is a perfect accompaniment.

1 cup sugar                                  ½ teaspoon ground cinna-
¼ cup orange juice                              mon

½ teaspoon ground nutmeg
4 large sweet potatoes,
    peeled and cut in half
    lengthwise and then in ½
    inch thick lengths

1 lemon, thinly sliced
¼ pound butter

Preheat the oven to 350°F.

In a small bowl, mix the sugar, orange juice, cinnamon, and nutmeg.

Arrange the potatoes in layers in a baking dish, moistening each
    layer with the sugar mixture, lemon slices, and bits of butter.
    Pour any remaining orange juice mixture over the top. Bake
    uncovered for 1¼ hours, basting often.

Yield: 6 servings

Can be prepared for baking the night before.

# ÉPINARDS À LA MORNAY
# (SPINACH WITH CHEESE SAUCE)

3 pounds cleaned spinach,
    stripped of stems
salt and pepper to taste
butter

2 cups Mornay sauce
½ cup grated Gruyère
    cheese

Preheat the oven to 400°F.

Cook the spinach in the water remaining on its leaves for 5 minutes
    or until just wilted. Drain, run under cold water, and squeeze
    out the excess moisture. Chop and season with salt and pepper.

Rub a gratin with butter and place the spinach in a medium thick
    layer. Pour the sauce over the top and sprinkle with the grated
    cheese. Bake for 20 minutes or until bubbly and golden.

Yield: 6 servings

Can be prepared for baking the day before.

# MAPLE-GLAZED CARROTS, PARSNIPS
# AND TURNIPS

1 pound carrots, cut in ba-
    tons

1 pound parsnips, cut in
    batons

1 pound turnip (rutabaga)
    cut in batons
6 tablespoons butter
2 tablespoons lemon juice

2 tablespoons maple syrup
1¼ teaspoons salt
¼ teaspoon cinnamon
pepper

Bring a large pot of salted water to a boil, cook the carrots until
    tender, and remove with a slotted spoon. In the same pot, cook
    the parsnips until tender and remove with a slotted spoon. Cook
    the turnips until tender and drain.
In a bowl, mix the butter, lemon juice, maple syrup, salt, cinnamon,
    and pepper. Add the hot vegetables and toss gently.
Reheat in a microwave at high power for 2 minutes, or in a skillet
    stirring often until just heated.

Yield: 8 to 10 servings

Can be prepared ahead and reheated.

# FRICASSÉE DE JARDINIÈRE (SAUTÉ OF TOMATOES, RED PEPPERS AND ZUCCHINI)

⅓ cup butter
1 cup chopped onions
½ teaspoon minced
    garlic
3 tomatoes, peeled, seeded,
    and chopped
2 zucchini, ¾ inch cubes

2 red peppers, peeled and
    cut in julienne
salt and pepper to taste
cayenne pepper to taste
2 tablespoons minced
    parsley
1 teaspoon minced
    basil

In a skillet, heat 3 tablespoons butter and sauté the onion and garlic
    until soft, but not brown. Add the tomato, and zucchini and
    cook, covered 12 minutes, stirring occasionally. Raise heat and
    cook until moisture evaporates. Fold in pepper strips and season
    with salt, pepper, and cayenne. Remove from heat and swirl in
    the remaining butter and sprinkle with the fresh herbs.

Yield: 4 servings

Can be prepared ahead and reheated. Add the minced herbs just
    before serving.

# EGGPLANT, ZUCCHINI AND RED PEPPER SAUTÉ

3½ tablespoons olive oil
1 small eggplant, cut in batons
1 red pepper, cut in batons

1 zucchini, cut in batons
2 tablespoons minced basil
1 tablespoon butter
salt and pepper to taste

In a skillet, heat 1½ tablespoons olive oil and sauté the eggplant until lightly browned and soft. Remove and set aside. Add another tablespoon of oil and sauté the red pepper for about 1 minute. Add remaining oil and the zucchini and sauté another minute. Return the eggplant to the pan with the parsley and butter and stir to mix. Season with salt and pepper. Cook until the vegetables are tender, but still crisp.

Yield: 4 servings

Can be prepared ahead and reheated, if undercooked.


# TORTINO TRICOLORE (THREE COLORED GRATIN)

As with so many other fine Italian dishes, this carries the colors of the Italian flag.

2 pounds zucchini, thinly sliced
1½ tablespoons butter
1 tablespoon olive oil
½ pound mozzarella, thinly sliced
2 ounces sliced Parmesan cheese

¾ pound tomatoes, peeled and thinly sliced
oregano to taste
salt and pepper to taste
3 tablespoons grated bread crumbs
2 ounces grated Parmesan cheese

Preheat the oven to 375°F.
In a large skillet, sauté the zucchini in 1 tablespoon of butter and olive oil for 15 minutes.
Butter a gratin dish and put half the zucchini in the bottom, cover with half the mozzarella and Parmesan slices. Layer the toma-

toes on top, season with salt, pepper, and oregano. Cover with
the remaining mozzarella, Parmesan, and zucchini slices.
In a bowl, mix the grated bread crumbs and Parmesan. Sprinkle
on top and dot with remaining ½ tablespoon butter. Bake about
20 minutes.

Yield: 6 servings

Can be prepared the day before and reheated.

## RICE FRITTERS

| | |
|---|---|
| 4 eggs | 4 teaspoons sugar |
| 6 tablespoons heavy cream | pinch of salt |
| 2 cups cooked rice | 1 cup bread crumbs |
| 2 tablespoons butter | oil for deep frying |

In a 1-quart saucepan, beat 3 eggs until frothy and add 4 tablespoons of cream and the rice. Cook over low heat, stirring until
thickened. Stir in the butter, sugar, and salt. Cool.
In a small bowl, mix the remaining eggs and cream and place the
bread crumbs in another bowl.
Form the cooled rice into small balls or flat cakes. Dip into the egg
and roll in the bread crumbs. Set aside on a rack.
Heat the oil to 375°F.
Fry the fritters until golden. Drain on paper toweling and serve
with honey, maple syrup, or jam.

Yield: 6 servings

Can be prepared for frying the night before.

## SFORMATO DI TAGLIATELLE E PROSCIUTTO (NOODLE AND PROSCIUTTO MOLD)

This is one the finest pasta dishes. Simple and elegant. It takes little
effort to assemble and yet looks and tastes extraordinary.

| | |
|---|---|
| 6 tablespoons butter | ½ cup tiny peas, parboiled |
| 8 slices prosciutto | 8 ounces Tagliatelle |
| ½ cup mushrooms, sliced | pasta |

salt to taste                          ½ cup grated Parmesan
                                          cheese

Preheat the oven to 350°F.

Butter a 7-inch soufflé dish with 1 tablespoon of butter. Line the mold, placing the narrower ends of the prosciutto in the center of the mold, and letting the wider ends overlap the edges. Set aside.

Melt 2 tablespoons of the butter in a skillet and cook the mushrooms and peas, covered, over high heat for 3 minutes. Set aside.

Cook the noodles in boiling salted water until just barely done. Drain. Immediately toss with 3 tablespoons butter, Parmesan, peas, and mushrooms and mix gently.

Pour into the prosciutto-lined mold and fold the ends over the filling. Place in the oven for 5 to 6 minutes to heat. Invert the mold onto a platter and let stand for 2 minutes to let it settle. Remove the mold and serve.

Yield: 6 servings

For the best flavor and texture, prepare shortly before serving.

NOTE

Buy or make the thinnest noodles for the best results.

# PENNE WITH GORGONZOLA AND TOMATO

3 tablespoons olive oil
1 onion, chopped
4 garlic cloves, chopped
14½ ounce can plum tomatoes, drained and chopped

½ cup chopped basil
½ cup butter
6 ounces Gorgonzola cheese
1 pound penne
1 cup grated Romano or Parmesan cheese

In a skillet, heat the oil and add the onion and garlic and sauté until soft, but not brown. Stir in the tomatoes and basil and cook until thickened, about 20 minutes.

In a small bowl, beat the butter and gorgonzola together with a spoon.

Cook pasta until tender and drain.

Whisk Gorgonzola into tomato sauce and stir into the pasta. Season with salt and pepper. Pass with grated cheese.

Yield: 6 servings

Both the tomato sauce and the Gorgonzola butter can be prepared the day before.

## VARIATION

Instead of Gorgonzola butter, make a sage butter mashing 1 tablespoon minced sage into the butter.

---

# RIGATONI WITH HOT ITALIAN SAUSAGE AND MUSHROOMS

1 ounce dried porcini mushrooms soaked in 1 cup
  hot water
1 tablespoon butter
1 onion, chopped
1¼ pounds hot Italian sausages, casings removed
1 pound mushrooms,
  sliced
½ teaspoon dried rosemary

½ cup white wine
1 bay leaf
1 cup beef stock
1 cup cream
1 pound rigatoni or
  penne
1½ cups grated Parmesan
salt and pepper
minced parsley

Drain the porcini, reserving the liquid. Chop the porcini, discarding any heavy stems. Set aside.

In a skillet, melt the butter and cook the onion until softened. Add the sausage and increase heat to high. Cook until no longer pink, breaking up the pieces. Add the sliced mushrooms and rosemary and cook, stirring until mushrooms begin to soften. Add the porcini, wine, and bay leaf, and cook until most of the liquid evaporates.

Add the stock and porcini liquid. Simmer until sauce is syrupy, stirring occasionally. Add cream and cook until slightly thickened. Cook pasta in boiling salted water until just tender. Drain and add to the sauce with 1½ cups grated Parmesan. Stir to mix and correct the seasoning with salt and pepper and serve with additional cheese.

Yield: 6 to 8 servings

The sauce can be prepared ahead and reheated.

# FETTUCCINE CON PROSCIUTTO DI PARMA E PANNA (FETTUCCINE WITH PROSCIUTTO AND CREAM)

1¾ cups heavy cream
¼ pound prosciutto, cut
    into thin strips
1½ cups grated Parmesan
    cheese

2 egg yolks
pepper
1 pound fresh pasta

In a large bowl, place the cream, ham, half the Parmesan, and the egg yolks and stir to blend. Place the bowl over a pan of boiling water and heat. Cook the fettuccine in boiling salted water until al dente. Drain and add to the sauce, toss well and serve with remaining cheese.

Yield: 4 to 6 servings

Cannot be prepared ahead.

# NOODLES AND TOMATOES AU GRATIN

4 tablespoons butter
½ cup chopped onions
2 cups drained canned to-
    matoes, chopped
salt and pepper to taste

1 tablespoon minced basil
½ cup cream
¾ cup green noodles
¼ cup grated Parmesan
    cheese

Preheat the broiler.
Butter a 6 cup baking dish.
Heat 2 tablespoons butter in a saucepan and cook the onions until wilted. Add the tomatoes, salt, pepper, and basil and cook, stirring 5 minutes. Add the cream and cook 2 minutes.
Cook the noodles in boiling salted water until tender. Drain and return to the kettle. Add remaining 2 tablespoons butter and stir to coat. Add tomato sauce, stir again and pour into the prepared baking dish and sprinkle with cheese. Brown under the broiler.

Yield: 6 servings

Can be prepared the day before. To reheat, bake at 350°F until bubbling hot and browned. Put under the broiler, if necessary.

## GNOCCHI ALLA ROMANO (SEMOLINA GNOCCHI BAKED WITH BUTTER AND CHEESE)

3 cups milk
1½ teaspoons salt
pinch of nutmeg
pepper to taste

¾ cup semolina flour
2 eggs
1 cup grated Parmesan
    cheese
4 tablespoons melted butter

Butter a baking sheet and set aside.

In a heavy 2- to 3-quart saucepan bring the milk, salt, nutmeg, and pepper to a boil. Gradually add the semolina so the mixture does not stop boiling, stirring constantly.

Cook stirring until the mixture is thick enough to support a spoon, about 10 minutes. Remove from the heat and beat in the eggs. Beat in ¾ cup of the cheese and mix well.

Spread the mixture about a half inch thick, on the baking sheet, and chill until firm.

Preheat the oven to 400°F.

Butter a shallow ovenproof serving dish.

With a round 1½ inch cookie cutter, cut circles of the mixture and place in the serving dish overlapping the circles slightly. Sprinkle with the remaining melted butter and cheese. Bake for 15 minutes until crisp and golden.

Yield: 6 servings

Can be prepared for the final baking the day before.

## LA PASTA DI CASAMICCIOLA ("DONKEY HOUSE" PASTA)

This is from Ischia, the island up the coast from Capri off the Italian mainland. There are no measurements, so you can prepare to your taste. Some people prefer more or less lemon juice, others add a pinch of garlic. This is never served with cheese.

Tomatoes, peeled, seeded,
    and chopped
olive oil

fresh basil
lemon juice

| salt and pepper to taste | 1 pound pasta cooked al dente |

In a bowl, mix the tomatoes, olive oil, basil, lemon juice, salt, pepper. Let macerate for 10 minutes to two hours.

Add the pasta. Correct seasoning with basil, lemon juice, salt, and pepper.

Yield: 4 to 6 Servings

NOTE

Think of the tomato mixture as a tomato salad and add an equal weight of pasta. I like to chill the tomato mixture and pour it over hot pasta so there is a hot/cool sensation with the first mouthful.

I suggest that you use small pasta such as shells instead of spaghetti or other long pasta shape since the sauce slides off long pastas.

Add other ingredients at will such as red or green peppers, diced mozzarella, diced salami or shreds of prosciutto, or hot pepper, if you prefer.

CHAPTER

*11*

*Fruits*

*D*essert is not part of breakfast and is not necessarily part of brunch. For those who want something sweet, fruit can provide the answer. You can serve fruit as a first course or just let guests eat it whenever they choose. A grapefruit, or melon half, or a bowl of berries accompanied with cream and sugar is often sufficient. There are also wonderful fruit compotes, macedoines, and other fruit preparations. Years ago, and in some homes still, pie appears at the table. New Englanders prefer apple or blueberry, but in other farming areas they prefer cherry or peach.

You can prepare many of these ahead, but fresh fruits, served simply often taste best served immediately. Strawberries, once hulled, start to look limp within a few hours and should be served shortly after preparing. Other sliced fruits, like peaches and banana turn brown quickly once exposed to air, while melon slices soon look tired if left uncovered unless mixed with other fruits or in a syrup.

Sugar syrup added to fruits often draws out the juices and "cooks" them, so time the maceration period accordingly. For crisp vibrant fruits, serve quickly, for more tender syrup-coddled flavors, let macerate up to 24 hours before serving.

The recipes are flexible. Macedoines and compotes may have a list of specific fruits, but you can substitute according to availability. Remember that similar fruits, apples, and pears can easily substitute one for another as can most berries. Use your imagination.

For the diehard sweet eater, you may want to make a simple sugar cookie, plain sponge cake dusted with confectioners' sugar, or a delicate butter cake. Recipes for those are in *The Book of Great Desserts*.

---

## MACERATED FRUITS

⅔ cup dry vermouth or orange juice
5 tablespoons sugar
½ teaspoon cinnamon

1 large pineapple cut into chunks
4 navel oranges, peeled and sectioned
2 pears, diced

In a bowl, mix the vermouth, sugar, and cinnamon and let stand for 1 hour, stirring occasionally. Strain, discarding any undissolved sugar. Prepare the fruits and place in a bowl. Pour the liquid over the fruits and macerate for at least 1 hour.

Yield: 6 servings

Can be prepared the night before.

## FRUITS RAFRAICHIS AU LIQUEURS (FRESH FRUITS WITH LIQUEURS)

Buy imported kirsch for the best flavor and greatest economy. A small amount will go a long way.

½ cup sugar
1 cup water
2 teaspoons lemon juice
pinch of salt
2 apricots, peeled and quartered

½ cup pineapple chunks
½ cup pitted cherries
½ cup strawberries, hulled
2 nectarines, peeled, and quartered
2 to 3 tablespoons kirsch, Cointreau or Framboise

In a small saucepan, simmer the sugar, water, lemon juice, and salt for 5 minutes. Cool. Place the fruits in a bowl and pour the syrup over just before serving. Sprinkle with the liqueur of choice and mix gently.

Yield: 6 servings

You can prepare the fruits the night before. Keep covered with plastic wrap.

## MACEDOINE DE FRUITS (FRESH FRUIT CUP)

1 small pineapple, diced
½ pound fresh peaches, peeled and diced
1 pint strawberries, halved

Sugar, if desired
1 teaspoon minced ginger
1 teaspoon minced lemon rind
¼ cup port

In a bowl, mix the fruits, add sugar if desired, and stir in the ginger, lemon rind, and port. Let macerate for at least 1 hour.

Yield: 6 servings

Can be prepared the night before.

---

## COMPOTE DE FRUITS (HOT FRUIT COMPOTE)

This old fashioned dessert always brings raves. Warm fruit on a cold winter's day served with a dollop of cream makes the world a lot nicer.

2 cups sugar
5 cups water
½ cup dried apricots
12 cup pitted prunes
½ cup dried figs

½ cup dried peaches
½ cup dried pears
1 teaspoon vanilla
½ cup slivered almonds, toasted

In a 3-quart saucepan, simmer the sugar and water for 4 minutes. Add the apricots, prunes, figs, peaches, and pears. Simmer until tender, about 20 minutes. Stir in the vanilla and almonds. Serve warm, preferably, or cold with a pitcher of heavy cream.

Yield: 6 to 8 servings

Can be prepared several days before.

NOTE

You can use any dried fruits, and some people like to add a thin slice or two of lemon for tartness.

---

## PASTEL DE MANZANA (APPLE MINT CRISP)

1 tablespoon butter
1 cup sugar
1 cup flour
½ teaspoon baking powder
1 egg

1 tablespoon dried mint leaves
1 tablespoon cinnamon
4 tart apples, peeled, cored, and sliced
1 cup heavy cream, whipped

Preheat the oven to 350°F.
Butter an 8-inch square baking dish and set aside.

In a bowl, mix the sugar, flour, and baking powder. Make a well in the
center and add the egg. Cut the ingredients together with a knife,
pastry blender, or your fingertips until it resembles coarse meal.
In another bowl, mix the mint and cinnamon. Add the apples and
toss until evenly coated.
Place apples in the baking dish and sprinkle the flour mixture over
the top. Bake for 45 minutes or until the topping is crusty. Let
cool to room temperature and serve with whipped cream.

Yield: 6 servings

Can be prepared the day before.

## LA FLAMUSSE AUX POMMES
## (BAKED APPLE PUDDING)

Another version of this dessert is to dip slices of apple in a crêpe
batter and spread them on buttered cabbage leaves and bake. The
leaves impart an extraordinary flavor.

2 tablespoons butter
8 large apples peeled and
  cut into thick slices
4 eggs

1 tablespoon flour
2 cups milk
3 tablespoons sugar
2 tablespoons dark rum

Preheat the oven to 350°F.
In a skillet, heat the butter and sauté the apple slices until tender.
In a bowl, beat the eggs, and beat in the flour, milk, sugar, and rum
until blended. Fold in the apple slices. Pour into a buttered
gratin and bake for 30 to 45 minutes. Serve warm.

Yield: 6 servings

NOTE

Best if prepared and served immediately.

## NERUPPU VAZHAI (BANANAS WITH
## COCONUT AND CARDAMON)

6 bananas, peeled
¼ cup orange juice

½ cup firmly packed brown
  sugar

1 cup grated coconut
½ cup silvered, blanched al-
    monds

1 teaspoon ground carda-
    mom
¼ cup melted butter

Preheat the oven to 400°F.
Butter a baking dish and arrange the bananas in one layer. Pour
    on the orange juice, sprinkle with the sugar, coconut, almonds,
    cardamom, and butter. Bake for 25 minutes or until the bananas
    are tender. Serve warm.

Yield: 6 servings

Can be prepared several hours ahead and reheated.

## BLUEBERRY CRUMBLE

1 quart blueberries
2 teaspoons lemon juice
⅓ cup sugar
⅓ cup dark brown sugar

4 tablespoons butter, cut up
½ cup flour
1¼ cups quick cooking oats

Preheat the oven to 350°F.
Butter an 8-inch baking dish.
Place berries in the dish and sprinkle with lemon juice and sugar.
    In a bowl, mix the brown sugar, flour, and oats, with your finger-
    tips and work in the butter until the mixture resembles crumbs.
    Sprinkle evenly over the blueberries. Bake for 40 minutes or
    until the topping is golden and the blueberries bubble around
    the edges. Serve with yogurt, sour cream, or heavy cream.

Yield: 6 servings

Can be prepared for baking the day before.

## LEMON CURD WITH BERRIES

1⅓ cups sugar
14 tablespoons butter
⅔ lemon juice

4 eggs
4 egg yolks

| 1 tablespoon grated lemon rind | 4 cups raspberries, black- berries, or other berries |

In a saucepan, stir the sugar, butter, lemon juice, eggs, egg yolks, and lemon rind over low heat until thick enough to coat the back of a spoon. Cool to room temperature. Fill parfait glasses with alternating layers of berries and lemon curd.

Yield: 6 servings

Can be prepared 2 weeks ahead and refrigerated.

NOTE

Serve with any berries of your choice.

## MELON WITH ORANGE AND RUM

| 1 large ripe cantaloupe | ½ cup orange juice |
| ¼ cup honey | 3 tablespoons rum |

Cut the melon in half and remove the seeds. Cut each half into 4 wedges. Remove skin from flesh and cut flesh into bite sized pieces, or prepare melon balls.
In a bowl, mix the honey, orange juice, and rum. Fold in the melon cubes and keep covered until ready to serve.

Yield: 4 to 6 servings

Can be prepared several hours ahead.

## SPICY ORANGES WITH CINNAMON AND CLOVES

| 12 amaretti cookies | ½ teaspoon ground cloves |
| 6 large oranges | ¼ cup sugar |
| ¼ teaspoon cinnamon | ½ cup orange liqueur |

Crush the cookies. Peel the oranges and slice thinly, reserving the juice. Put oranges in a serving bowl and toss with cinnamon, cloves, and sugar. Chill at least 1 hour.

Sprinkle with amaretti crumbs, reserved orange juice, and liqueur.

Yield: 6 servings

Can be prepared the day before.

## ARANCI CARAMELATI (CARAMELIZED ORANGES)

6 navel oranges
1½ cups sugar

3 tablespoons cognac
½ cup diced candied fruit, optional

With a zester remove the zest from two oranges. Blanch the strips in boiling water for 5 minutes. Drain, refresh under cold water, and drain again. Peel the oranges, removing any white pith. Set aside.

In a saucepan, simmer 1 cup water and ½ cup sugar for 10 minutes. Add the orange strips and cook 10 minutes longer. Transfer the zest to a plate and set aside. Reserve the syrup.

In another saucepan, cook the remaining 1 cup of sugar and 5 tablespoons water until a deep golden caramel. Stir in ½ cup of reserved syrup and simmer 3 minutes. Remove from the heat and add the cognac. (Be careful of splattering.)

Arrange the oranges, whole or sliced, in a shallow dish and pour the caramel mixture over the top. Sprinkle with the reserved zest and candied peel and spoon the syrup over often. Chill.

Yield: 6 servings

## PERE AI MIRTILLI (STEWED PEARS WITH BLUEBERRIES)

6 pears, peeled, stems intact
2¼ cups red wine
⅔ cup sugar

grated peel of ½ lemon
2 cups blueberries

Peel the pears, leaving on the stems. Place in a saucepan or casserole with the wine, sugar, and lemon peel, cover and simmer 10 minutes, or until pears are just tender. Remove pears to a serving dish.

Purée the berries in a processor. Reduce the cooking liquid by ¾ and stir in the berries. Pour over the pears and cool.

Yield: 6 servings

Can be prepared the day before.

## GOURMANDISE DOMFRONTAISE (FRESH PEARS BAKED WITH PEAR BRANDY AND CREAM)

4 Anjou pears, peeled, halved, and cored
1 tablespoon Poire William (pear eau de vie)
¼ cup plus 1 tablespoon sugar

3 eggs
pinch of salt
pinch of cinnamon
½ cup heavy cream
1 tablespoon flour

Preheat the oven to 350°F.

Cut each pear into 8 sections. Arrange in the bottom of a large casserole. Sprinkle with Poire William and 1 tablespoon sugar. Bake for 15 minutes.

Meanwhile mix the ¼ cup sugar and the eggs until lemon colored. Stir in the cinnamon, heavy cream, and flour. Pour over the pears and bake 35 to 40 minutes or until lightly browned.

Yield: 6 servings

Can be prepared ahead and reheated.

## PLUM HAZELNUT CRISP

3 pounds red plums, pitted and thickly sliced
9 tablespoons sugar
1½ tablespoons flour
¾ teaspoon vanilla

⅛ to ¼ teaspoon cinnamon
¾ cup rolled oats
⅔ cup light brown sugar
½ cup flour
¼ teaspoon cinnamon

pinch of salt                     ½ cup toasted hazelnuts
½ cup butter, diced

Preheat the oven to 375°F.
Butter one 2- to 2½-quart baking dish with 3-inch sides.
In a bowl, mix the plums, sugar, flour, vanilla, and cinnamon. Let macerate for 30 minutes, stirring occasionally.
In a food processor, mix the oats, light brown sugar, flour, cinnamon, and salt and process with a couple of turns. Add the butter with on/off turns until the mixture resembles coarse meal. Add the hazelnuts and chop coarsely.
Stir the plum mixture and turn into the dish. Sprinkle with topping and bake for 45 minutes or until brown and bubbly. Serve with heavy or whipped cream, or ice cream.

Yield: 6 servings

Can be prepared ahead and reheated.

---

## CROÛTES AUX PRUNES (FRESH PLUM TOASTS)

This is a simple but delicious dessert made from a few simple ingredients. Serve with heavy or whipped cream if desired.

6 to 12 slices bread,            12 tablespoons butter
   ½-inch thick                 6 tablespoons brown
12 to 18 plums, stoned          sugar

Preheat the oven to 350°F.
Butter the bread slices well on both sides. Place in a baking dish and arrange 5 to 6 plum halves on each slice, cut side up. Dot with remaining butter and sprinkle with sugar. Press the plum halves onto the bread slices.
Cover with foil and bake for 30 minutes, or until the bread is crispy and the plums have a syrupy coating. If necessary, remove the foil and bake another 10 minutes.

Yield: 6 servings

Can be prepared for baking the night before.

NOTE

Substitute pears, peaches or apricots.

# RHUBARB FOOL

"Fool" comes from the French verb *fouler*, to crush.

| | |
|---|---|
| 1 pound rhubarb, trimmed and cut in half inch pieces | 1 cup heavy cream |
| ½ cup sugar | 2 tablespoons confectioners' sugar |
| grated rind of 1 lemon | |

Put the rhubarb into a heavy saucepan with the sugar, lemon rind, and ½ tablespoon of cold water. Cover and simmer for 15 minutes or until the rhubarb is tender and will form a purée when whisked. Stir the rhubarb to break it up and taste for sugar. Chill.

Beat the cream with the confectioners' sugar to form soft peaks. Fold in the puréed rhubarb, taking care to leave large streaks for a marbled effect. Transfer to 4 chilled cups or glasses and chill until ready to serve.

Yield: 6 servings

Can be prepared the day before.

# STRAWBERRY RHUBARB COBBLER

| | |
|---|---|
| 1 cup flour | 3 cups strawberries, cut up |
| ¼ teaspoon baking powder | 3 tablespoons quick-cooking tapioca |
| ½ teaspoon baking soda | |
| 4 tablespoons butter | 1 tablespoon butter |
| 2 tablespoons sugar | 3 tablespoons sugar |
| ⅓ cup buttermilk | grated rind of 1 orange |
| 3 cups sliced rhubarb | sugar |

Preheat the oven to 425°F.
Butter a 2-quart baking dish.
Sift the flour, baking powder, and soda into a bowl. Cut in the

butter until the mixture resembles coarse crumbs. Add the sugar and stir in the buttermilk to form a dough. Knead just to gather together.

In a bowl, mix the rhubarb, strawberries, tapioca, sugar, and orange rind and turn into the prepared dish.

On a lightly floured board, pat and press the dough until it is as large as the dish. Lay the dough on top of the filling and press directly onto the fruit, pressing the edges against the sides of the dishes. Sprinkle with the sugar. Cut slits in the top of the dough and place on a baking sheet with sides.

Bake 40 minutes, Cover loosely with foil if the top gets too dark. Serve warm.

Yield: 6 servings

Can be prepared ahead and reheated.

## FRAISES MARINÉES AUX CALVADOS (STRAWBERRIES MARINATED IN CALVADOS)

4 cups small strawberries
2 tablespoons calvados
¼ cup sugar

1 cup heavy cream
cinnamon

In a bowl, toss the strawberries with the calvados and let macerate for 1 hour. Add the sugar and mix gently and set aside. Whip the cream to stiff peaks and place a bed on each plate. Sprinkle the edges of the cream with cinnamon and put the strawberries in the center.

Yield: 6 to 8 servings

## MANSIKKALUMI (FINNISH STRAWBERRY SNOW)

2 cups strawberries, hulled
½ cup sugar
4 egg whites

pinch of salt
¾ cup heavy cream, whipped
12–16 strawberries

In a food processor, purée the berries and stir in the sugar. In a mixing bowl, beat the egg whites and salt until they hold stiff peaks. Fold in the strawberry purée and whipped cream. Turn into serving glasses and garnish with a strawberry.

Yield: 6 servings

Serve within 4 hours.

CHAPTER

*12*

*Basic Sauces and Preparations*

*E*very cookbook uses sauces for more than one recipe. They also may provide for a particular dish to use as the base for several different recipes. For instance, you can use eggplant provencale as the base for several egg dishes, a filling for crêpes, an omelet filling, or as a vegetable. Rather than leave it in the vegetable chapter where it might get lost, I chose to put it here were it may jog your thoughts to use it in other ways.

The basic sauces listed here provide a ready reference for recipes that you might well use often, but need a memory jog to get to the specifics. You probably make béchamel sauce often, but do not always remember the specific measurements, so here they are. Some of these sauces such as Lime Hollandaise, may not be part of your repertoire, until after you have read it here.

In many books, we use the section on composed butters only when directed by another recipe. In this book, since many of these are suitable as a spread for muffins, breads, pancakes, and waffles, you may find this section worth reading in its own right.

## COMPOSED BUTTERS

For a composed butter, mix butter with other ingredients. This is a simple idea, but one worth noting. Waffles with strawberry butter, cranberry muffins with cranberry butter, pancakes with raspberry butter all sound delicious and they are, but we tend to think of butter as butter first, and we need some help to remember to make flavored butters. Fruit based butters are not the only type possible. There are many savory butters. In this book one recipe calls for lobster butter. You could omit it, but intense lobster flavor would be missing from the recipe. Shellfish butters seem daunting at first, but once you make one, you will realize how easy they are to prepare.

## BASIC FRUIT-FLAVORED BUTTER

6 tablespoons butter
⅓ cup fruit purée

¼ cup confectioners' sugar

In a food processor, electric mixer or by hand, cream the butter and work in the fruit purée and the sugar. Chill until semi-firm.

Yield: ½ cup

Can be prepared ahead and frozen.

NOTE:

Use blueberry, cherry, cranberry, raspberry, or strawberry purées.

## VARIATIONS

Instead of, or in addition to, the fruit purées, add 2 tablespoons minced ginger to the butter.

Instead of the fruit purées, add 2 tablespoons grated orange rind, or 1 tablespoon grated lemon rind and 1 teaspoon lemon juice.

Use the same quantity of honey instead of the sugar.

Add 1 tablespoon minced mint to honey butter.

Add ¼ teaspoon ground cinnamon to the butter.

Add ¼ teaspoon ground cinnamon, ⅛ teaspoon ground nutmeg, and a pinch of ground cloves to the butter.

# FRUIT TOPPINGS

Maple syrup, honey, and molasses are the traditional toppings for pancakes and waffles. Fruit toppings are not only a delicious addition to this grouping, they may be more appealing to the health-conscious.

Many fruit macedoines and cups in this chapter make delightful toppings.

# APPLE TOPPING

2 pounds apples, peeled and cored
2 tablespoons butter
¼ cup sugar

½ teaspoon ground cinnamon
¼ teaspoon ground nutmeg

In a large skillet, sauté the apples in the butter until soft, but still hold their shape. Sprinkle with the sugar, cinnamon, and nutmeg and mix gently. Serve warm or at room temperature.

Yield: 3 cups

Can be prepared ahead and reheated.

## BLUEBERRY TOPPING

1 pint blueberries           grated rind of 1 lemon
½ cup sugar

In a saucepan, mix the blueberries, sugar, and lemon rind. Simmer
for 5 minutes. Serve hot or at room temperature.

Yield: 2 cups

Can be prepared ahead and refrigerated for several days.


## CHERRY TOPPING

2 cups pitted cherries       ½ teaspoon ground cinna-
½ cup brown sugar          mon

In a saucepan, simmer the cherries, ½ cup water, and the sugar until
the cherries are soft. Stir in the cinnamon. Serve hot or cold.

Yield: 2 cups

Can be prepared several days ahead.


## PEACH TOPPING

2 pounds peaches, peeled     ½ cup maple syrup
    and chopped               pinch of ground cloves

In a saucepan, simmer the peaches in the syrup with the cloves
until very tender. With a wire whisk, beat the peaches into a
lumpy sauce. Serve hot or at room temperature.

Yield: 3 cups

Can be prepared ahead and reheated.


## APRICOT ORANGE TOPPING

2 pounds apricots, peeled     ½ cup orange marmalade
½ cup water                  1 teaspoon lemon juice

In a saucepan, simmer the apricots in the water until very tender. Stir in the marmalade and simmer 5 minutes. Let cool.

In a food processor, purée the apricot mixture. Taste and add sugar and lemon juice to taste. Serve hot or at room temperature.

Yield: 3 cups

Can be prepared ahead and reheated.

# PEAR CARAMEL TOPPING

1 cup water
½ cup sugar
1 stick cinnamon

2 pounds pears, peeled, cored and sliced
1 cup heavy cream

In a saucepan, bring the water, sugar, and cinnamon stick to a boil. Add the pears and simmer until tender. With a slotted spoon remove the pears and reserve.

Cook the liquid until it begins to caramelize, about 5 minutes, and turns a medium golden brown. Remove from the heat and stir in the cream. Return the pears to the sauce and reheat gently. Serve hot.

Yield: 3 cups

Can be prepared ahead and reheated.

# PINEAPPLE YOGURT GINGER SAUCE

This is a cold sauce that is also low in calories.

1 pineapple, peeled, cored, and chopped
2 cups yogurt

1 tablespoon sugar, or to taste
1 teaspoon minced ginger, or to taste

In a bowl, mix the pineapple, yogurt, sugar, and ginger. Let macerate for at least 3 hours in the refrigerator. Serve cold.

Yield: 4 cups

Can be prepared 2 days ahead.

## PLUM TOPPING

2 pounds plums, pitted
½ cup brown sugar, firmly
  packed

1 tablespoon grated orange
  rind
pinch of cinnamon

In a saucepan, simmer the plums, sugar, orange rind, and cinnamon until the plums are very soft. Serve hot or at room temperature.

Yield: 3 cups

Can be prepared ahead and reheated.


## RASPBERRY TOPPING

2 cups raspberries
¼ cup honey

1 tablespoon lemon juice

In a saucepan, simmer the raspberries, honey, and lemon juice for 2 minutes. Serve hot or at room temperature.

Yield: 2 cups

Can be prepared ahead and reheated.


## STRAWBERRY TOPPING

1 pint strawberries, hulled
  and sliced
2 tablespoons butter

¼ cup sugar
½ cup heavy cream

In a skillet, sauté the strawberries in the butter until they begin to exude their juices. Add the sugar and cook, stirring gently, until the sugar dissolves. Add the cream and bring to a boil. Serve hot.

Yield: 2½ cups

Can be prepared ahead and reheated.

# BÉCHAMEL SAUCE

The major differences between béchamel sauce and standard cream sauce are: you cook béchamel much longer to remove any floury taste, and you strain it through a fine sieve to make it smooth.

| | |
|---|---|
| 2 tablespoons butter | ¼ teaspoon salt |
| 1 tablespoon onion, minced | 3 peppercorns |
| 4 tablespoons flour | sprig of parsley |
| 3 cups milk, scalded | pinch of grated nutmeg |

In a saucepan, melt the butter and sweat the onion until soft, but not brown. Add the flour and cook the roux, slowly, stirring constantly until it just starts to turn golden.

Add the milk stirring vigorously with a wire whisk until thickened and smooth.

Add the salt, peppercorns, parsley, and nutmeg and simmer over low heat, stirring often for about 30 minutes, or until reduced to ⅔ of the original quantity. Strain.

Yield: 2 cups

Can be prepared ahead and frozen.

# SAUCE CRÈME (CREAM SAUCE)

This is the French cream sauce which is a child of béchamel, not the standard cream sauce.

| | |
|---|---|
| 2 cups béchamel | salt to taste |
| ½ cup heavy cream | lemon juice to taste |

Reduce 2 cups béchamel sauce to 1½ cups and add the heavy cream. Correct the seasoning with the salt. For a more piquant sauce, and especially when using with fish, add a few drops of lemon juice.

Yield: 2 cups

Can be prepared ahead and frozen.

## SAUCE AURORE (AURORA SAUCE)

¼ cup tomato purée                    2 cups hot cream sauce

In a saucepan, mix the tomato purée and cream sauce and heat until hot.

Yield: 2¼ cups

Can be prepared ahead and frozen.


## SAUCE MORNAY (CHEESE SAUCE)

Note that this famous French sauce is a child of béchamel and uses Gruyère or Parmesan instead of cheddar cheese.

3 egg yolks                    2 tablespoons butter
½ cup heavy cream              2 tablespoons grated
2 cups hot béchamel              Gruyère

In a small bowl, mix the egg yolks and cream. In a small saucepan heat the béchamel. Cook, stirring constantly, until the sauce just reaches the boiling point. Stir in the cheese and swirl in the butter just before using. Heat only enough to melt the cheese without boiling.

Yield: 2½ cups

Can be prepared ahead and frozen. Reheat gently.


## VELOUTÉ SAUCE

This is the "other" cream sauce in fine French cooking. The principal difference is that you use stock instead of milk.

2 tablespoons butter            salt to taste
4 tablespoons flour             sprig of parsley
3 cups boiling stock            ½ cup mushroom peelings
3 white peppercorns               and stems

In a saucepan, melt the butter, add the flour, and cook the resulting roux over medium heat, stirring constantly with a wire whisk until it just starts to turn golden.

Gradually add the stock, stirring vigorously, and bring to a boil. Add the peppercorns, salt, parsley, and mushrooms. Simmer, stirring often until reduced to two-thirds of the original quantity or 2 cups. Strain and correct the seasoning.

Yield: 2 cups

Can be prepared ahead and frozen.

## SAUCE SUPRÊME (SUPREME SAUCE)

2 cups chicken stock
3 sliced mushrooms
1 cup velouté

1 cup heavy cream
salt to taste
cayenne pepper to taste

In a saucepan, boil the chicken stock and mushrooms until the liquid reduces to one-third of the original quantity or ⅔ cup. Add the velouté and simmer until reduced to 1 cup. Stir in the heavy cream and correct the seasoning with salt and cayenne pepper. Strain.

Yield: 2 cups

Can be prepared ahead and frozen.

## HOLLANDAISE SAUCE

3 egg yolks
1 tablespoon water
½ cup butter

salt to taste
lemon juice to taste

In a saucepan, beat the egg yolks and water with a wire whisk, until light and fluffy. Beat in the butter, bit by bit, until the sauce thickens and is smooth. Add the butter carefully and make sure that it is fully incorporated before adding more. When the butter is all added, correct the seasoning with salt and lemon juice. Keep warm in a double boiler if necessary.

Yield: 1 cup

Best if prepared just before serving.

## NOTE

If the sauce should curdle, beat in 1 tablespoon hot water. If that does not work, beat in 1 tablespoon very cold water. If that does not work, place an egg yolk in a warm bowl and beat in the curdled sauce, drop by drop until the sauce emulsifies. Continue adding the curdled sauce until all the sauce is added.

This sauce can also be prepared by the *processor method*. Place eggs, water, and lemon juice in a processor, melt the butter. With the machine running, slowly add the melted butter until emulsified. Proceed as described above. Keep warm over hot, not simmering water.

Remember that the sauce can never be hot, only warm. Too much heat and it will turn into scrambled eggs floating in buttery oil.

## VARIATIONS

### SAUCE MALTAISE (ORANGE-FLAVORED HOLLANDAISE)

1 cup hollandaise sauce
3 tablespoons orange juice

½ teaspoon grated orange
    rind
red food coloring, optional

Add the orange juice and rind to the sauce and, if desired, tint with the red food coloring until slightly pink. The food coloring replaces the natural red coloring of blood oranges. It may be omitted.

Yield: 1 cup

Best if prepared just before serving.

### LIME HOLLANDAISE

Prepare hollandaise using 1½ tablespoons lime juice, 1 teaspoon grated lime rind, and Tabasco to taste.

### MUSTARD HOLLANDAISE

Add enough Dijon mustard to sauce to give it a definite, but not overpowering mustard flavor, about 1 tablespoon.

## SAUCE MOUSSELINE (WHIPPED CREAM LIGHTENED HOLLANDAISE SAUCE)

Fold 3 tablespoons heavy cream, whipped until stiff, into warm Hollandaise.

## TARRAGON-FLAVORED SAUCE MOUSSELINE

Add 1 tablespoon minced fresh, or 1 teaspoon dried, tarragon to mousseline sauce.

---

# BÉARNAISE SAUCE

1 teaspoon tarragon
1 teaspoon chervil
2 shallots, minced
¼ cup tarragon
   vinegar
¼ cup white wine
3 egg yolks

1 tablespoon water
½ pound butter
salt to taste
pinch of cayenne
1 teaspoon tarragon
1 teaspoon chervil

In a small saucepan, simmer the tarragon, chervil, shallots, tarragon vinegar, and white wine until reduced to a thick paste. Let cool slightly.

Put the tarragon paste into a larger saucepan with the egg yolks and water and whisk until foamy. Put over low heat and beat in the butter 1 tablespoon or so at a time, until the sauce emulsifies and thickens slightly. Do not add more than ⅓ of the butter at a time. Correct the seasoning with salt and cayenne pepper. Strain the sauce into a clean saucepan or double boiler and add the remaining tarragon and chervil. Reheat if necessary.

Yield: 2 cups

Best if prepared and served.

## NOTE

The reason to strain the sauce is to remove the "deadwood" of shallots, tarragon, and chervil that have imparted all their flavor already, and add additional flavor with the fresh herbs.

## VARIATIONS
### SAUCE CHORON

Add ¼ cup hot, not boiling tomato purée to the Béarnaise.

---

# TOMATO SAUCE

| | |
|---|---|
| 1 quart tomatoes, prefera-<br>   bly plum tomatoes | ¼ pound butter, optional |
| 1 onion, halved | 1 teaspoon sugar |
| 1 teaspoon salt | salt and pepper to<br>   taste |

Cut the tomatoes into chunks and place in a 3-quart saucepan.
   Cover and simmer over medium heat for 10 minutes, stirring
   occasionally. In a food mill, preferably, or in a food processor,
   purée the tomatoes. Strain and discard the seeds and skins.
In a clean pot, simmer the tomatoes, onion, salt, butter (if using),
   and sugar for 45 minutes, or until thickened. Discard the onion
   and correct the seasoning with salt and pepper.

Yield: 3 cups

Can be prepared and frozen.

---

# TOMATO FONDUE

| | |
|---|---|
| ¼ cup minced shallots | ½ teaspoons salt |
| 1 garlic clove, crushed | pinch of sugar |
| 2 tablespoons butter | pinch of pepper |
| 5 tomatoes, peeled, seeded,<br>   and chopped | 1 tablespoon minced<br>   parsley |

In a saucepan, cook the shallots and garlic in the butter until soft
   but not brown. Add the tomatoes, salt, sugar, and pepper and
   cook over high heat until most of the liquid evaporates. Stir in
   the parsley. The sauce should be dry and pulpy. Do not stir too
   often to make it smooth.

Yield: 2 cups

Can be prepared ahead and frozen.

# MAYONNAISE

2 egg yolks
½ teaspoon salt
white pepper to taste
½ teaspoon dry mustard, or
  to taste

2 tablespoons vinegar or
  lemon juice, or to taste
1 cup oil (see below)

In a bowl, whisk the egg yolks, salt, and pepper with the dry mustard and 1 teaspoon of vinegar until it thickens slightly. Slowly beat in the oil, drop by drop, until about ¼ cup of oil has been incorporated and the sauce thickens. Add ½ teaspoon vinegar and continue beating, adding half the oil in a thin steady stream. Add another teaspoon of vinegar and continue to add the oil until finished. Correct the seasoning with salt, pepper, mustard, and vinegar or lemon juice.

Yield: 1½ cups

**Processor Method.**   Instead of 2 egg yolks, use 1 whole egg. Put egg into bowl with salt, pepper, mustard, and vinegar and turn on machine. With motor running, add the oil in a steady stream. Correct the seasoning.

Yield: 1½ cups

NOTE

All olive oil makes a strongly flavored mayonnaise and all salad oil such as cottonseed, soybean, or corn oil makes a bland oil. I recommend using half olive oil and half other vegetable oil.

# MAYONNAISE COLLÉE (JELLIED MAYONNAISE)

The gelatin aids this sauce in setting molded dishes and also helps to coat other foods.

1 tablespoon unflavored gelatin

¼ cup cold water
2 cups mayonnaise

In a small saucepan, sprinkle the gelatin on the water and let stand
for 3 minutes, or until softened. Place over low heat and stir
until the gelatin dissolves. Stir into the mayonnaise.

Yield: 2 cups

NOTE

This will set quickly. Use soon after making. Refrigerate the coated
food. It will protect the surface from drying for 24 to 36 hours.
The sauce can turn rubbery if kept longer.

## SAUCE TARTARE

1½ cups mayonnaise
2-3 tablespoons minced
  cornichons
4 shallots, minced
2 anchovies, minced
1 tablespoon minced
  capers
1 tablespoon minced parsley

1 teaspoon minced dill
1 tablespoon minced
  chervil
1 teaspoon dry mustard
heavy cream, optional
lemon juice to taste
salt and pepper to taste

In a bowl, mix the mayonnaise, cornichons, shallots, anchovies,
capers, parsley, dill, chervil, and mustard. Add cream to thin if
needed, and stir in lemon juice, salt, and pepper to taste.

Yield: 2 cups

Can be made several days ahead.

## VINAIGRETTE (OIL AND VINEGAR DRESSING)

2 tablespoons red or white
  wine vinegar
6 tablespoons olive oil
1 teaspoon Dijon mustard

1 teaspoon lemon juice, optional
1 teaspoon salt
pepper to taste

In a bowl, with a wire whisk, vigorously mix the vinegar, oil,
mustard, lemon juice, salt, and pepper until slightly thickened.

Yield: about 1½ cups

Will keep refrigerated for 2 weeks.

NOTE

Rapid whisking emulsifies the liquids so that the sauce thickens. Use the sauce immediately. If allowed to sit the emulsion will break.

**VARIATIONS**

Flavor the dressing with ½ teaspoon minced garlic, 1 tablespoon of minced fresh herbs, or ¼ to ½ cup of crumbled Roquefort cheese.

# EGGPLANT PROVENÇALE

¾ cup olive oil
1 large eggplant, cubed
2 zucchini, diced
3 onions, sliced
1 green pepper, thinly sliced
1 red pepper, thinly sliced
4 tomatoes, peeled, seeded, and chopped

1 tablespoon minced basil
¼ teaspoon minced oregano
2 tablespoons minced parsley
2 garlic cloves, minced
salt and pepper to taste

In a 12-inch skillet, sauté the eggplant in ½ cup olive oil until browned. Set aside in a colander to drain. Sauté the zucchini in the remaining oil until browned and add to the eggplant.

Add the onions, peppers, and tomatoes to the skillet and simmer until the juices evaporate. Season with basil, oregano, parsley, garlic, salt, and pepper. Return the eggplant and zucchini to the skillet and simmer 5 minutes or until tender.

Yield: 4 cups

Can be frozen and reheated.

# DUXELLES (MUSHROOM SAUCE)

Serve duxelles as the filling for crêpes or rolled soufflés, or add a little cream to thin, if needed, and serve as a sauce.

1 tablespoon minced shallot
3 tablespoons butter

1 pound mushrooms,
  minced
1 cup béchamel sauce

In a large skillet, sauté the shallot in the butter until soft. Stir in the mushrooms and cook until the liquid evaporates. Stir in the béchamel sauce and reheat.

Yield: 2 cups

Can be frozen and reheated.

# CARROT PURÉE

2 cups peeled, chopped carrots
¼ teaspoon salt
2 teaspoons sugar
1 tablespoon butter

¼ cup raw rice
2 cups water
1 tablespoon butter
heavy cream

In a 1-quart saucepan, simmer the carrots, salt, sugar, 1 tablespoon butter, rice, and water for 30 minutes, or until the rice and carrots absorb the water and are very tender. Force through a food mill or purée in a food processor. Return to the saucepan and heat to dry the purée. Stir in the remaining butter and enough cream to get the desired consistency.

Yield: 3 cups

Can be prepared ahead and frozen.

# CAULIFLOWER PURÉE

1 large head cauliflower, in florets
¼ cup mashed potatoes, optional

2 tablespoons butter
salt and pepper to taste
1 to 2 tablespoons heavy cream

In a saucepan of boiling salted water, cook the cauliflower until very tender. Drain well and force through a food mill or purée in a processor.

Stir in the mashed potatoes, if desired. Return to the saucepan and cook, stirring to dry the purée. Stir in the butter and correct the seasoning with salt and pepper. Add cream to thin to desired consistency.

Yield: 3 cups

Can be prepared ahead and frozen.

---

# LIMA BEAN PURÉE

2 10 ounce packages frozen
  lima beans
¼ cup heavy cream

salt and pepper to taste
1 to 2 tablespoons butter

In a saucepan, cook the lima beans in water to cover until very tender. Drain and purée the beans in a food mill or processor. If using a processor, force the purée through a fine sieve to remove any tough skins. Place in a saucepan and heat to dry if needed. Stir in the cream, salt, pepper, and butter.

Yield: 2½ cups

Can be prepared ahead and frozen.

---

# SPINACH PURÉE

3 pounds spinach,
  stripped
3 tablespoons butter

salt and pepper to taste
nutmeg to taste

Wash the spinach well and drain. In a saucepan, cook the spinach, covered, with the water on its leaves until wilted. Drain well and squeeze out excess moisture. Purée in a food mill or blender. Return to the saucepan, and cook to evaporate excess moisture. Stir in the butter, salt, pepper, and nutmeg.

Yield: 3 cups

Can be prepared ahead and frozen.

## VARIATION

For a more velvety purée, add ¼ cup heavy cream, or to taste.

---

# CROÛTES AND CROÛTONS (TOASTED BREAD)

Croûtes are full slices of bread, sautéed in butter or oil. If cut into small dice, they may be called croutons.

6 slices white bread, ½-inch         2 to 3 tablespoons butter
thick

Remove the crusts from the bread, if you want. Cut into rounds, triangles, or other shapes if desired. In a large skillet, heat the butter until hot but not brown and sauté the bread until golden on both sides. Drain on paper towels.

Yield: 6 croutes

Best when prepared shortly before serving.

---

# CROUSTADES (TOAST CUPS)

2 loaves unsliced bread         6 cups melted butter

Preheat the oven to 350°F. Remove the crusts from the bread and cut the bread into blocks, 2½-inches wide, 4-inches long, and 2½-inches high. Cut the center out of each block, leaving ½-inch thick walls. Brush the bread on all sides with melted butter and place on a baking sheet. Bake about 20 minutes, or until crisp and golden brown.

Yield: 6 croustades

Best when served shortly after baking.

---

# BUTTERED BREAD CRUMBS

1 slice white bread         2 teaspoons butter

In a food processor, with on/off turns, grate the bread into fine crumbs. Add the butter and with on/off turns, cut it into the bread crumbs. Do not overprocess.

Yield: about ½ cup buttered crumbs

Prepare just before using.

## PÂTE BRISÉE ORDINAIRE

3½ cups flour
2 teaspoons salt
¼ teaspoon sugar
9 ounces or 2½ sticks butter

2½ ounces or 5 tablespoons lard
1 cup iced water

In a bowl, mix the flour, sugar, and salt. Cut in the butter and lard to form a coarse meal. Add the liquid and mix gently with a fork until it starts to form a ball. It will not be smooth.
Perform the *fraisage*, or smearing. Press the palm of your hand into the edge of dough farthest from you and smear it out about 6 inches, bring your hand back to the edge of the dough and repeat until you smear all the dough.
Shape it into a ball, flatten the ball and wrap in waxed paper. Refrigerate at least 20 minutes.
Remove from the refrigerator cut the dough into quarters and roll each quarter on a lightly floured board to the desired size and line the pie molds.
If there is time, freeze for 20 minutes before baking.
Prick the bottom of the shell and line with foil. Fill with dried beans. Bake at 425°F for 10 minutes, or until the sides are firm enough to support themselves. Remove the beans and bake until lightly browned, about 25 minutes or fully cooked about 40 minutes.

Yield: 4 9- to 10-inch pie shells or 2 two-crust pies

NOTE

When rolling the dough, think of a fabric with a warp and woof. Roll from the middle away from you and then the middle back toward you. Give the pastry a quarter turn and repeat. The dough will roll into a square. Rolling it into a circle stretches the dough in all directions and can toughen it.

# PÂTE BRISÉE II (PASTRY FOR SINGLE PIE)

1½ cups flour                    3½ tablespoons water
8 tablespoons butter             1 teaspoon salt
4 tablespoons lard

In a bowl, place the flour and make a well in the center. With your
    fingertips or a pastry blender, or two knives, cut in the butter
    and lard until the mixture resembles coarse meal. Add the water
    and salt and mix gently into a dough.
Turn onto a board and perform the *fraisage* (see previous recipe).
    Wrap in plastic wrap and chill for at least 20 minutes.

Yield: dough for 1 pie shell

Can be prepared ahead and frozen before baking. Bake directly
    from the freezer.


# PROCESSOR PASTRY DOUGH

2 cups flour                     4 tablespoons lard
½ teaspoon salt                  5 tablespoons iced water
7 tablespoons butter

In a food processor, place the flour, salt, butter, and lard. Turn
    the processor on and off rapidly several times until the mixture
    looks like coarse meal.
Add the water and process until the mixture is moistened and starts
    to come together. Do not let it form a ball on top of the blades.
    Place the mixture into a plastic bag, press into a flat cake, and
    chill at least 20 minutes.

Yield: enough dough for a 9-inch, 2-inch crust pie

Can be prepared, shaped, and frozen before baking.


# PÂTE SABLE (SANDTORTE PASTRY)

This pastry makes a crispier more cookie-like dough than the
previous recipes.

¼ pound butter                       1½ cups flour
¼ cup sugar                          1 teaspoon baking
2 egg yolks, or 1 egg                   powder

Place all the ingredients into a bowl and work the mixture with
   your hand until it feels waxy and holds together. Chill for 20
   minutes. Roll between sheets of waxed paper.
Line a tart shell with the pastry and line the pastry with foil and fill
   the shell with dried beans. Bake at 400°F. for 15 minutes,
   remove the beans and foil, and bake until half- or fully-cooked
   according to the recipe.

Yield: 1 pie shell

Can be molded and frozen before baking.

---

## EGG WASH

An egg wash is a wash brushed onto pastries to help them brown
and to give them a sheen. The richer the egg wash, the deeper the
color and the glossier the finish. Egg washes can be prepared from
salted water; water and egg white; whole egg and salt; water, salt,
and whole egg; milk and whole egg; milk and egg yolks; cream and
while egg; and cream and egg yolks. For the pastries in this book,
an equal mixture of milk or cream and whole egg or egg yholk
makes the most attrractive glaze. When the pastries have been
shaped, brush with the egg wash, refrigerate for 10 minutes, and
brush again. For a more devcorative finish, use the point of a small
knife to score the surface of the pastry after the second brushing.
After it is baked, the scoring will show through the glaze.

# Index